Collins

NEW MATHS FRAMEWORKING

Matches the revised KS3 Framework

Kevin Evans, Keith Gordon, Trevor Senior, Brian Speed

Contents

Introduction

Learning objectives

See what you are going to cover and what you should already know at the start of each chapter. The purple and blue boxes set the topic in context and provide a handy checklist.

National Curriculum levels

Know what level you are working at so you can easily track your progress with the colour-coded levels at the side of the page.

Worked examples

Understand the topic before you start the exercises by reading the examples in blue boxes. These take you through how to answer a question step-by-step.

Functional Maths

Practise your Functional Maths skills to see how people use Maths in everyday life.

 Look out for the Functional Maths icon on the page.

Extension activities

Stretch your thinking and investigative skills by working through the extension activities. By tackling these you are working at a higher level.

Level booster

Progress to the next level by checking the Level boosters at the end of each chapter. These clearly show you what you need to know at each level and how to improve.

National Test questions

Practise the past paper Test questions to feel confident and prepared for your KS3 National Curriculum Tests. The questions are levelled so you can check what level you are working at.

Extra interactive National Test practice

Watch and listen to the audio/visual National Test questions on the separate Interactive Book CD-ROM to help you revise as a class on a whiteboard.

Look out for the computer mouse icon on the page and on the screen.

Functional Maths activities

Put Maths into context with these colourful pages showing real-world situations involving Maths. You are practising your Functional Maths skills by analysing data to solve problems.

Extra interactive Functional Maths questions and video clips

Extend your Functional Maths skills by taking part in the interactive questions on the separate Interactive Book CD-ROM. Your teacher can put these on the whiteboard so the class can answer the questions on the board.

See Maths in action by watching the video clips and doing the related Worksheets on the Interactive Book CD-ROM. The videos bring the Functional Maths activities to life and help you see how Maths is used in the real world.

Look out for the computer mouse icon on the page and on the screen.

NEW
Hone your Functional Maths skills further by doing the four exciting tasks given in the new chapter – Functional Maths Practice.

CHAPTER 1 · Algebra 1 & 2

This chapter is going to show you

- How to find the *n*th term of a linear sequence
- How to describe a sequence derived from a geometrical pattern
- How to find a second difference
- How to find inverse functions
- The limits of some series

What you should already know

- How to continue a given pattern
- How to graph a simple relationship

Sequences

Arsenal had a sequence of 43 games in which they scored in every game. Is it possible to predict how many goals they would score in their next game?

A **sequence** is an ordered set of numbers or terms, such as the positive integers, 1, 2, 3... . Every number or term in a sequence is given by applying the same rule throughout the sequence. Look at Examples 1.1 and 1.2.

Example 1.1 ▷ What is the next number in the following sequence?

10, 100, 1000, 10 000, ...

It is 100 000.

What is the term-to-term rule for the sequence? Multiply by 10.

Example 1.2 ▷ What is the next number in this sequence?

1, 2, 4, 7, 11, 16, …

It is 22.

Show the differences between consecutive terms. They are: 1, 2, 3, 4, 5,… .

The position of a term in a sequence can sometimes be used to find its value. The idea is to try to find a general term which represents the pattern. This is usually written as the *n*th term, or as *T*(*n*).

A sequence is usually defined by its *n*th term. Look at Examples 1.3 to 1.5 to see how this works.

Example 1.3 ▷ Write down the first four terms of the sequence whose *n*th term is given by $T(n) = 4n + 2$.

The first term, $T(1)$, is given by $n = 1$. Hence, $4 \times 1 + 2 = 6$.
The second term, $T(2)$, is given by $n = 2$. Hence, $4 \times 2 + 2 = 10$.
The third term, $T(3)$, is given by $n = 3$. Hence, $4 \times 3 + 2 = 14$.
The fourth term, $T(4)$, is given by $n = 4$. Hence, $4 \times 4 + 2 = 18$.

So, the first four terms are 6, 10, 14, 18.

Example 1.4 ▷ Write down the *n*th term of the sequence 2, 5, 8, 11, … .

First, find the differences between consecutive terms. The sequence has the same difference, 3, between consecutive terms. This shows that the sequence is in the form $An + B$.

Since the common difference is 3, then $A = 3$.

So, in order to get the first term of 2, –1 must be added to 3. Hence $B = -1$.

That is, the *n*th term is given by $T(n) = 3n - 1$.

When a sequence has the same difference between consecutive terms, it is called a **linear sequence**. A linear sequence can be defined by a general term that will be in the following form:

$$T(n) = An + B$$

where A is the common difference between consecutive terms, B is the value which is added to A to give the first term, and n is the number of the term (that is, first, second, …).

Example 1.5 ▷ Write down the *n*th term of the sequence 5, 9, 13, 17, 21, … .

The difference between consecutive terms is 4.

To get the first term of 5, 1 must be added to 4.

Hence, the *n*th term is $T(n) = 4n + 1$

Check this as follows: $T(1) = 4 \times 1 + 1 = 5$
$T(2) = 4 \times 2 + 1 = 9$
$T(3) = 4 \times 3 + 1 = 13$

So, $T(n) = 4n + 1$ is correct.

Exercise 1A

① Find the next three terms in each of the following sequences.

a 1, 5, 9, 13, …   **b** 3, 8, 13, 18, …   **c** 2, 9, 16, 23, …
d 4, 10, 17, 25, …   **e** 6, 14, 24, 36, …   **f** 5, 8, 13, 20, …

② Write down the first four terms of each of the following sequences whose *n*th term is given below.

a $2n + 3$ **b** $3n - 2$ **c** $4n + 5$ **d** $5n - 3$
e $3n - 1$ **f** $4n - 5$ **g** $2n - 4$

3 Find the *n*th term of each of the following sequences.

   a   6, 10, 14, 18, 22, …   **b**   8, 15, 22, 29, 36, …

   c   21, 19, 17, 15, 13, …   **d**   32, 28, 24, 20, 16, …

4 Find the *n*th term of each of the following sequences.

   a   43, 51, 59, 67, 75, …   **b**   57, 50, 43, 36, 29, …

   c   35, 48, 61, 74, 87, …   **d**   67, 76, 85, 94, 103, …

5 Find the *n*th term of each of the following sequences.

   a   9, 4, –1, –6, –11, …   **b**   –11, –9, –7, –5, –3, …

   c   –1, –5, –9, –13, –17, …   **d**   –15, –12, –9, –6, –3, …

6 Find the *n*th term of each of the following sequences.

   a   2.4, 2.6, 2.8, 3.0, 3.2, …   **b**   1.7, 2.0, 2.3, 2.6, 2.9, …

   c   6.8, 6.3, 5.8, 5.3, 4.8, …   **d**   5.3, 4.9, 4.5, 4.1, 3.7, …

7 Find the *n*th term of each of the following sequences of fractions.

   a $\frac{1}{2}, \frac{2}{5}, \frac{3}{8}, \frac{4}{11}, \frac{5}{14}, \ldots$ **b** $\frac{3}{4}, \frac{5}{9}, \frac{7}{14}, \frac{9}{19}, \frac{11}{24}, \ldots$

8 Look at each of the following sequences of squares.

     Shape 1   **Shape 2**   **Shape 3**   **Shape 4**

   a   Find the number of squares in the *n*th shape.

   b   Find the number of squares in the 50th shape in the pattern.

9 Look at each of the following sequences of lines (blue) and crosses (green).

   Diagram 1   **Diagram 2**   **Diagram 3**   **Diagram 4**

   a   Find the number of lines in the *n*th shape.

   b   Find the number of crosses in the 50th shape in the pattern.

   c   Find the number of crosses in the *n*th shape in the pattern.

Extension Work

The *n*th term of a sequence is given by $\frac{1}{2}n(n + 1)$.

1   Work out the first five terms of the sequence.

2   Write down the term-to-term rule for the sequence.

3   Continue the sequence for 10 terms.

4   What special name is given to this sequence of numbers?

Quadratic sequences

You have already met the sequence of square numbers:

1, 4, 9, 16, 25, 36, ...

The nth term of this sequence is n^2.

Many sequences have nth terms that include n^2.

These are called quadratic sequences.

Example 1.6 ▷ The nth term of a quadratic sequence is given by $n^2 + 3n + 2$.

    a Work out the first five terms of the sequence.

    b Write down the term-to-term rule for this sequence.

    c Continue the sequence for ten terms.

    d What is the 100th term in the sequence?

    a Substituting $n = 1, 2, 3, 4$ and 5 into the expression for the nth term gives the first five terms of the sequence: 6, 12, 20, 30, 42

    b The sequence increases by 6, 8, 10 and 12 so the term-to-term rule is 'goes up in even numbers starting with 6'.

    c Carry on adding 14, 16, ... to give:

        6, 12, 20, 30, 42, 56, 72, 90, 110, 132, ...

    d The 100th term is $100^2 + 3 \times 100 + 2 = 10\ 302$

Example 1.7 ▷ Write down the nth term of the following sequences.

    a 1, 4, 9, 16, 25, ...   **b** 3, 6, 11, 18, 27, ...

    c 2, 8, 18, 32, 50, ...   **d** $\frac{1}{2}$, 2, $4\frac{1}{2}$, 8, $12\frac{1}{2}$, ...

    a This is the square number sequence, nth term = n^2

    b This is 2 more than the square number sequence, nth term = $n^2 + 2$

    c This is twice the square number sequence, nth term = $2n^2$

    d This is half the square number sequence, nth term = $\frac{1}{2}n^2$

Exercise 1B

1 Write down the first four terms of each of the following sequences whose nth term is given below.

    a n^2 **b** $n^2 + 1$ **c** $n^2 + n$ **d** $n^2 + 3n + 4$

2 For each of the following nth terms:

    i work out the first five terms of the sequence.

    ii write down the term-to-term rule for this sequence.

    iii continue the sequence for ten terms.

    a $n(n + 3)$ **b** $3n^2$ **c** $n^2 + 5$

    d $(n + 1)^2$ **e** $(n + 3)(n - 2)$ **f** $2n^2 + n + 1$

7

3 Write down the *n*th term of the following sequences.

a   1, 4, 9, 16, 25, …   b   2, 5, 10, 17, 26, …

c   5, 20, 45, 80, 125, …   d $\frac{1}{4}$, 1, $2\frac{1}{4}$, 4, $6\frac{1}{4}$, …

4 Look at the way straight lines can intersect one another.

1 line   2 lines   3 lines   4 lines
0 intersections 1 intersection   3 intersections   6 intersections

The maximum number of intersections for each set of lines is shown in the table below.

Number of lines	1	2	3	4
Maximum number of intersections	0	1	3	6

a   Before drawing a diagram, can you predict, from the table, the maximum number of intersections you will have for five lines?

b   Draw the five lines so that they all intersect one another. Count the number of intersections. Were you right?

c   Now predict the maximum number of intersections for six and seven lines.

d   Draw the diagram for six lines to confirm your result.

e   Which of the following is the *n*th term of the sequence?

$\frac{1}{2}n(n + 1)$ $(n - 1)(n + 1)$ $\frac{1}{2}n(n - 1)$

5 Look at the following polygons. Each vertex is joined to every other vertex with a straight line, called a diagonal.

3 sides   4 sides   5 sides   6 sides   7 sides
0 diagonals   2 diagonals   5 diagonals   9 diagonals   14 diagonals

The table below shows the number of diagonals drawn inside each polygon.

Number of sides	3	4	5	6	7
Number of diagonals	0	2	5	9	14

a   Before drawing a diagram, can you predict, from the table, the number of diagonals you will have for a polygon with eight sides?

b   Draw an eight-sided polygon and put in all the diagonals. Count the number of diagonals. Were you right?

c   Now predict the number of diagonals for polygons with nine and ten sides.

d   Check your results for part **c** by drawing the polygons with their diagonals and seeing how many diagonals there are in each case.

e Which of the following is the nth term of the sequence?

$\frac{1}{2}(n + 2)(n - 1)$ $\qquad$ $\frac{1}{2}n^2 + \frac{1}{2}n - 1$ $\qquad$ $\frac{1}{2}(n^2 + n - 2)$

6 Write down the first five terms of each of the following sequences.

a $T(n) = (n + 1)(n + 2)$ $\qquad\qquad$ **b** $T(n) = (n - 1)(n - 2)$

c $T(n) = n + (n - 1)(n - 2)$ $\qquad$ **d** $T(n) = 2n + (n - 1)(n - 2)(n - 3)$

e $T(n) = 3n + (n - 1)(n - 2)(n - 3)(n - 4)$

Extension Work

What is the pattern of second differences in $T(n) = n^2$?

The first six terms of the sequence $T(n) = n^2$, where $T(1) = 1$, are:

1, 4, 9, 16, 25, 36

The first differences are those between consecutive terms. These are:

```
1   4   9   16   25   36
  3   5   7    9   11
```

The second differences are those between consecutive first differences, as shown below:

```
3   5   7   9   11
  2   2   2   2
```

Every quadratic sequence has second differences which are the same throughout the sequence, as shown above.

1 a Find the second differences for each of the following sequences by writing down the first six terms.

    i $T(n) = n^2 + 3n + 4$ $\qquad\qquad$ **ii** $T(n) = n^2 + 4n + 3$

  b What do you notice about each second difference?

2 a Find the second differences for each of the following sequences by writing down the first six terms.

    i $T(n) = 2n^2 + 3n + 4$ $\qquad\qquad$ **ii** $T(n) = 2n^2 + 4n + 3$

  b What do you notice about each second difference?

  c What do you expect the second difference to be for $T(n) = 3n^2 + 3n + 4$?

Functions

A **function** is a rule which changes one number, called the **input**, to another number, called the **output**. For example, $y = 2x + 1$ is a function. So, when $x = 2$, a new number $y = 5$ is produced. Another way of writing this function is:

$x \rightarrow 2x + 1$

Identity function $\qquad$ $x \rightarrow x$ is called the **identity function** because it maps any number onto itself. In other words, it leaves the inputs unaltered.

$$0 \rightarrow 0$$
$$1 \rightarrow 1$$
$$2 \rightarrow 2$$
$$3 \rightarrow 3$$
$$4 \rightarrow 4$$

Inverse function

Every linear function has an **inverse function** which reverses the direction of the operation. In other words, the output is brought back to the input.

Example 1.8 ▷

The inverse function of $x \rightarrow 4x$ is seen to be $y \rightarrow \frac{y}{4}$.

$$
\begin{array}{ccccc}
x & \rightarrow & 4x & & \\
0 & \rightarrow & 0 & \rightarrow & 0 \\
1 & \rightarrow & 4 & \rightarrow & 1 \\
2 & \rightarrow & 8 & \rightarrow & 2 \\
3 & \rightarrow & 12 & \rightarrow & 3 \\
& & y & \rightarrow & \frac{y}{4}
\end{array}
$$

Note that the inverse function is sometimes written as $x \rightarrow \frac{x}{4}$, but we will use the letter y for inverse functions to avoid confusion.

Example 1.9 ▷

The inverse function of $x \rightarrow x + 3$ is seen to be $y \rightarrow y - 3$.

$$
\begin{array}{ccccc}
x & \rightarrow & x+3 & & \\
0 & \rightarrow & 3 & \rightarrow & 0 \\
1 & \rightarrow & 4 & \rightarrow & 1 \\
2 & \rightarrow & 5 & \rightarrow & 2 \\
3 & \rightarrow & 6 & \rightarrow & 3 \\
& & y & \rightarrow & y-3
\end{array}
$$

When a function is built up from two or more operations, you will need to consider the original operations and work backwards through these to find the inverse.

Example 1.10 ▷

Find the inverse function of $x \rightarrow 4x + 3$.

The sequence of operations for this function is:

Input $\longrightarrow$ ☐ × 4 $\longrightarrow$ ☐ + 3 $\longrightarrow$ Output

Reversing this sequence gives:

Input $\longleftarrow$ ☐ ÷ 4 $\longleftarrow$ ☐ − 3 $\longleftarrow$ Output

Then give the output the value y:

$$\frac{y-3}{4} \leftarrow y - 3 \leftarrow y$$

So, the inverse function is:

$$y \rightarrow \frac{y-3}{4}$$

Self-inverse function

The inverse functions of some functions are the functions themselves. These are called **self-inverse functions**.

Example 1.11 ▷

The inverse function of $x \rightarrow 8 - x$ can be seen to be itself, as $y \rightarrow 8 - y$.

$$
\begin{array}{ccccc}
x & \rightarrow & 8-x & & \\
0 & \rightarrow & 8 & \rightarrow & 0 \\
1 & \rightarrow & 7 & \rightarrow & 1 \\
2 & \rightarrow & 6 & \rightarrow & 2 \\
3 & \rightarrow & 5 & \rightarrow & 3 \\
4 & \rightarrow & 4 & \rightarrow & 4 \\
5 & \rightarrow & 3 & \rightarrow & 5 \\
& & y & \rightarrow & 8-y
\end{array}
$$

Exercise 1C

1. Write down the inverse function of each of the following functions.

   a $x \rightarrow 2x$ b $x \rightarrow 5x$ c $x \rightarrow x + 6$

   d $x \rightarrow x + 1$ e $x \rightarrow x - 3$ f $x \rightarrow \frac{x}{5}$

2. For each of the following functions:
   i   draw the flow diagram for the function.
   ii   draw the flow diagram for the inverse function.
   iii write down the inverse function in the form $y \rightarrow \dots$

   a $x \rightarrow 2x + 3$ b $x \rightarrow 3x + 1$ c $x \rightarrow 4x - 3$

   d $x \rightarrow 5x - 2$ e $x \rightarrow 4x + 7$ f $x \rightarrow 6x - 5$

3. Show that the following are self-inverse functions.

   a $x \rightarrow 6 - x$ b $x \rightarrow \frac{2}{x}$

4. Write down the inverse function of each of the following functions.

   a $x \rightarrow 2(x + 3)$ b $x \rightarrow 3(x - 4)$ c $x \rightarrow \frac{(x + 3)}{4}$

   d $x \rightarrow \frac{(x - 2)}{5}$ e $x \rightarrow \frac{1}{2}x + 3$ f $x \rightarrow \frac{1}{2}x - 7$

Extension   Work

1. The function $x \rightarrow 2x$ can also be expressed as $y = 2x$. Show this to be true by considering the input set {1, 2, 3, 4, 5}.
   a   What is the output set from {1, 2, 3, 4, 5} with the function $x \rightarrow 2x$?
   b   Find the values of y when x has values {1, 2, 3, 4, 5}, where $y = 2x$.
   c   Are the two sets of values found in parts **a** and **b** the same? If so, then you have shown that $y = 2x$ is just another way of showing the function $x \rightarrow 2x$.

2. Draw a graph of the function $x \rightarrow 2x$ by using $y = 2x$. On the same pair of axes, draw the graph of the inverse function of $x \rightarrow 2x$.

3. On the same pair of axes, draw the graphs representing the function $x \rightarrow 4x$ and its inverse function.

4. On the same pair of axes, draw the graphs representing the function $x \rightarrow 5x$ and its inverse function.

5. Look at the two lines on each graph you have drawn for Questions **2**, **3** and **4**. Do you notice anything special about each pair of lines?

Graphs

The distance–time graph on the right illustrates three people in a race.

The graph shows how quickly each person ran, who was ahead at various times, who won and by how many seconds.

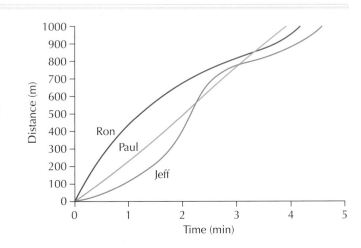

Paul

Notice that Paul's graph is a straight line. This means that he ran at the same speed throughout the race. Paul won the race, finishing about 20 seconds in front of Ron.

Ron

The shape of Ron's graph indicates that he started quickly and then slowed down. He was in the lead for the first 850 m, before Paul overtook him.

Jeff

Jeff started slowly, but then picked up speed to overtake Paul for a minute before running out of steam and slowing down to come in last, about 30 seconds behind Ron.

Note: The steeper the graph, the faster the person is running.

Exercise 1D

 1 Look at the distance–time graph, which illustrates how two rockets flew during a test flight. Rocket D flew higher than Rocket E.

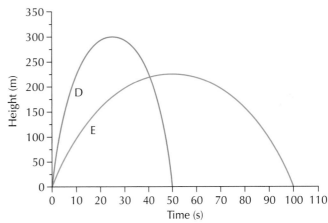

a Estimate the height reached by Rocket D.

b Estimate how much higher than Rocket E Rocket D went.

c How long after the launch were both rockets at the same height?

d For how long was each rocket higher than 150 m?

e Can you tell which rocket travelled further? Explain your answer.

 2 Look at the graph below, which illustrates the amount of water in a bath after it has started to be filled.

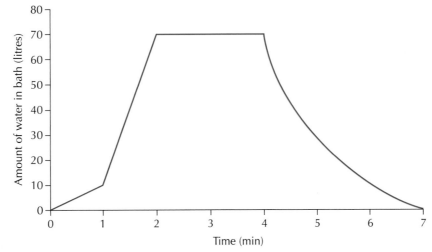

a Explain what might have happened 1 minute after the start.

b When was the plug pulled out for the bath to start emptying?

c Why do you think the graph shows a curved line while the bath was emptying?

d How long did the bath take to empty?

3 Water drips steadily into the container shown on the right. The graph shows how the depth of water varies with time.

Sketch similar graphs for bottles with the following shapes.

a   **b**   **c**   **d**

 4 Suggest which graph below best fits each situation given.

a   **b**   **c**

A The distance travelled by a train moving at a constant speed.

B The distance travelled by a motorbike accelerating to overtake.

C The distance travelled by an old car, which starts well, but gradually slows down.

5 Suggest which graph below best fits each situation given.

a   **b**   **c**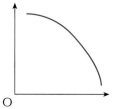

A The amount of fuel left in the tank of my car as I travel from Sheffield to Cornwall.

B The amount of infection in a body as it responds to medicine will first reduce gradually and then more quickly until it has all gone.

C The rate of cooling of a hot drink starts quickly and then slows down.

 6 Sketch graphs to illustrate each of the following situations.

a The number of euros that can be purchased with £x

b The temperature during the 24 hours of 21st July

c The temperature during the 24 hours of 12th February

d The number of empty car-park spaces in a supermarket on a Saturday between 8 am and 8 pm

e The amount of daylight each day of the year from 21st June to next 20th June

The UK population has been increasing over the last 200 years. The following table shows the population every 20 years.

a Draw a graph to show how the population has increased since 1801.

b From the graph, estimate what the population was in 2001.

c Try to find out what the actual population was in 2001.

Year	Population (millions)	Year	Population (millions)
1801	12	1901	38
1821	15.5	1921	44
1841	20	1941	47
1861	24.5	1961	53
1881	31	1981	56

Limits of sequences

Some sequences go on forever, as you have seen. These are called **infinite sequences**. Other sequences finish after so many numbers or terms. These are called **finite sequences**. Follow through Example 1.12, which shows an infinite sequence.

Example 1.12

Using the term-to-term rule 'Divide by 5 and add 4', find the first 10 terms of this sequence, which starts at 1.

This rule generates the following sequence:

1, 4.2, 4.84, 4.968, 4.9936, 4.998 72, 4.999 744, 4.999 948 8, 4.999 989 76, 4.999 997 952

Notice that the sequence gets closer and closer to 5, which is called the **limit** of the sequence.

Exercise 1E

1 a Using the term-to-term rule 'Divide by 2 and add 3' to build a sequence and starting at 1, find the first 12 terms generated by this sequence. Use a calculator or a spreadsheet.

b To what value does this sequence get closer and closer?

c Use the same term-to-term rule with different starting numbers. What do you notice?

2 Repeat Question 1, but change the 'add 3' in the term-to-term rule to 'add 4'.

3 Repeat Question 1, but change the 'add 3' in the term-to-term rule to 'add 5'.

4 a Look at your answers to Questions 1 to 3. See whether you can estimate to what value the sequence will get closer and closer when you change the 'add 3' in Question 1 to 'add 6'.

b Work out the sequence to see whether you were correct in part a.

5 Repeat Question 1, but change the 'divide by 2' to 'divide by 3'.

6 Repeat Question 5, but change the 'add 3' to 'add 4'.

7 Repeat Question 5, but change the 'add 3' to 'add 5'.

8 a Look at your answers to Questions **5** to **7**. See whether you can estimate to what value the sequence will get closer and closer when you change the 'add 3' in Question **5** to 'add 6'.

b Work out the sequence to see whether you were correct in part **a**.

8

Extension Work

Continue the above investigation to see whether you can predict the limiting number that each sequence reaches from the term-to-term rule 'Divide by *A* and add *B*'.

LEVEL BOOSTER

5 I can predict the next terms in a linear sequence of numbers.

I can write down and recognise the sequence of square numbers.

I know the squares of all numbers up to 15^2 and the corresponding square roots.

I can find any term in a sequence given the first term and the term-to-term rule.

I can find any term in a sequence given the algebraic rule for the *n*th term.

6 I can find the *n*th term of a sequence in the form $an + b$.

7 I can find any term in a sequence given the algebraic rule for the *n*th term, where the *n*th term contains the term n^2.

I can recognise and give the *n*th term of a sequence based on the square number sequence.

I can work out the second difference of a quadratic sequence and use this to continue the sequence.

I can work out the inverse function of a function of the form $x \rightarrow ax + b$.

I can recognise and sketch graphs of real-life situations.

National Test questions

1 *2005 Paper 2*

a The *n*th term of a sequence is $3n + 4$

What is the **8th** term of this sequence?

b The *n*th term of a different sequence is $\dfrac{n - 2}{n^2}$

Write the first **three** terms of this sequence.

2 *1999 Paper 1*

Each term of a number sequence is made by adding 1 to the numerator and 2 to the denominator of the previous term. Here is the beginning of the number sequence:

$$\frac{1}{3}, \frac{2}{5}, \frac{3}{7}, \frac{4}{9}, \frac{5}{11}, \cdots$$

a Write an expression for the *n*th term of the sequence.

b The first five terms of the sequence are shown on the graph.

The sequence goes on and on for ever. Which of the four graphs below shows how the sequence continues?

i

ii

iii

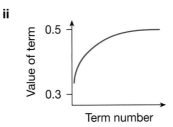

iv

c The *n*th term of a different sequence is $\dfrac{n}{n^2 + 1}$.

The first term is $\frac{1}{2}$.

Write down the next three terms.

d This new sequence also goes on and on for ever. Which of these four graphs shows how the sequence continues?

i

ii

iii

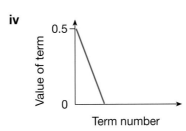

iv

Mobile phone tariffs

Pick your plan

Mix & match plans		Inclusive UK minutes and texts	Free 3 to 3 minutes	Free voicemail	Free Instant Messaging	Free Skype
£12 a month	£12 Promotional Tariff	**100** Anytime any network minutes or texts or any mix of the two	**300** 3 to 3 minutes	✔	✔	✔
£15 a month	Mix & match 300	**300** Anytime any network minutes or texts or any mix of the two	**300** 3 to 3 minutes	✔	✔	✔
£18 a month	Mix & match 500	**500** Anytime any network minutes or texts or any mix of the two	**300** 3 to 3 minutes	✔	✔	✔
£21 a month	Mix & match 700	**700** Anytime any network minutes or texts or any mix of the two	**300** 3 to 3 minutes	✔	✔	✔
£24 a month	Mix & match 900	**900** Anytime any network minutes or texts or any mix of the two	**300** 3 to 3 minutes	✔	✔	✔
£27 a month	Mix & match 1100	**1100** Anytime any network minutes or texts or any mix of the two	**300** 3 to 3 minutes	✔	✔	✔
Texter plans		**Texts**	**Minutes**	**Free voicemail**	**One-Off Cost**	**Unlimited Skype**
£15 a month	£15 Texter	**600**	**75** Anytime, any network			
£20 a month	£20 Texter	**1000**	**100** Anytime, any network			

- Pay by voucher or direct debit

- If you pay by voucher, service is suspended once the monthly allowance is reached

- If you pay by direct debit, any minutes or texts over the allowance are charged at 15p per minute or 15p per text

- 10% discount if you pay by direct debit

- All tariffs do not include VAT which is charged at $17\frac{1}{2}\%$

Use the information on Mobile phone tariffs to help you answer these questions.

1 Ed has the 'Mix and match 700' tariff and pays by voucher each month.
   a How much does this cost a month before VAT is added?
   b How much does this cost a month when VAT is added at $17\frac{1}{2}\%$?

2 Sean has the 'Mix and match 900' tariff and pays by debit card each month.
   a How much does this cost a month before VAT is added?
   b How much does this cost a month when VAT is added at $17\frac{1}{2}\%$?

3 Sandra has the 'Mix and match 500' tariff. She uses all of her any network minutes and all of her free '3 to 3' minutes. How many minutes did she talk in total? Give your answer in hours and minutes.

4 Gordon has the '£12 promotional' tariff. So far he has used 24 minutes on voice calls and sent 19 texts. How many more minutes or texts can he send before he gets charged extra?

5 Dave has the '£15 texter' tariff. He pays by direct debit. In one month he uses 750 texts and 100 minutes of voice calls. What is his bill for that month?

6 Andy has the '£20 texter' tariff. He pays by direct debit. In one month he uses all of his 100 anytime, any network voice calls and makes x texts. His bill for the month before discount and VAT is £23. What is the value of x?

Once a tariff has been chosen there are offers on phones.
This table shows the monthly costs of phones and their extra features.

£5 a month	**Sony Ericsson K850i with 50 video calling minutes** The K850i is a true photographer's phone. With a 5 megapixel camera, auto lens cover, autofocus and Xenon flash, it allows perfect pictures all the time.	5 megapixel	40 MB internal, 512 MB M2 included	■ Extra video minutes charged at 20p per minute
£9 a month	**LG U990 Viewty with 90 video calling minutes** The complete camera phone. 5 megapixels and large touch sensitive screen.	5 megapixel	100 MB internal, MicroSD expandable	■ 10% discount if you pay by direct debit
FREE	**Sony Ericsson K800i** Cyber-Shot camera and phone.	3.2 megapixel	Expandable with M2 card	■ All tariffs do not include VAT which is charged at $17\frac{1}{2}\%$

7 Lucy has the '£15 texter' tariff. She pays by direct debit. In one month she makes y minutes of voice calls and 540 texts. Her bill for the month before discount and VAT is £24.90. What is the value of y?

8 Ann has the 'Mix and match 300' tariff and the Sony Ericsson K850i phone. She pays by voucher.

  a How much does this cost a month before VAT is added?

  b How much does this cost a month when VAT is added at $17\frac{1}{2}\%$?

9 Steve has the 'Mix and match 500' tariff and the LG U990 Viewty phone. He pays by direct debit.

  a How much does this cost a month before VAT is added?

  b How much does this cost a month when VAT is added at $17\frac{1}{2}\%$?

10 Ben has the 'Mix and match 500' tariff and an LG U990 Viewty phone. He pays by direct debit. In one month he makes 400 minutes of voice calls, sends 150 texts and sends 100 minutes of videos. How much is his bill for the month?

11 Coryn has a 'Mix and match 300' tariff and a Sony Ericsson K800i phone. He pays by voucher. Coryn knows that his average voice calls per month are 220 minutes and he sends an average of 40 texts. He sees this advertisement.

Special offer for existing customers
'Mix and match 250'
250 anytime any network minutes or texts or any mix of the two.
Only £13.00 per month *including* VAT.
Extra minutes or texts 15p.

If Coryn changes to the 'Mix and match 250' tariff, will he save money in an average month?
You must show your working to justify your answer.

12 Robin has a 'Mix and match 100' tariff and a Sony Ericsson K850i phone. He pays by direct debit. In one month he makes 80 minutes of voice calls, sends x texts and sends y minutes of video. He notices that he sends 10 more minutes of videos than the number of texts. His bill for the month before discount and VAT is £27.

What are the values of x and y?

This chapter is going to show you	What you should already know
● How to multiply and divide fractions ● How to calculate with percentages in more complicated problems, such as compound interest ● How to solve problems using ratios ● What reciprocals are ● Connection between enlargement of length, area and volume	● How to add and subtract simple fractions ● How to cancel simple fractions and ratios ● How to work out simple percentages of quantities

The four rules governing fractions

You met the addition and subtraction of fractions in Year 8. This section will show you how to solve all types of problem involving the addition, subtraction, multiplication and division of fractions.

Example 2.1 ▶

Work out the answer to each of these.

a $3\frac{1}{3} + 1\frac{2}{5}$ **b** $4\frac{3}{8} - 1\frac{2}{3}$

a When adding mixed numbers, you can convert them to improper (top-heavy) fractions and add them using a common denominator. If appropriate, cancel and/or convert the answer to a mixed number.

So, you have:

$$3\frac{1}{3} + 1\frac{2}{5} = \frac{10}{3} + \frac{7}{5}$$
$$= \frac{50}{15} + \frac{21}{15} = \frac{71}{15} = 4\frac{11}{15}$$

As this method involves large numbers, it is easy to make a mistake. A better method is to split up the problem:

$$3\frac{1}{3} + 1\frac{2}{5} = 3 + 1 + \frac{1}{3} + \frac{2}{5}$$

The whole-number part gives $3 + 1 = 4$, and the fraction part gives:

$$\frac{1}{3} + \frac{2}{5} = \frac{5}{15} + \frac{6}{15} = \frac{11}{15}$$

Hence, the total is:

$$4 + \frac{11}{15} = 4\frac{11}{15}$$

b Using the method of splitting up the calculation, you have:

$$4\frac{3}{8} - 1\frac{2}{3} = 4 + \frac{3}{8} - 1 - \frac{2}{3}$$
$$= 4 - 1 + \frac{3}{8} - \frac{2}{3}$$
$$= 3 + \frac{9}{24} - \frac{16}{24}$$
$$= 3 - \frac{7}{24} = 2\frac{17}{24}$$

So far, you have seen how to add and to subtract fractions. Now you will multiply and divide fractions.

Example 2.2 ▷ Jan's watering can is $\frac{3}{5}$ full. She waters her roses and uses half of this water. How full is her watering can now?

As you can see from the diagram, Jan's watering can is $\frac{3}{10}$ full after she has watered the roses. How can you calculate this result?

One half of $\frac{3}{5}$ is written as:

$$\frac{1}{2} \times \frac{3}{5} = \frac{1 \times 3}{2 \times 5} = \frac{3}{10}$$

This shows that when a fraction is multiplied by another fraction, the new numerator is found by multiplying together the two original numerators, and the new denominator by multiplying together the two original denominators.

Example 2.3 ▷ Work out each of these.

  a $\frac{3}{4} \times \frac{2}{9}$ **b** $2\frac{3}{7} \times 2\frac{4}{5}$

  a Following Example 2.2, you can calculate mentally that the answer is $\frac{6}{36}$, which can be cancelled to $\frac{1}{6}$. However, this is an example of where it is easier to cancel before you complete the multiplication.

   When numerators and denominators have factors in common, you can cancel them. In this example, 3 and 9 will cancel, as do 2 and 4. The calculation is therefore given like this:

$$\frac{\overset{1}{\cancel{3}}}{\underset{2}{\cancel{4}}} \times \frac{\overset{1}{\cancel{2}}}{\underset{3}{\cancel{9}}} = \frac{1}{6}$$

   The remaining numbers are multiplied together to give the new numerator and the new denominator. When the fractions are cancelled properly, the final answer will not cancel.

  b Convert the mixed numbers to improper (top-heavy) fractions and cancel when possible. Change the answer to a mixed number if appropriate.

   Hence, you have:

$$2\frac{3}{7} \times 2\frac{4}{5} = \frac{17}{\underset{1}{\cancel{7}}} \times \frac{\overset{2}{\cancel{14}}}{5}$$

$$= \frac{34}{5} = 6\frac{4}{5}$$

Example **2.4**

Work out each of these.

a $\frac{3}{5} \div \frac{1}{4}$ **b** $\frac{15}{24} \div \frac{9}{16}$ **c** $2\frac{2}{7} \div 1\frac{11}{21}$

a When you are dividing by a fraction, always use the following rule:

Turn the dividing fraction upside down and multiply by it.

So, you have:

$$\frac{3}{5} \div \frac{1}{4} = \frac{3}{5} \times \frac{4}{1} = \frac{3 \times 4}{5 \times 1} = \frac{12}{5} = 2\frac{2}{5}$$

b When possible, cancel during the multiplication.

$$\frac{15}{24} \div \frac{9}{16} = \frac{\cancel{15}^5}{\cancel{24}_3} \times \frac{\cancel{16}^2}{\cancel{9}_3} = \frac{5 \times 2}{3 \times 3} = \frac{10}{9} = 1\frac{1}{9}$$

c Convert the mixed numbers to improper (top-heavy) fractions. Turn the dividing fraction upside down, put in a multiplication sign and cancel if possible. Then change the result to a mixed number if appropriate.

$$2\frac{2}{7} \div 1\frac{11}{21} = \frac{16}{7} \div \frac{32}{21}$$

$$= \frac{\cancel{16}^1}{\cancel{7}_1} \times \frac{\cancel{21}^3}{\cancel{32}_2} = \frac{3}{2} = 1\frac{1}{2}$$

6

Exercise 2A

1 Convert each of the following pairs of fractions to a pair of equivalent fractions with a common denominator. Then work out the answer, cancelling down or writing as a mixed number if appropriate.

   a $1\frac{2}{3} + 1\frac{1}{4}$ **b** $2\frac{2}{5} + 2\frac{1}{6}$ **c** $2\frac{1}{3} + 1\frac{2}{5}$ **d** $2\frac{1}{3} + 1\frac{1}{2}$

   e $4\frac{1}{5} + 1\frac{3}{4}$ **f** $5\frac{1}{2} + 1\frac{5}{6}$ **g** $6\frac{5}{6} + 2\frac{1}{9}$ **h** $7\frac{1}{6} + 3\frac{7}{8}$

2   **a** $3\frac{1}{3} - 1\frac{1}{4}$ **b** $4\frac{2}{5} - 1\frac{1}{6}$ **c** $2\frac{2}{5} - 1\frac{1}{3}$ **d** $3\frac{1}{2} - 1\frac{1}{3}$

   e $3\frac{2}{5} - 1\frac{3}{4}$ **f** $5\frac{1}{2} - 1\frac{5}{6}$ **g** $7\frac{5}{6} - 2\frac{8}{9}$ **h** $6\frac{5}{6} - 3\frac{7}{8}$

3 Work out each of the following.

   a $\frac{3}{4} + \frac{9}{14}$ **b** $\frac{2}{9} + \frac{4}{21}$ **c** $\frac{11}{28} + \frac{9}{35}$

   d $\frac{5}{12} - \frac{2}{21}$ **e** $\frac{31}{48} - \frac{15}{32}$ **f** $\frac{19}{25} - \frac{7}{15}$

4 Work out each of the following. Cancel before multiplying when possible.

   a $\frac{1}{3} \times \frac{2}{5}$ **b** $\frac{3}{4} \times \frac{3}{4}$ **c** $\frac{2}{7} \times \frac{5}{8}$ **d** $\frac{3}{8} \times \frac{4}{9}$

   e $\frac{5}{8} \times \frac{12}{25}$ **f** $\frac{5}{6} \times \frac{3}{5}$ **g** $\frac{1}{2} \times \frac{6}{11}$ **h** $\frac{1}{4} \times \frac{8}{15}$

   i $\frac{3}{4} \times \frac{8}{9}$ **j** $\frac{3}{5} \times \frac{15}{22} \times \frac{11}{18}$

5 Work out each of the following. Write as improper (top-heavy) fractions and cancel before multiplying when possible.

   a $1\frac{3}{5} \times 2\frac{1}{8}$ **b** $2\frac{3}{4} \times 3\frac{1}{5}$ **c** $2\frac{1}{2} \times 1\frac{3}{5}$ **d** $1\frac{1}{4} \times 1\frac{4}{5}$

   e $2\frac{1}{5} \times \frac{10}{21}$ **f** $3\frac{1}{2} \times \frac{8}{35}$ **g** $\frac{1}{2} \times 3\frac{3}{5}$ **h** $2\frac{2}{7} \times 2\frac{4}{5}$

   i $1\frac{5}{6} \times 2\frac{2}{5}$ **j** $4\frac{1}{2} \times 2\frac{3}{5}$

6 Work out each of the following. Cancel at the multiplication stage when possible.

a $\frac{1}{2} \div \frac{1}{8}$ **b** $\frac{2}{3} \div \frac{3}{5}$ **c** $\frac{5}{6} \div \frac{2}{3}$ **d** $\frac{1}{3} \div \frac{6}{7}$

e $\frac{4}{5} \div \frac{3}{10}$ **f** $\frac{5}{8} \div \frac{15}{16}$ **g** $\frac{2}{7} \div \frac{7}{8}$ **h** $\frac{3}{4} \div \frac{9}{13}$

i $\frac{1}{2} \div \frac{3}{5}$ **j** $\frac{1}{4} \div \frac{3}{8}$

7 Work out each of the following. Write as improper (top-heavy) fractions and cancel at the multiplication stage when possible.

a $1\frac{1}{4} \div \frac{5}{8}$ **b** $3\frac{1}{2} \div 1\frac{3}{5}$ **c** $2\frac{1}{2} \div 1\frac{1}{4}$ **d** $1\frac{2}{3} \div 1\frac{3}{5}$

e $2\frac{5}{6} \div 1\frac{7}{12}$ **f** $1\frac{1}{2} \div 2\frac{3}{8}$ **g** $4\frac{1}{2} \div \frac{3}{5}$ **h** $4\frac{1}{2} \div \frac{8}{9}$

i $\frac{7}{8} \div 2\frac{3}{4}$ **j** $3\frac{1}{2} \div \frac{3}{4}$

8 A rectangle has sides of $\frac{3}{7}$ cm and $\frac{14}{27}$ cm. Calculate its area.

9 A rectangle has sides of $5\frac{1}{4}$ cm and $4\frac{5}{8}$ cm. Calculate its area.

10 How many $\frac{2}{3}$-metre lengths of cloth can be cut from a roll that is $3\frac{2}{9}$ metres long?

11 A rectangle has an area of $7\frac{4}{5}$ m². Its length is $3\frac{1}{4}$ m. What is its width?

$7\frac{4}{5}$ m²

$3\frac{1}{4}$ m

This is a fractional magic square.

What is the magic number?

Find the missing values in the cells.

$\frac{2}{15}$		
$\frac{7}{15}$	$\frac{1}{3}$	$\frac{1}{5}$

Percentages and compound interest

If you put £100 in a bank and it earns 5% interest each year, which graph do you think represents the way the amount of money in the bank changes as time passes – assuming you don't spend any of it!

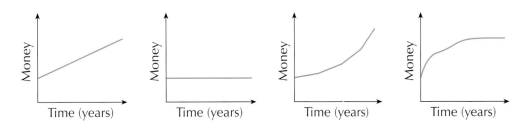

Example 2.5 ▷ Jenny puts £100 in a bank and it earns 5% interest per annum (Latin for 'each year'). How much will she have after 3 years?

Making calculations such as this are sometimes called **compound interest** problems. There are two ways to solve such problems.

Method 1 *Increase and add on*

Calculate the amount of interest earned after each year and add it to the previous year's total, as shown below.

After first year: 5% of £100 = £5, which gives Jenny £100 + £5 = £105

After second year: 5% of £105 = £5.25, which gives Jenny £105 + £5.25
                            = £110.25

After third year: 5% of £110.25 = £5.51, which gives Jenny £110.25 + £5.51
                            = £115.76

The last amount of interest has been rounded to the nearest penny. As you can see, the increase gets bigger year by year.

Method 2 *Use a multiplier*

When dealing with percentage increase, the multiplier is found by adding the percentage increase expressed as a decimal to 1, which represents the original value. So, in this case, the multiplier is given by 1 + 0.05 = 1.05

(When dealing with a percentage decrease, the multiplier is found by subtracting the decrease from 1, which gives a value for the multiplier of less than 1.)

So, you have:

After first year: £100 × 1.05 = £105

After second year: £105 × 1.05 = £110.25

After third year: £110.25 × 1.05 = £115.76

This can also be done using the power key on the calculator as:
£100 × $(1.05)^3$ = £115.7625 ≈ £115.76

The second method is good if you use a calculator as you get the final answer very quickly. Make sure you write down your calculation in case you make a mistake.

Example 2.6 ▷ A petri dish containing 200 000 bacteria is treated with a new drug. This reduces the number of bacteria by 16% each day.

a   How many bacteria remain after 7 days?

b   How long does it take to reduce the bacteria to below a safe level of 20 000?

a   The method of calculating the decrease and subtracting it day by day will take too long. It is quicker to use a multiplier. For a 16% decrease, the multiplier is 0.84.

Key into your calculator:

$$\boxed{2}\ \boxed{0}\ \boxed{0}\ \boxed{0}\ \boxed{0}\ \boxed{0}\ \boxed{\times}\ \boxed{(}\ \boxed{0}\ \boxed{.}\ \boxed{8}\ \boxed{4}\ \boxed{)}\ \boxed{x^{\blacksquare}}\ \boxed{7}\ \boxed{=}$$

You may not need the brackets and your power key may be different.

This gives an answer of 59 018.069 31, which can be rounded to 59 000 bacteria.

b Using trial and improvement to make this calculation, gives these rounded values:

168 000, 141 120, 118 541, 99 574, 83 642, 70 260, 59 018,

49 575, 41 643, 34 980, 29 383, 24 682, 20 733, 17 416

So, it takes 14 days to get below 20 000.

Check by calculating $200\,000 \times 0.84^{13}$ and $200\,000 \times 0.84^{14}$.

Compound interest does not only concern money. It can be applied to, for example, growth in population and increases in the body weight of animals. It can also involve reduction by a fixed percentage, such as decrease in the value of a car, pollution losses and water losses.

Exercise 2B

1 Write down the multiplier which is equivalent to each of these.

a	12% increase	**b**	5% decrease	**c**	8% decrease
d	7% increase	**e**	4% decrease	**f**	2% increase
g	3.2% increase	**h**	$2\frac{1}{2}$% increase	**i**	15% decrease
j	6% increase	**k**	2.6% decrease	**l**	$\frac{1}{2}$% increase
m	24% decrease	**n**	7% decrease	**o**	$17\frac{1}{2}$% increase

You may want to check your answers, as they will help you with the rest of the questions.

2 How much would you have in the bank if you invest:

a £200 at 2% interest per annum for 4 years?

b £3000 at 3.2% interest per annum for 7 years?

c £120 at 6% interest per annum for 10 years?

d £5000 at 7% interest per annum for 20 years?

e £75 at $2\frac{1}{2}$% interest per annum for 3 years?

3 Investments (including stocks and shares) can decrease in value as well as increase. How much would your investments be worth in each of the following cases?

a You invested £3000 which lost 4% each year for 6 years.

b You invested £250 which lost 2.6% each year for 5 years.

c You invested £4000 which lost 24% each year for 4 years.

4 To decrease the rabbit population in Australia, the disease mixomatosis was introduced into rabbit colonies. In one colony, there were 45 000 rabbits. The disease decreased the population by 7% each month. How many rabbits were left in that colony after: **a** 4 months? **b** a year?

FM **5** Some Internet sales sites will decrease the price of a product by a certain percentage each day until someone buys it.

Freda is interested in buying a computer. She has £1500 to spend. An Internet site has the computer Freda wants but it is £2000. The price is to be decreased by 5% per day. How many days will Freda have to wait until she can afford the computer?

FM **6** During a hot spell, a pond loses 8% of its water each day due to evaporation. It has 120 gallons in it at the start of the hot spell. How many days will it take before the pond's volume of water falls to 45 gallons?

Extension Work

FM

Jane started drinking a bottle of cola a day, which cost her £1.50.

Her brother Jack put £1.50 into a jar each day and took the money (£45) to the bank each month.

The bank paid Jack $\frac{1}{2}$% compound interest each month.

1 How much does Jane spend on cola in a year (365 days)?

2 The first £45 that Jack pays in earns 11 months of interest. How much does the first £45 increase to over the 11 months?

3 The second £45 that Jack pays in earns 10 months of interest. How much does the second £45 increase to over the 10 months?

4 Now work out the value of each £45 that Jack pays in. For example, the third £45 is in the bank for 9 months and the final £45 is paid in on the last day of the year, so gets no interest.

5 Add up the answers to parts **2**, **3** and **4** to find out how much Jack has in the bank at the end of the year.

A computer spreadsheet is useful for this activity.

Reverse percentages and percentage change

In Britain, most prices in shops include VAT. In the USA, a sales tax (similar to VAT) has to be added to the displayed price.

Which camera is cheaper if the exchange rate is $1.96 to one pound?

Cost £175.25
(including 17½% VAT)

Cost $350.00
(not including 6% sales tax)

Example 2.7 ▷ After a 10% pay rise, John now gets £5.50 an hour. How much per hour did he get before the pay rise?

Making calculations such as this are sometimes called **reverse percentage** problems. There are two ways to solve such problems.

Method 1 *Unitary method*

A 10% pay rise means that he now gets 100% + 10% = 110%

   £5.50 represents 110%

   £0.05 represents 1% (dividing both sides by 110)

   £5.00 represents 100% (multiplying both sides by 100)

So, before his pay rise, John was paid £5.00 an hour.

Method 2 *Use a multiplier*

10% = 0.1

A 10% increase is represented by the multiplier 1 + 0.1 = 1.1

To work backwards to find John's hourly rate of pay before his pay rise, divide £5.50 by the multiplier.

This gives: £5.50 ÷ 1.1 = £5.00

Example 2.8 ▶

In a sale the price of a coat is reduced by 20%. It now costs £40. How much did it cost before the sale?

Unitary method

In the sale, the price of the coat is 80% (100% – 20%) of the original cost.

So £40 represents 80%

0.50 represents 1% (dividing both sides by 80)

£50 represents 100% (multiplying both sides by 100)

So the price of the coat before the sale was £50.

Example 2.9 ▶

The number of fish in a pond increased to 3750 in one year. This was a 25% increase. How many fish were in the pond originally?

Multiplier method

A 25% increase is represented by the multiplier 1 + 0.25 = 1.25

To work backwards to find the number of fish in the pond originally, divide 3750 by the multiplier.

This gives: 3750 ÷ 1.25 = 3000

$$\text{Percentage change} = \frac{\text{Change}}{\text{Original amount}} \times 100$$

Example 2.10 ▶

The price of a hi-fi system increases from £189 to £199. What percentage of the original price is the increase?

The increase is £10 and the original price was £189. So, the percentage increase is:

$$\frac{\text{Increase}}{\text{Original amount}} \times 100 = \frac{10}{189} \times 100 = 5.3\%$$

Example 2.11 ▶

A shop's offer is shown on the right.

Explain why this is misleading.

A $17\frac{1}{2}$% increase on £510 is £599.25 but an £89 reduction on £599 is:

$$\frac{\text{Reduction}}{\text{Original amount}} \times 100 = \frac{89}{599} \times 100 = 14.9\%$$

So, the reduction is only about 15%.

> We will pay your VAT of $17\frac{1}{2}$%.
>
> **Typical example**
> A sofa costing £599 including VAT will cost you £510.
>
> This is a $17\frac{1}{2}$% reduction on the normal price!

1 The label on a packet of soap powder states it is 25% bigger! The packet now contains 1500 g. How much did it weigh before?

2 After a 10% price increase, a trombone now costs £286. How much was it before the increase?

3 This table shows the cost of some goods after $17\frac{1}{2}$% VAT is added. Work out the cost of the goods before VAT is added.

Item	Cost (inc VAT)	Item	Cost (inc VAT)
Camera	£223.25	Dishwasher	£293.75
Heater	£70.50	Sofa	£528.75
Printer	£82.25	Computer	£2115.00

4 A suit is on sale at £96, which is 75% of its original price. What was the original price?

5 There was a 20% discount in a sale. Elle bought a pair of boots for £40 in the sale. What was the original price of the boots?

6 In 2002, the Prime Minister's salary went up from £114 600 to £162 000. What percentage increase is that?

7 Adina asked for a 40% pay rise. In the end, her pay went up from £21 500 to £22 400 per annum. What percentage increase is that?

8 In the second year it was open, the attendance at the Magna exhibition went up by 30% to 1 230 000 visitors. How many visitors were there in the first year it was open?

9 I bought a CD in a sale and saved £2.25 off the normal price. This was a 15% reduction. What was the normal price of the CD?

10 The table shows the average price of detached houses, semi-detached houses, terraced houses and flats in September 2006 and September 2007. Calculate the percentage increase for each type.

Type	Price in September 2006 (£)	Price in September 2007 (£)
Detached	257 000	277 000
Semi-detached	160 000	178 000
Terraced	131 000	144 000
Flats	158 000	174 000

Credit card companies and loan companies quote the Annual Percentage Rate or APR. This is the equivalent over a year to the interest which they charge monthly.

For example, if 2% is charged each month on a loan of £1000, the amount owed after 12 months will be £1000 × $(1.02)^{12}$ = £1268, which is equivalent to 26.8% APR (because £1000 increased by 26.8% gives £1268).

 1 Work out the APR for companies which charge an interest rate of:

     a 1.5% per month   **b** 0.9% per month

     c 1% per month   **d** 5% per month

 2 Work out the monthly interest rate for an APR of 30%. [*Hint:* Try trial and improvement.]

A computer spreadsheet is useful for this activity.

Direct and inverse proportion

Example 2.12 Six tubes of toothpaste have a total mass of 972 g. What is the mass of 11 tubes?

If six tubes have a mass of 972 g, one tube has a mass of:
972 ÷ 6 = 162 g

Hence, 11 tubes have a mass of 11 × 162 = 1782 g = 1.782 kg

Example 2.13 A guitarist plays for 40 minutes with 400 people in the audience. How long would it take him to play the same set if there were only 300 people in the audience?

It takes exactly the same time of 40 minutes! The number of people in the audience does not affect the length of the performance.

Example 2.14 Six girls take 4 days to paint a fence. How long will it take eight girls?

If it takes six girls 4 days to paint the fence, it would take one girl 6 × 4 = 24 days to paint the fence.

Hence, eight girls will take 24 ÷ 8 = 3 days to paint the fence.

Example 2.15 Four men take 5 days to lay a pipeline that is 300 m long. What length of pipe could be laid by six men working for 8 days?

It takes 4 × 5 = 20 man-days to lay 300 m of pipe.

Hence, 1 man-day would lay 300 ÷ 20 = 15 m of pipe.

So, 6 × 8 = 48 man-days would lay 48 × 15 = 720 m of pipe.

Example 2.16 ▷

Six shirts hanging on a washing line take 2 hours to dry. How long would it take three shirts to dry?

It would take the same time! The number of shirts on the line does not make any difference.

Be careful! Some of these questions may trip you up.

You may use a calculator for this exercise.

1 In 5 hours a man earns £28. How much does he earn in 7 hours?

2 A girl walks 3 miles in 1 hour. How long would it take her to walk 5 miles?

3 Four men lay a pipeline in 5 days. How long would 10 men take?

4 Travelling at 8 miles an hour, a boy takes 5 hours for a cycling trip. How long would he take at a speed of 12 miles per hour?

5 Seven chocolate bars cost £1.82. How much would 11 chocolate bars cost?

6 In two days my watch loses 4 minutes. How much does it lose in one week (7 days)?

7 It takes 6 minutes to hard-boil three eggs in a pan. How long would it take to hard-boil two eggs in the same pan?

8 I have three cats who eat a large bag of cat food every 4 days. If I get another cat how long will the bag of food last now?

9 In 20 minutes an aircraft travels 192 miles. How far would it travel in 25 minutes at the same speed?

10 Four buckets standing in a rain shower take 40 minutes to fill. How long would three buckets standing in the same rain shower take to fill?

11 Nine men build a wall in 20 days. How long will the job take 15 men?

12 A distance of 8 km is represented by a distance of 12.8 cm on a map.
  a How many centimetres would represent a distance of 14 km?
  b What distance is represented by 7 cm on the map?

13 My motorbike travels 120 miles on 10 litres of petrol.
  a How many miles will it travel on 12 litres?
  b How many litres will I need to travel 55 miles?

14 Four taps fill a bath in 36 minutes. How long would it take three taps to fill the same bath?

15 An electric light uses 5 units of electricity in 120 minutes. If 9 units of electricity have been used, how long has it been switched on?

16 It takes 12 seconds to dial the 12-digit number of a friend who lives 100 miles away.

  a How long will it take to dial the 12-digit number of a friend who lives 50 miles away?

  b How long will it take to dial the 6-digit number of a friend who lives 10 miles away?

17 At peak times, a phone card gives 120 minutes of calls. At off-peak times, the cost is one-third of the cost at peak times. How many minutes of calls will the phone card give at off-peak times?

18 A box of emergency rations can feed 12 men for six days. For how long would the box of rations feed eight men?

19 A man takes 10 minutes to hang out a load of washing. How long would it take two men?

20 One woman went to mow a meadow. It took her 15 minutes to walk there. If two women went to mow a meadow how long would it take them to walk there?

21 Some tins of beans are packed into seven boxes each of which holds 12 tins. If I pack them into four boxes instead, how many tins will be in each box?

22 Two men can paint a room in 6 hours. How long would five men take?

23 A shelf is filled with 20 books each 3.5 cm thick. If the books are replaced by 28 books of equal thickness, how thick would they have to be to fill the shelf?

24 From the top of a hill, two girls can see 20 miles. How far would three girls be able to see from the top of the same hill?

25 A 2.5 gallon cylinder of gas will keep a patio heater burning at full power for 30 hours. How many hours will a 1.5 gallon cylinder of gas keep the heater burning at half power?

26 Three women building a patio lay 30 m² in 4 days. How many days would it take two women to lay a patio that is 45 m²?

27 A family use four tubes of toothpaste in nine weeks, brushing their teeth twice a day. They decide to give a four-week trial to brushing their teeth three times a day. How many tubes of toothpaste will they use in that time?

28 A haulage company charges £240 to transport four pallets a distance of 300 miles. How far would they transport five pallets for a cost of £180?

29 Seven men can pack 2352 boxes of chocolate bars in a 4-hour shift. How long would it take five men to pack 3150 boxes of chocolate bars?

30 In 1 hour, eight teachers can mark 90 exam papers. How many exam papers can 15 teachers mark in one and a half hours?

Extension | Work

You are told that:

$a \times b \times c = d$

1 What would the answer be if a were doubled?

2 What would the answer be if b were trebled?

3 What would the answer be if c were halved?

4 What would the answer be if, at the same time, a were doubled, b trebled and c halved?

5 What would the answer be if, at the same time, a were doubled, b doubled and c doubled?

6 What would the answer be if, at the same time, a were halved, b halved and c halved?

Ratio in area and volume

Investigation

These three blocks are similar. This means that the ratio height : length : width is the same for all three blocks.

a Work out the area of the front face of each block.

b Work out the volume of each block.

Work out each of the following ratios and write it in the form $1 : n$.

c **i** Length of block A to length of block B
   ii Area of the front face of block A to area of the front face of block B
   iii Volume of block A to volume of block B

d **i** Length of block A to length of block C
   ii Area of the front face of block A to area of the front face of block C
   iii Volume of block A to volume of block C

e **i** Length of block B to length of block C
   ii Area of the front face of block B to area of the front face of block C
   iii Volume of block B to volume of block C

Look at your answers to parts **c**, **d** and **e**. What do you notice?

Explain the connection between the ratio of the lengths, areas and volumes of similar shapes.

Exercise 2E

1 You will have found out that two similar shapes with their lengths in the ratio $1 : a$ have areas in the ratio $1 : a^2$.

The following shapes are similar. The drawings are not to scale. For each shape, you are given the width. You are also given the area of shape P.

P $A = 5$ cm²

2 cm

Q

4 cm

R

6 cm

S

10 cm

Copy and complete the following. (The first has been done for you.)

a **i** The ratio of lengths of shapes P and Q is 1 : 2.
  ii The ratio of areas of shapes P and Q is 1 : 4.
  iii The area of shape Q is 4 × area of shape P. So, area of Q = 4 × 5 = 20 cm²

b **i** The ratio of lengths of shapes P and R is 1 : ….
  ii The ratio of areas of shapes P and R is 1 : ….
  iii The area of shape R is … × area of shape P. So, area of R = … × 5 = … cm²

c **i** The ratio of lengths of shapes P and S is 1 : ….
  ii The ratio of areas of shapes P and S is 1 : ….
  iii The area of shape S is … × area of shape P. So, area of S = … × 5 = … cm²

2 You will have found out that two similar shapes with their lengths in the ratio $1 : a$ have volumes in the ratio $1 : a^3$.

The following shapes are similar. The drawings are not to scale. For each shape you are given the width. You are also given the volume of shape J.

J $V = 6$ cm³

2 cm

K

4 cm

L

8 cm

M

10 cm

Copy and complete the following. (The first has been done for you.)

a **i** The ratio of lengths of shapes J and K is 1 : 2.
  ii The ratio of volumes of shapes J and K is 1 : 8.
  iii The volume of shape K is 8 × volume of shape J.
    So, volume of K = 8 × 6 = 48 cm³

b **i** The ratio of lengths of shapes J and L is 1 : ….
  ii The ratio of volumes of shapes J and L is 1 : ….
  iii The volume of shape L is … × volume of shape J.
    So, volume of L = … × 6 = … cm³

c **i**   The ratio of lengths of shapes J and M is 1 : ....
   ii The ratio of volumes of shapes J and M is 1 : ....
   iii The volume of shape M is ... × volume of shape J.
       So, volume of M = ... × 6 = ... cm³

3 The following pair of shapes, A and B, are similar. The drawings are not to scale.
   Work out the area of shape B.

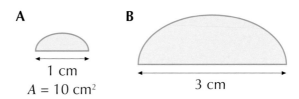

A

B

1 cm

3 cm

A = 10 cm²

4 Two similar shapes, P and Q, are shown below. The drawings are not to scale. Work
   out the area of shape P.

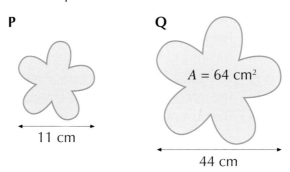

P

Q

A = 64 cm²

11 cm

44 cm

5 The following pair of solids, C and D, are similar. The drawings are not to scale.
   Work out the volume of solid D.

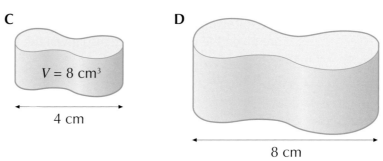

C

D

V = 8 cm³

4 cm

8 cm

6 Two similar solids, R and S, are shown below. The drawings are not to scale. Work
   out the volume of solid R.

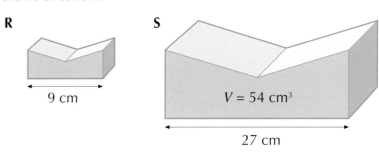

R

S

9 cm

V = 54 cm³

27 cm

7 The sides of a cube are reduced by a half.

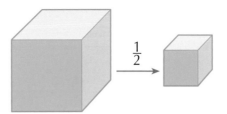

    a By what fraction is the area of a face reduced?

    b By what fraction is the volume of the cube reduced?

8 A one-centimetre cube is placed alongside a metre cube.

    a What is the ratio of the lengths of the two cubes?

    b What is the ratio of the areas of a face of the two cubes?

    c What is the ratio of the volumes of the two cubes?

Extension Work

Three cylinders have the dimensions shown.

1 Explain how you know that the cylinders are similar.

2 For cylinders A, B and C work out each of the following.

    a The area of the circular end

    b The volume of the cylinder (Formula for the volume is $\pi r^2 h$.)

3 Work out each of the following ratios.

    a End area of A : End area of B

    b End area of A : End area of C

    c Volume of A : Volume of B

    d Volume of A : Volume of C

4 Another similar cylinder, D, has a radius of 15 cm. Write down each of the following ratios.

    a End area of C : End area of D

    b Volume of C : Volume of D

The special numbers −1, 0 and 1 divide the number line shown above into four sets of numbers: A, B, C and D.

A contains all the numbers less than −1. B contains all the numbers between −1 and 0. C contains all the numbers between 0 and 1 and D contains all the numbers greater than 1.

Example 2.17 ▷

a What happens when a number from set A is multiplied by a number from set D?

b What happens when a number from set B is divided by 1?

a Choose any number from set A, say −2. Choose any number from set D, say +3. Multiply them together:

$$-2 \times +3 = -6$$

The answer belongs to set A.

Try other combinations of numbers from set A and set D. For example:

$$-4 \times +4 = -16 \quad -1.5 \times 5 = -7.5 \quad -5 \times 1.5 = -7.5$$

They all belong to set A. So, a number from set A multiplied by a number from set D always gives a number in set A.

b Pick numbers from set B and divide each one by 1. For example:

$$-0.4 \div 1 = -0.4 \quad -\tfrac{2}{3} \div 1 = -\tfrac{2}{3} \quad -0.03 \div 1 = -0.03$$

The answers are the same as the values from set B. So, they all give numbers in set B.

7

Exercise 2F

1 Copy and complete this table, which shows the result of multiplying the first number by the second number. The result from Example 2.17, part **a**, has been filled in along with some other results.

Second number

×	Set A	−1	Set B	0	Set C	1	Set D
Set A			C or D			Set A	Set A
−1						−1	
Set B							
0	0						
Set C	A or B						
1						1	
Set D							

First number

2) Copy and complete this table, which shows the result of dividing the first number by the second number. The result from Example 2.17, part **b**, has been filled in along with some other results. One thing you cannot do in maths is to divide by zero. So, this column has been deleted.

Second number

	÷	Set A	−1	Set B	0	Set C	1	Set D
First number	Set A	C or D						
	−1						−1	
	Set B			C or D		A or B	Set B	
	0	0						
	Set C							
	1							
	Set D							

3) Use your tables to answer each of the following. Choose one answer.

a When any positive number is divided by a number between 0 and 1, the answer is:
  i the same.   **ii** always bigger.
  iii always smaller.   **iv** sometimes bigger, sometimes smaller.

b When any positive number is divided by a number bigger than 1, the answer is:
  i the same.   **ii** always bigger.
  iii always smaller.   **iv** sometimes bigger, sometimes smaller.

c When any positive number is multiplied by a number between 0 and 1, the answer is:
  i the same.   **ii** always bigger.
  iii always smaller.   **iv** sometimes bigger, sometimes smaller.

d When any positive number is multiplied by a number bigger than 1, the answer is:
  i the same.   **ii** always bigger.
  iii always smaller.   **iv** sometimes bigger, sometimes smaller.

4) In each case, give an example to show that the statement is not true. (Such an example is called a **counter-example**.)

a When you divide any number by −1, the answer is always negative.

b When you multiply any number by a number less than −1, the answer is always bigger.

c Dividing any number by a number between −1 and 1 (except 0) always gives a bigger number.

d Multiplying any number by a number between −1 and 1 (except 0) always gives a smaller number.

Extension Work

Repeat Example 2.17 but this time add and subtract the numbers from each set.
Can you reach any definite conclusions?

Reciprocal of a number

The reciprocal of a number is the number divided into 1. For example, the reciprocal of 2 is $1 \div 2 = 0.5$.

On a calculator, the reciprocal key is usually marked in one of the ways shown below.

x^{-1} $1/x$ $^1/x$

Example 2.18

Find the reciprocals of: **a** 25   **b** 0.625

Using the reciprocal key on your calculator, or dividing the number into 1, you will get:

a $1 \div 25 = 0.04$

b $1 \div 0.625 = 1.6$

8

Exercise 2G

1 a Find, as a decimal, the reciprocal of each and every integer from 1 to 20.

b Which of the reciprocals are terminating decimals?

2 Find the reciprocal of each of the following numbers. Round your answers if necessary.

a	30	**b**	0.005	**c**	80	**d**	0.001 25
e	2000	**f**	0.002	**g**	100	**h**	10^6

3 Investigation

Using a calculator and its fraction key, find the reciprocals of some fractions.

For example, $\frac{2}{3}$ has a reciprocal of $1 \div \frac{2}{3} = 1\frac{1}{2} = \frac{3}{2}$

You will need to convert any mixed numbers to improper fractions.

Repeat this until you can write down a rule for quickly finding the reciprocal of a fraction.

4 Investigation

The grid shows five pairs of lines.

a What is the geometrical relationship between each pair of lines?

b Copy and fill in the following table. Some values have been filled in.

Pair	Gradient line 1	Gradient line 2
A	$\frac{1}{2}$	
B		
C		$-\frac{2}{3}$
D		
E	3	

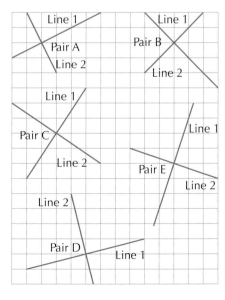

c Look at the values of the gradients of each pair of lines. What is the relationship between them?

Copy and complete the following statement.

When a pair of lines is...... their gradients are the .... of each other.

5 Calculate the sum of each of the following numbers with its reciprocal.

a 1   **b** −1

Is it always true that the sum of a number and its reciprocal is the positive value of the sum of the negative number and its reciprocal? Investigate.

6 Is there a reciprocal of zero ?

Extension Work

The powers of two are 2, 2^2, 2^3, 2^4, ..., which are equal to 2, 4, 8, 16, ...

1 Use a calculator to find the negative powers of two, namely: 2^{-1}, 2^{-2}, 2^{-3}, ...

2 Use your calculator to investigate the relationship between the reciprocals of positive powers of two and those of negative powers of two.

Rounding and estimation

Example 2.19 ▶ Round each of the following numbers to one significant figure.

a 582   **b** 0.0893   **c** 0.732   **d** 0.291

When rounding to one significant figure, you need to find the nearest number which has just one digit followed or preceded by zeros. This gives:

a 582 ≈ 600 (1 sf)   **b** 0.0893 ≈ 0.09 (1 sf)

c 0.732 ≈ 0.7 (1 sf)   **d** 0.291 ≈ 0.3 (1 sf)

Example 2.20 ▶ By rounding the numbers to one significant figure, estimate the value of each of the following.

a $(3124 \times 0.476) \div 0.283$ **b** $0.067 \times (0.82 - 0.57)$

a Round each number to one significant figure. Then proceed with the calculation using the rules which you have already learnt.

$$(3124 \times 0.476) \div 0.283 \approx (3000 \times 0.5) \div 0.3$$
$$= 1500 \div 0.3$$
$$= 15\,000 \div 3 = 5000$$

b Proceed as in part **a**.

$$0.067 \times (0.82 - 0.57) \approx 0.07 \times (0.8 - 0.6)$$
$$= 0.07 \times 0.2 = 0.014$$

Exercise 2H

1. Round each of the following numbers to one significant figure.

   a 598   b 0.312   c 0.06734   d 109

   e 0.327   f 0.092   g 345   h 0.378

   i 0.65   j 0.609   k 888   l 0.98

2. Work out each of the following.

   a 200×400 b 300×5000 c 60×70 d 80×2000

   e 90×90 f 0.6×0.3 g 0.09×0.7 h 0.05×0.8

   i 2000×0.05 j 200×0.7 k 0.08×3000 l 0.6×700

3. Work out each of the following.

   a $300 \div 50$ b $600 \div 0.2$ c $2000 \div 400$ d $24000 \div 60$

   e $800 \div 20$ f $1500 \div 30$ g $200 \div 0.4$ h $300 \div 0.5$

   i $20 \div 0.05$ j $4 \div 0.08$ k $60 \div 0.15$ l $0.09 \div 0.3$

4. By rounding values to one significant figure, estimate the answer to each of the following. Show your working.

   a 0.73×621 b $278 \div 0.47$

   c $3127 \div 0.58$ d 0.062×0.21

   e $(19 \times 0.049) \div 0.38$ f $(0.037 + 0.058) \times (0.067 + 0.083)$

   g $(211 \times 0.112) \times (775 \div 0.018)$ h $0.475 \times (33.66 \div 0.41)$

   i $4.8^2 \times 7.8 \div 0.19^2$ j $(19.7 \times 0.38) \div (1.98 + 0.46)$

5. Estimate the answer to each of the following.

   a $\dfrac{231 \times 0.615}{0.032}$ b $\dfrac{298 + 376}{0.072}$ c $\dfrac{185^2}{0.38^2}$

   d $\dfrac{0.831 \times 0.478}{387}$ e $\dfrac{715 \times 0.723}{341 \times 0.058}$ f $\dfrac{632}{0.41} + \dfrac{219}{0.46}$

Extension **Work**

You can round to any number of significant figures. For example, rounding to three significant figures is very common in trigonometry problems, which you will meet later.

Take, for example, 253.78, which has five significant figures.

$253.78 \approx 253.8$ (4 sf) ≈ 254 (3 sf) ≈ 250 (2 sf) ≈ 300 (1 sf)

Now, take as an example 0.098 54, which has four significant figures.

$0.098\,54 \approx 0.0985$ (3 sf) ≈ 0.099 (2 sf) ≈ 0.1 (1 sf)

Round each of the following to the accuracy shown.

a 347 (2 sf)   b 4217 (3 sf)   c 4217 (2 sf)

d 0.6187 (3 sf)   e 0.6187 (2 sf)   f 302 (1 sf)

g 4698 (2 sf)   h 4698 (3 sf)   i 0.0785 (2 sf)

j 978.32 (4 sf)   k 978.32 (3 sf)   l 978.32 (2 sf)

6
I can change fractions to decimals.
I can add and subtract fractions with different denominators.
I can solve problems involving ratio.
I can use percentages to solve real-life problems.
I can use brackets correctly.
I can solve questions involving proportions.

7
I can multiply and divide by numbers between 0 and 1.
I can solve problems by multiplying and dividing with numbers of any size.
I can understand and use percentage change using multiplier methods.
I can follow a method to calculate reverse percentages.
I can round numbers to one significant figure.

8
I can solve compound interest problems.
I can solve reverse percentage problems.
I understand and can use ratios to solve problems involving areas and volumes.
I can work out the reciprocal of a number.

National Test questions

1 *2007 Paper 1*

a In this design, the ratio of **grey to black** is **3 : 1**

What **percentage** of the design is **black**?

b In this design, **60%** is **grey** and the rest is black.

What is the ratio of **grey to black?**

Write your ratio in its simplest form.

2 *2005 Paper 1*

a Look at this information.

Two numbers **multiply** to make zero.

One of the statements below is true.

Write it down.

Both numbers must be zero.
At least one number must be zero.
Exactly one number must be zero.
Neither number can be zero.

b Now look at this information.

> Two numbers **add** to make zero.

If **one** number is **zero**, what is the other number?

If **neither** number is **zero**, give an example of what the numbers could be.

3 *2002 Paper 2*

a One calculation below gives the answer to the question:

What is 70 increased by 9%?

Choose the correct one.

> 70×0.9 70×1.9 70×0.09 70×1.09

Choose one of the other calculations. Write a question about percentages that this calculation represents.

Calculation chosen: ......

Question it represents: ......

Now do the same for one of the remaining two calculations:

Calculation chosen: ......

Question it represents: ......

b Fill in the missing decimal number.

To decrease by 14%, multiply by ......

4 *2006 Paper 1*

a Give an example to show the statement below is **not** correct.

> When you multiply a number by 2, the answer is always greater than 2.

b Now give an example to show the statement below is **not** correct.

> When you subtract a number from 2, the answer is always less than 2.

c Is the statement below correct for all numbers?

> The square of a number is greater than the number itself.

Explain how you know.

5 *2004 Paper 1*

a Calculate $\frac{5}{6} \times \frac{3}{5}$

Show your working.

Write your answer as a fraction in its **simplest form.**

b Four-fifths of the members of a club are female.
Three-quarters of these females are over 20 years old.

What fraction of the members of the club are females over 20 years old?

Show your working.

6 *2007 Paper 2*

Here is part of a newspaper report about wildlife in a country in Africa.

> The number of gorillas has **fallen by 70%** in the last ten years.
>
> Only about **5000 gorillas** are left.

About how many gorillas were there in this country ten years earlier?

7 *2006 Paper 2*

Since 1952 the total number of people living in Wales has increased by about **one-eighth**. The total number of people living in Wales now is about **3 million**.

About how many people lived in Wales in 1952?

8 *2005 Paper 2*

   a   Each side of a square is **increased** by **10%**.

         By what percentage is the **area** increased?

   b   The length of a rectangle is **increased** by **20%**.
         The width is **decreased** by **20%**.

         By what percentage is the area changed?

 9 *2001 Paper 2*

A shop had a sale. All prices were reduced by 15%.

A pair of shoes cost £38.25 in the sale. What price were the shoes before the sale? Show your working.

10 *2003 Paper 2*

Find the values of t and r.

$$\frac{2}{3} = \frac{t}{6} \qquad\qquad t = \ldots\ldots$$

$$\frac{2}{3} = \frac{5}{r} \qquad\qquad r = \ldots\ldots$$

11 *2002 Paper 1*

I fill a glass with orange juice and lemonade in the ratio 1 : 4.

I drink $\frac{1}{4}$ of the contents of the glass, then I fill the glass using orange juice. Now what is the ratio of orange juice to lemonade in the glass?

Show your working, and write the ratio in its simplest form.

 12 *2002 Paper 2*

A 10% increase followed by another 10% increase is not the same as a total increase of 20%.

What is the total percentage increase? Show your working.

FM   The London Olympics 2012

Olympic village

Beds provided for 17 320 athletes and officials during Olympics.

Beds provided for 8756 athletes and officials during Paralympics.

The dining hall will cater for 5500 athletes at a time.

After the Games, the village will provide 4000 homes.

Tickets

Number of tickets for sale

- 8 million for the Olympics
- 1.6 million for the Paralympics

Tickets include free travel on London Transport.

Cost

75% of tickets will cost less than £50.

Organisers expect to sell 82% of all Olympic tickets and 63% of all Paralympics tickets.

Athletics

Ticket prices start from £15.

20 000 big screen tickets available for £10.

Travel

90% of venues will have three or more forms of public transport including:

- Docklands light railway
- 'Javelin' rail link from St Pancras to Olympic park
- London Underground
- New rail links
- Buses – The iBus: an automatic vehicle location system
- Cycle lanes and footpaths
- Two major park and ride sites off the M25 with a combined capacity of 12 000 cars

During the Games, up to 120 000 passengers will arrive and depart through Stratford station each day.

1 How many beds are there for athletes and officials during the Olympics? Give your answer to two significant figure.

2 The Olympic stadium will have 80 000 seats.
If for an event the stadium is 85% full, how many seats will be empty?

3 **a** How many passengers will arrive and depart through Stratford station over the 17 days?

b 45% of all spectators visiting the games each day will arrive and depart through Stratford station.

Work out the number of spectators that are expected at the games each day. Give your answer to the nearest 10 000.

4 Boccia is a Paralympic sport.

The aim of the game is to throw red or blue leather balls as close as possible to a white target ball.

At the end of every round, the competitor whose ball is closest to the target ball scores one point for every one of his balls that is closer than his opponent's.

a At the end of a game, the blue team has 8 points and the red team has 4 points. Write the number of points as a ratio in its simplest form.

b At the end of another game 15 points have been scored altogether. The points are divided between the blue team and the red team in the ratio 3 : 2.

How many points does each team have?

5 Here are some men's long jump world record distances and the years in which they occurred.

8.90 metres   8.95 metres   7.98 metres   8.13 metres   8.21 metres

1991   1968   1931   1960   1935

a Copy and complete the table by putting the distances and years in the correct order. Two of the answers have already been filled in.

Name	Year	World record
Mike Powell	1991	
Bob Beamon		
Ralph Boston		
Jesse Owens		
Chuhei Nambu		7.98 metres

b Ralph Boston broke Jesse Owens' world record.

For how long did Jesse Owens' world record stand before it was broken?

6 **a** How many tickets for the Olympics will cost less than £50?

b How many tickets for the Olympics that cost less than £50 do the organisers expect to sell?

CHAPTER 3

Algebra **3**

This chapter is going to show you	What you should already know
<ul><li>How to construct and solve different types of linear equation</li><li>How to use trial and improvement</li><li>How to solve problems involving direct proportion</li></ul>	<ul><li>How to solve simple linear equations</li><li>How to find the square root of a number</li></ul>

Equations, formulae and identities

Equations

An **equation** is formed when an expression is made equal to a number or another expression.

As a general rule, an equation can be solved.

You will be expected to deal with equations which have only one **variable** or letter in them. For example:

$$3x + 2 = 7 \qquad x^2 = 24 \qquad y + 3 = 4y - 2$$

The **solution** to an equation is that value of the variable which makes the equation true. For example:

$$2x + 6 = 18$$

for which the solution is $x = 6$.

Always check that the answer makes the equation true. In this case:

$$2 \times 6 + 6 = 18$$

which is correct.

Example 3.1 ▷

Solve $4(2x - 3) = 3(x + 11)$

Expand both brackets to obtain:

$$8x - 12 = 3x + 33$$

Subtract $3x$ from both sides, which gives:

$$5x - 12 = 33$$

Add 12 to both sides to obtain:

$$5x = 45$$

Dividing both sides by 5 gives the solution:

$$x = 9$$

Formulae

Although it may look like an equation, a formula states the connection between two or more quantities. Each quantity is represented by a different letter.

Every formula has a **subject**, which is the variable (letter) which stands on its own, usually on the left-hand side of the 'equals' sign. For example:

$$P = 2l + 2w \qquad A = lw$$

where P and A are the subjects.

Example 3.2 ▷

The formula for the volume of a cylinder is $V = \pi r^2 h$.

Giving your answers in terms of π, calculate the volume when:

a $r = 5$ and $h = 8$ **b** $r = r$ and $h = 2r$

a $V = \pi \times 5^2 \times 8 = 200\pi$

b $V = \pi \times r^2 \times 2r = 2\pi r^3$

Identities

An identity is an algebraic equation or formula which is true for all values whether numerical or algebraic. It has a special sign $\equiv$.

Example 3.3 ▷

Show that $(a + b)^2 \equiv a^2 + 2ab + b^2$ is an identity by substituting the following values.

a $a = 3$ and $b = 5$ **b** $a = x$ and $b = 2x$

a   Substitute into the left-hand side:
$$(a + b)^2 = (3 + 5)^2 = 8^2 = 64$$
Substitute into the right-hand side:
$$a^2 + 2ab + b^2 = 3^2 + 2 \times 3 \times 5 + 5^2 = 9 + 30 + 25 = 64$$
Both sides give the same value of 64.

b   Substitute into the left-hand side:
$$(a + b)^2 = (x + 2x)^2 = (3x)^2 = 9x^2$$
Substitute into the right hand side:
$$a^2 + 2ab + b^2 = x^2 + 2 \times x \times 2x + (2x)^2 = x^2 + 4x^2 + 4x^2 = 9x^2$$
Both sides give the same value of $9x^2$.

Exercise 3A

① Solve each of the following equations.

   a $5(x - 1) = 4(x + 1)$ **b** $3(x - 2) = 2(x + 2)$

   c $5(x + 3) = 3(x + 5)$ **d** $3(2x + 1) = 2(4x + 3)$

   e $4(3x - 2) = 5(2x + 3)$ **f** $6(2x - 1) = 4(2x + 5)$

② Solve each of the following equations.

   a $3(m - 1) - 2(m + 4) = 0$ **b** $4(k + 3) - 3(k - 7) = 0$

   c $5(y + 2) - 4(y + 3) = 0$ **d** $2(5x - 4) - 3(2x + 5) = 1$

   e $4(3p - 2) - 2(5p + 3) = 0$ **f** $7(2w - 3) - 5(3w - 1) = 0$

3 a Look at each of the following statements.

A an equation

B a formula

C an identity

Note: None of the identities below carry a $\equiv$ sign.

Match either **A** or **B** or **C** to each of the following.

i $3x + 5 = x - 9$ **ii** $y = 4x + 3$ **iii** $t = u + st$

iv $p = 3d$ **v** $\sqrt{x} \times \sqrt{y} = \sqrt{xy}$ **vi** $m + 3 = 5m - 4$

vii $y = mx + c$ **viii** $ax + ay = a(x + y)$ **ix** $t = 3w + 5$

b Write a brief explanation about the difference between an equation, a formula and an identity.

4 The formula $A = 180(n - 2)$ is used to calculate the sum of the angles inside a polygon with n sides.

a Use the formula to calculate the sum of the angles for:

     i an octagon.   **ii** a dodecagon.

b A polygon has an angle sum of 1440°. How many sides does it have?

FM **5** DJ Dave uses the following formula to work out how much to charge for his gigs:

$$C = £55 + £3N + £5T + £10E$$

where:

     N is the number of people attending the gig

     T is the number of hours worked before midnight

     E is the number of hours worked after midnight

Calculate the cost of each of the following gigs.

a A teenager's party with 25 people from 7 pm to 11 pm

b A wedding reception with 60 people from 9 pm to 2 am

6 Show that $2(a + b) \equiv 2a + 2b$ is an identity by substituting the values below into both sides.

a $a = 5$ and $b = 4$ **b** $a = 5x$ and $b = 2x$

7 Show that $(a + b)(a - b) \equiv a^2 - b^2$ is an identity by substituting the values below into both sides.

a $a = 7$ and $b = 4$ **b** $a = 3x$ and $b = x$

Extension Work

The area of this rectangle is 6.4 cm².

Find its perimeter.

$3x + 1$

$8x$

Simultaneous equations

Simultaneous equations are equations for which we want the same solution. Therefore, we solve them together.

The simultaneous equations you will meet are always in pairs and are always linear.

For example, $x + y = 8$ has many solutions:

$x = 2, y = 6$ $x = 3, y = 5$ $x = 4, y = 4$ $x = 5, y = 3$ ...

Also, $2x + y = 13$ has many solutions:

$x = 2, y = 9$ $x = 3, y = 7$ $x = 4, y = 5$ $x = 5, y = 3$ ...

But only *one* solution, $x = 5$ and $y = 3$, satisfies both equations at the same time.

One way to solve pairs of simultaneous equations is by the elimination method.

Elimination method   Follow through the Examples 3.4 and 3.5 to see how this method works.

Example 3.4 ▷

Solve $5x + y = 23$
        $2x + y = 11$

First, number the equations:

    $5x + y = 23$ (i)
    $2x + y = 11$ (ii)

Since both equations have the same y-term, subtract equation (ii) from equation (i). This eliminates y to give:

    $3x = 12$
     $x = 4$ (Divide both sides by 3)

Now substitute $x = 4$ into one of the original equations (usually that with the smallest numbers).

So, substitute $x = 4$ into (ii): $2x + y = 11$
which gives: $8 + y = 11$
                      $y = 11 - 8$
                      $y = 3$

Next, test the solution in equation (i). So, substitute $x = 4$ and $y = 3$ into $5x + y$, which gives:

    $20 + 3 = 23$

This is correct, so we can confidently say that the solution is $x = 4$ and $y = 3$.

Example 3.5 ▷ Solve $4x + 3y = 34$
$$2x - 3y = 8$$

First number the equations:

$4x + 3y = 34$ (i)

$2x - 3y = 8$ (ii)

Since both equations have the same y-term but different signs, add equations (i) and (ii). This eliminates y to give:

$6x = 42$

$x = 7$ (Divide both sides by 6.)

Now substitute into equation (i).

So, put $x = 7$ into (i): $4x + 3y = 34$

This gives: $28 + 3y = 34$

$3y = 6$

$y = 2$ (Divide both sides by 3)

Test the solution by putting $x = 7$ and $y = 2$ into the equation (ii), $2x - 3y$. This gives:

$14 - 6 = 8$

This is correct. So, the solution is $x = 7$ and $y = 2$.

In both Example 3.4 and Example 3.5, the y-term was eliminated. But with other pairs of equations, it could be easier to eliminate the x-term. See, for example, Questions 7, 8 and 10 in Exercise 3B.

Exercise 3B

Solve each pair of simultaneous equations.

1 $5x + y = 21$
$2x + y = 9$

2 $6x + 2y = 14$
$2x + 2y = 10$

3 $3x + y = 10$
$5x - y = 14$

4 $4x + 2y = 24$
$2x - 2y = 6$

5 $5x - 4y = 31$
$x - 4y = 3$

6 $4x + 2y = 26$
$7x - 2y = 29$

7 $x + 4y = 12$
$x + 3y = 10$

8 $2x + 4y = 20$
$2x + 3y = 16$

9 $5x - y = 10$
$3x + y = 14$

10 $2x + 5y = 19$
$2x + 3y = 13$

11 $5x - 3y = 11$
$2x + 3y = 17$

12 $6x - y = 26$
$3x - y = 11$

Solve each of the following problems by expressing it as a pair of simultaneous equations, for which you find the solution.

1 The two people in front of me in the post office bought stamps. One bought 10 second-class and five first-class stamps at a total cost of £3.35. The other bought 10 second-class and 10 first-class stamps at a total cost of £4.80.

How much would I pay for:

   a   one first-class stamp?   b   one second-class stamp?

2 In a fruit shop, one customer bought five bananas and eight oranges at a total cost of £2.85. Another customer bought five bananas and 12 oranges at a total cost of £3.65.

If I bought two bananas and three oranges, how much would it cost me?

Solving by substitution

Simultaneous equations can be solved another way. When one or other of the two variables can be easily made the subject of either of the two equations, it can be easier to substitute that variable in the other equation.

Example 3.6

Solve $3x + 2y = 18$
$2x - y = 5$

First number the equations:
$3x + 2y = 18$ (i)
$2x - y = 5$ (ii)

Take equation (ii) and add y to both sides, which gives:
$2x - y = 5$
$2x = 5 + y$

Subtracting 5 from both sides gives:
$2x - 5 = y$

By convention, this is written as:
$y = 2x - 5$

Substitute $y = 2x - 5$ into equation (i), which gives:
$3x + 2(2x - 5) = 18$

Expand the bracket to obtain:
$3x + 4x - 10 = 18$
$7x - 10 = 18$

Add 10 to both sides, which gives:
$7x = 28$
$x = 4$ (Divide both sides by 7.)

Now substitute $x = 4$ into the equation with y as the subject, $y = 2x - 5$, giving:
$y = 2 \times 4 - 5 = 3$

Hence, the solution is $x = 4$ and $y = 3$.

Solve each of the following pairs of simultaneous equations by first changing the subject of one of the equations to give an equal term. Then, by addition or subtraction, eliminate the equal term.

1 $5x + 3y = 23$
$2x - y = 7$

2 $3x + y = 9$
$4x + 5y = 23$

3 $5x - 2y = 14$
$x - y = 1$

4 $4x + 3y = 37$
$2x + y = 17$

5 $2x + y = 9$
$6x + 2y = 22$

6 $10x - 3y = 19$
$x + 2y = 18$

7 $4x + 5y = 13$
$x + 3y = 5$

8 $3x + y = 14$
$4x - 2y = 2$

9 $5x - 2y = 24$
$3x + y = 21$

10 $5x - 2y = 36$
$x + 6y = 20$

11 $x + 3y = 16$
$4x + 7y = 39$

12 $3x - y = 7$
$5x + 6y = 50$

Extension Work

Work out each of the following problems by expressing it as a pair of simultaneous equations, which are then solved.

1 At a local tea room, I couldn't help noticing that at one table, where the people had eaten six buns and had three teas, the total cost was £1.65.

At another table, the people had eaten 11 buns and had seven teas at a total cost of £3.40.

My guests and I had five buns and had six teas. What would it cost me?

2 A chef uses this formula to cook a roast: $T = a + bW$

where T is the time it takes (minutes), W is the weight of the roast (kg), and both a and b are constants.

The chef says it takes 2 hours 51 minutes to cook a 12 kg roast, and 1 hour 59 minutes to cook an 8 kg roast.

How long will it take to cook a 5 kg roast?

Equations involving fractions

When you have to solve an equation which involves a fraction, you have to use the rules for working out ordinary fractions.

For example, to solve $\frac{x}{3} = 5$, you first multiply both sides by 3 in order to remove the denominator:

$$\frac{x}{3} \times 3 = 5 \times 3$$

which gives: $x = 15$

Follow through Examples 3.7 to 3.9, which show you how to remove the fractional part of equations.

Example 3.7 ▷

Solve $\dfrac{4x + 5}{3} = 7$

First, multiply both sides by 3 to obtain:

$\quad 4x + 5 = 21$

Subtract 5 from both sides, which gives:

$\quad 4x = 16$

Dividing both sides by 4 gives the solution:

$\quad x = 4$

Example 3.8 ▷

Solve $\dfrac{x - 1}{2} = \dfrac{2x + 8}{6}$

The product of the two denominators is 12. So, multiply both sides by 12 which, after cancelling, gives:

$\quad 6(x - 1) = 2(2x + 8)$

Expand both sides to obtain:

$\quad 6x - 6 = 4x + 16$

which simplifies to:

$\quad 2x = 22$

$\quad\ \ x = 11$

So, $x = 11$ is the solution.

Example 3.9 ▷

Solve $\frac{4}{5}(2x + 1) = \frac{2}{3}(x - 3)$

Multiply both sides by the product of the denominators of the fractions, which is $5 \times 3 = 15$. This gives:

$\quad 15 \times \frac{4}{5}(2x + 1) = 15 \times \frac{2}{3}(x - 3)$

Cancelling the fractions leaves:

$\quad 3 \times 4(2x + 1) = 5 \times 2(x - 3)$

$\quad 12(2x + 1) = 10(x - 3)$

Multiply out both brackets to obtain:

$\quad 24x + 12 = 10x - 30$

which simplifies to:

$\quad 14x = -42$

Dividing both sides by 14 gives the solution:

$\quad x = -3$

Exercise 3D

1 Solve each of these equations.

a $\dfrac{4x}{5} = 12$ **b** $\dfrac{2t}{5} = 6$ **c** $\dfrac{3m}{8} = 9$ **d** $\dfrac{2x}{3} = 8$ **e** $\dfrac{3w}{4} = 6$

2 Solve each of the following equations.

a $\dfrac{(2x+1)}{5} = \dfrac{(x-4)}{2}$ **b** $\dfrac{(3x-1)}{3} = \dfrac{(2x+3)}{4}$ **c** $\dfrac{(2x-3)}{2} = \dfrac{(3x-2)}{5}$

3 Solve each of the following equations.

a $\frac{3}{4}(x+2) = \frac{1}{2}(4x+1)$ **b** $\frac{1}{2}(2x+5) = \frac{3}{4}(3x-2)$

c $\frac{3}{5}(2x+3) = \frac{1}{2}(3x-6)$ **d** $\frac{2}{3}(4x-1) = \frac{3}{4}(2x-4)$

4 Solve each of the following equations.

a $\dfrac{4}{(x+1)} = \dfrac{7}{(x+4)}$ **b** $\dfrac{5}{(x+3)} = \dfrac{4}{(x-1)}$ **c** $\dfrac{3}{(x+2)} = \dfrac{2}{(x-5)}$

d $\dfrac{7}{(x-3)} = \dfrac{5}{(x+4)}$ **e** $\dfrac{6}{(5x+1)} = \dfrac{2}{(2x-1)}$ **f** $\dfrac{2}{(4x+3)} = \dfrac{3}{(5x-1)}$

Extension Work

1 Solve each of the following equations.

a $4(2t+3) = 3(4t+1) - 5(3t-2)$ **b** $2(5h+4) = 6(2h+3) - 3(5h+1)$

c $5(3m+1) = 4(5m-2) - 4(2m-3)$ **d** $7(8g-5) = 5(6g+4) - 2(3g+4)$

e $3(4k-2) = 5(3k+1) - 2(4k-3)$ **f** $4(3x-1) = 3(5x-2) - 4(2x-7)$

2 Solve each of the following equations.

a $5(t+0.3) = 2(t+1.6) - 4(t-0.2)$ **b** $2(h+1.4) = 5(h+3.1) + 3(h+1.1)$

c $6(m+1.3) = 3(m-0.2) - 3(m-3.2)$ **d** $5(g-0.5) = 4(g+1.4) - 2(3g+0.4)$

e $4(4k-0.2) = 4(k+1.1) - 2(4k-3.1)$ **f** $3(2x-1.3) = 2(3x-2.1) - 3(x-0.7)$

Inequalities

$5x + 6 \geq 10$ is a linear inequality. It looks and behaves similarly to linear equations which you have already met, but instead of an equals sign, it contains one of the four inequality signs. It is important that you are familiar with them:

> $>$ is greater than
> $\geq$ is greater than or equal to
> $<$ is less than
> $\leq$ is less than or equal to

The same rules are used to solve linear inequalities as linear equations. However, the solutions to linear inequalities can be expressed graphically on a number line as well as using standard inequality notation, as examples 3.10 and 3.11 show.

Example 3.10 ▷

Solve $5x + 6 \geq 10$

Subtract 6 from both sides to give: $5x \geq 4$
Divide both sides by 5 to obtain: $x \geq 0.8$

The solution expressed on a number line is shown below. To show that 0.8 is included in the solution, a filled in circle is used.

Example 3.11 ▷

Solve $\frac{1}{2}t - 1 < 4$

Add 1 to both sides to give: $\frac{1}{2}t < 5$
Multiply both sides by 2 to obtain: $t < 10$

The solution expressed on a number line is shown below. An empty circle is used to show that the 10 is not included in the solution.

So:

$$\bullet\!\!\leftarrow\!\! x\leq \qquad \bullet\!\!\rightarrow\!\! x\geq$$
$$\circ\!\!\leftarrow\!\! x< \qquad \circ\!\!\rightarrow\!\! x>$$

Exercise 3E

1 Solve the following inequalities and illustrate their solutions on number lines.

a	$x + 3 < 5$	**b**	$x - 2 \geq 7$	**c**	$t - 4 < 2$
d	$2t + 3 > 7$	**e**	$3t - 1 \leq 8$	**f**	$5x + 3 < 8$
g	$3x + 5 > 2$	**h**	$4t + 7 \leq -1$	**i**	$2x - 4 \geq 4$
j	$7t + 3 \geq 3$	**k**	$3(x + 4) \geq 6$	**l**	$2(x - 2) \leq 8$
m	$\frac{x}{4} > 3$	**n**	$\frac{1}{2}x + 1 < 3$	**o**	$4(2x - 3) \geq 12$

2 Write down the values of x that satisfy the conditions given.

a $x + 11 < 20$, where x is a positive integer
b $x + 15 \leq 20$, where x is a positive, odd number
c $2x - 3 < 14$, where x is a positive, even number
d $5(3x + 4) < 100$, where x is a positive, prime number
e $2x + 1 \leq 50$, where x is a positive, square number
f $4x - 1 \leq 50$, where x is a positive, prime number
g $5x + 3 < 60$, where x is a positive, multiple of three

3 Solve the following linear inequalities.

a $\frac{x + 3}{2} \leq 4$ 　　　　　　　　　　　**b** $\frac{x - 4}{3} > 7$

c $\frac{3x + 1}{5} < 2$ 　　　　　　　　　　　**d** $\frac{2x - 5}{3} \geq 5$

④ Solve the following linear inequalities, illustrating their solutions on number lines.

a $2x + 4 < 17$ and $x > 3$ **b** $4(x - 3) \leq 0$ and $x > -2$

c $5x - 4 > 18$ and $x \leq 8$ **d** $2(5x + 7) \geq 15$ and $x < 1$

e $1 \leq 3x + 2 \leq 17$ **f** $1 \leq 4x - 3 < 13$

Extension Work

Much like linear equations, linear inequalities can also be plotted on a graph. The result is a region that lies on one side of a straight line or the other, which is usually shaded.

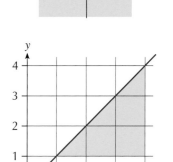

1 Show each of the following inequalities as a graph.

a $y \geq 6$ **b** $x \leq 4$ **c** $y \leq 3x + 2$

2 The shaded area shown on the graph on the right shows a region that satisfies more than one inequality.

Write down the three inequalities which describe the shaded area.

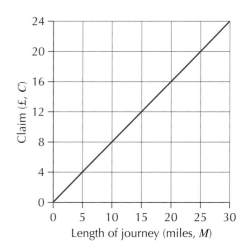

Graphs showing direct proportion

When Mr Shah uses his car for business he gets paid 80p per mile by his company.

The table below shows the amounts he claims for different lengths of journeys.

Length of journey (miles, M)	5	10	15	20	25	30
Claim (£, C)	4.00	8.00	12.00	16.00	20.00	24.00

The information can be graphed, as shown on the right. Because the amount claimed is in direct proportion to the length of journey, the graph is a straight line.

Note that the equation of the graph is $C = 0.8M$, where C is the amount claimed in pounds and M is the number of miles travelled. The gradient of the line, 0.8, is the amount paid per mile.

Straight-line graphs that pass through the origin show the relationship between two variables that are in direct proportion. This means that for every unit that one variable increases the other variable increases by a fixed amount.

Not all graphs that show the relationship between two variables are in direct proportion.

For example, taxi fares have a fixed charge to start then the rest of the cost of the journey is in direct proportion to the mileage travelled.

Example 3.12

Mr Evans wants to convert the scores on a written French test to a standard percentage. All of his class already have 20 percent on an oral test.

Written test score (F)	0	30	60
Final Percentage (P)	20	60	100

The table above shows data he wants to use.

a Create a graph which Mr Evans could use as a conversion graph from his French scores to percentage scores.

b What is the equation of this graph?

a Use the three points given above to draw a straight-line graph. Then use that graph to make a conversion graph.

b The gradient of the line is approximately 1.33, so the equation is $P = 20 + 1.33F$.

1 One morning in Scotland, Jenny recorded the temperature every hour from 8 am until noon. Her results are shown below.

Time	8 am	9 am	10 am	11 am	12 noon
Temperature (°C)	4	5.5	7	8.5	10

a Plot the points on a graph and join them up with a suitable line.

b On this morning, are the temperature rises above 4° directly proportional to the number of hours after 8 am?

c Write down the equation of the line showing the relationship between the number of hours after 8 am, t, and temperature, C.

d If the relationship held all day, what would be the temperature at 4 pm, when $t = 8$?

2 Thousands of fans pour into a stadium ready to watch Joe King. A count is kept of the number of fans in the stadium after various time intervals.

Time (pm)	1.30	1.45	2.00	2.15
Number of fans	14 000	26 000	38 000	50 000

a Plot the points on a graph and join them up with a suitable line.

b For this hour, is the increase in the number of fans above the initial 14 000 directly proportional to the time after 1.30 pm?

c Write down the equation of the line showing the relationship between the number of minutes added after 1.30 pm, *t*, and the number of fans, *f*.

d If the relationship held all afternoon, when did the first fan enter the stadium?

3 Given in the table below is the length of a stretched spring with each of a series of different weights hanging from it.

Weight (g)	0	200	400	600	800	1000
Length (cm)	10	12	14	16	18	20

a Plot the points on a graph and join them up with a suitable line.
b Is the extension directly proportional to the weight?
c Write down the equation of the line showing the relationship between hanging weight, *w*, and length, *L*.
d If the relationship continued to hold, what would be the hanging weight when the length of the spring is 27 cm?

4 Tea is served at a garden party between 3.00 pm and 5.30 pm. The number of cups of tea sold during the afternoon is shown in the table below.

Time (pm)	3.00	3.15	4.00	4.45	5.00	5.30
Cups of tea	0	13	52	91	104	130

a Plot the points on a graph and join them up with a suitable line.
b On this afternoon, is the number of cups of tea sold during a time interval directly proportional to the length of time?
c Write down the equation of the line showing the relationship between the length of time, *t*, and the number of cups of tea sold, *S*.
d If the relationship held all day and the garden party continued, how many cups of tea would have been sold by 9.30 pm, when *t* = 6.5?

5 An experiment was done with a bouncing tennis ball. A tennis ball was dropped from different heights and the height of the first bounce was measured. The results are given in the table below.

Height of drop (cm)	25	50	75	100	125	150	175	200
Bounce (cm)	15	31	48	66	82	98	113	130

a Plot the points on a graph and join them up with a suitable line.
b Is the bounce directly proportional to the height of drop?
c Write down the equation of the line showing the relationship between height of drop, *h*, and bounce, *b*.
d If the relationship held, from what height would you need to drop the ball in order to have a bounce of 5 m?

Solve this problem by drawing a graph.

Two women are walking on the same long, straight road towards each other. One sets off at 9.00 am at a speed of 4 km/h. The other also sets off at 9.00 am, 15 km away, at a speed of 5 km/h. At 9.10 am, a butterfly leaves the shoulder of the quicker woman and flies to the other woman at 20 km/h. It continues to fly from one woman to the other until they both meet, and take a photograph of it.

a   At what time will the butterfly be photographed?

b   How many times will the butterfly have landed on the woman walking at 4 km/h?

Solving simultaneous equations by graphs

Every equation can be graphed. Every pair of coordinates on the graph represent a possible solution for the equation. Hence, when the graphs of two equations are drawn between the same axes, where they intercept gives a solution which satisfies both equations.

Example 3.13 ▷ By drawing their graphs on the same grid, find the solution of these simultaneous equations:

$$3x + 5y = 25$$
$$5x - 3y = 2$$

First, number the equations:

$$3x + 5y = 25 \quad \text{(i)}$$
$$5x - 3y = 2 \quad \text{(ii)}$$

Equation (i) is drawn by plotting the points where the graph crosses both axes:

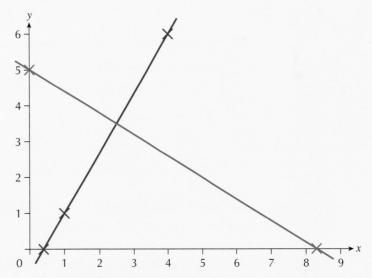

When $x = 0$, $y = 5$, giving the coordinates (0, 5).
When $y = 0$, $x = 8.3$, giving the coordinates (8.3, 0).

Equation (ii) is drawn by plotting three points for y and substituting:

When $y = 0$, $x = 0.4$, giving the coordinates (0.4, 0).
When $y = 1$, $x = 1$, giving the coordinates (1, 1).
When $y = 6$, $x = 4$, giving the coordinates (4, 6).

The point where the graphs intercept is (2.5, 3.5). So, the solution to the simultaneous equations is $x = 2.5$ and $y = 3.5$.

Exercise 3G Solve each pair of simultaneous equations by drawing their graphs. Give your solutions to one decimal place.

1 $x + y = 5$
$y = 5x - 4$

2 $x + y = 4$
$2y = 4x - 7$

3 $y = x - 1$
$y = 8 - x$

4 $x + y = 5$
$x = 8 - 3y$

5 $y = 6x - 5$
$x + y = 4$

6 $y = 3x - 5$
$2x + y = 6$

7 $4y = 12 + x$
$3x = 2y - 3$

8 $x + y = 4$
$5y - 3x = 3$

Extension   Work

Solve each pair of simultaneous equations by drawing their graphs.

1 $y = x^2 - 1$ and $5x + 4y = 20$

2 $y = x^2 + x$ and $8x + 3y = 12$

LEVEL BOOSTER

6
I can expand and simplify expressions involving brackets.
I can solve linear equations with brackets where the solution may be fractional or negative.
I can solve equations involving a fraction where the solution may be negative.
I can draw and interpret graphs that show direct proportion.

7
I can solve equations with more than one fraction where the solution may be negative.
I can solve linear inequalities and represent their solution on a number line.
I can solve a pair of linear simultaneous equations by elimination of one variable.
I can solve a pair of linear simultaneous equations by drawing graphs.

8
I can solve a pair of linear simultaneous equations by substitution of one equation into the other.

1   *2007 Paper 2*

Look at the equation in the box.

$$x + (x + 1) + (x + 2) = y$$

Use it to help you write the missing expressions **in terms of y**.

The first one is done for you.

$$5 + x + (x + 1) + (x + 2) = y + 5$$

$$(x + 5) + (x + 6) + (x + 7) =$$

$$2x + 2(x + 1) + 2(x + 2) =$$

$$(x + a) + (x + 1 + a) + (x + 2 + a) =$$

2   *2006 Paper 1*

Solve these simultaneous equations using an algebraic method.

$$3x + 7y = 18$$
$$x + 2y = 5$$

You must show your working.

3   *2007 Paper 1*

Look at the simultaneous equations.

$$x + 2y = a$$
$$x + y = b$$

a   Write an expression for y in terms of a and b.

b   Now write an expression for x in terms of a and b.

Write your expression as simply as possible.

CHAPTER 4

Geometry and Measures **1**

This chapter is going to show you

- How to use Pythagoras' theorem
- How to find the locus of a point using more complex rules
- How to recognise congruent triangles
- Some important circle theorems
- How regular polygons tessellate
- The difference between a practical demonstration and a proof

What you should already know

- How to find the square and the square root of a number
- How to find the locus of a point
- How to construct the perpendicular bisector of a line segment and the bisector of an angle
- How to recognise congruent shapes
- The definition of a circle and the names of its parts
- How to calculate the interior and exterior angles of a polygon

Pythagoras' theorem

Thousands of years ago, the builders of the pyramids in Egypt used a rope with 12 equally spaced knots, which, when stretched out as shown on the right, formed a right-angled triangle.

This helped the builders make sure that any right angles required in the construction of the Pyramids were accurate.

In a right-angled triangle, the longest side opposite the right angle is called the **hypotenuse**.

Hypotenuse

Activity

Make accurate copies of the three right-angled triangles below.

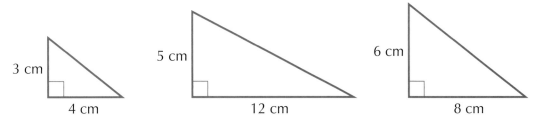

Next, measure the length of the hypotenuse of each one. Then copy and complete the table below.

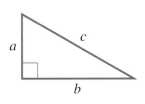

a	b	c	a^2	b^2	c^2
3	4				
5	12				
6	8				

Can you see a pattern in the last three columns? If you can, you have just rediscovered **Pythagoras' theorem.**

Pythagoras was a Greek philosopher and mathematician, who was born in about 581 BC on the island of Samos, just off the coast of Turkey. The following famous theorem about right-angled triangles is attributed to him.

> In any right-angled triangle, the square of the hypotenuse is equal to the sum of the squares of the other two sides.

Pythagoras' theorem is usually written as:

$$c^2 = a^2 + b^2$$

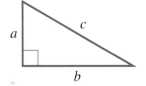

The following two examples will show you how to use Pythagoras' theorem.

Example 4.1 ▷

Finding the length of the hypotenuse

Calculate the length x in the triangle shown on the right.

Using Pythagoras' theorem:

$$x^2 = 6^2 + 5^2$$
$$= 36 + 25$$
$$= 61$$

So, $x = \sqrt{61} = 7.8$ cm (1 dp)

You should be able to work this out on a scientific calculator. Try the following sequence of keystrokes:

[6] [x^2] [+] [5] [x^2] [=] [$\sqrt{\blacksquare}$] [=]

This may not work on some makes of calculator, and you may need to ask your teacher to help you.

Example 4.2 ▷ **Finding the length of a shorter side**

Calculate the length x in the triangle shown on the right.

Using Pythagoras' theorem:
$$x^2 + 7^2 = 9^2$$
$$x^2 = 9^2 - 7^2$$
$$= 81 - 49$$
$$= 32$$
So, $x = \sqrt{32} = 5.7$ cm (1 dp)

Try the following sequence of keystrokes:

9 x^2 − 7 x^2 = $\sqrt{\blacksquare}$ =

Exercise 4A

1 Calculate the length of the hypotenuse in each of the following right-angled triangles. Give your answers to one decimal place.

a

3 cm, a, 5 cm

b
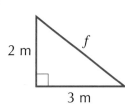
b, 6 cm, 7 cm

c

9 cm, 8 cm, c

d
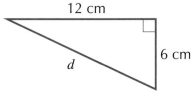
12 cm, 6 cm, d

e
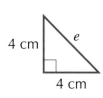
4 cm, e, 4 cm

f

2 m, f, 3 m

g
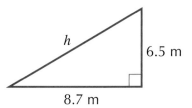
1 m, 4 m, g

h

h, 6.5 m, 8.7 m

2 Calculate the length of the unknown side in each of the following right-angled triangles. Give your answers to one decimal place.

a
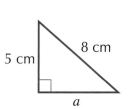
8 cm, 5 cm, a

b

15 cm, b, 11 cm

c

c, 10 cm, 12 cm

d

18 cm, 20 cm, d

e
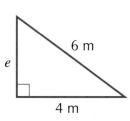
6 m, e, 4 m

f

f, 5.6 m, 3.9 m

g
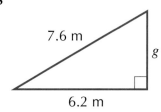
7.6 m, g, 6.2 m

h

1 m, h, 4.5 m

3 Calculate the lengths of x, y and z in the diagram on the right. Give your answers to one decimal place.

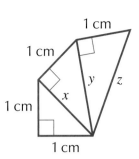

4 Calculate the length of the diagonal AC in the rectangle ABCD. Give your answer to one decimal place.

5 Calculate the length of the diagonal of a square with side length 5 cm. Give your answer to one decimal place.

Extension Work

The table below shows the lengths, in centimetres, of the three sides of six triangles.

Construct each one accurately, using a ruler and a pair of compasses. Label it as in the triangle on the right.

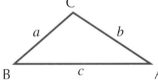

a	b	c	a^2	b^2	c^2	a^2+b^2	Is $a^2 + b^2 = c^2$? Is $a^2 + b^2 > c^2$? Is $a^2 + b^2 < c^2$? Write =, > or <	Is $\angle C$ right-angled, acute or obtuse?
3	4	5						
4	5	7						
5	6	7						
5	12	13						
4	8	10						
7	8	9						

Copy and complete the table. Then, write down a rule using the results in the last two columns.

Test your rule by drawing triangles with different lengths for a, b and c.

Solving problems using Pythagoras' theorem

Pythagoras' theorem can be used to solve various practical problems.

When solving such a problem:

- Draw a diagram for the problem, clearly showing the right angle.
- Decide whether the hypotenuse or one of the shorter sides needs to be found.
- Label the unknown side x.
- Use Pythagoras' theorem to calculate x.
- Round your answer to a suitable degree of accuracy.

Example 4.3 ▷

A ship sails 4 km due east. It then sails for a further 5 km due south. Calculate the distance the ship would have travelled had it sailed a direct route.

First, draw a diagram to show the distances sailed by the ship. Then label the direct distance, x.

Now use Pythagoras' theorem:
$$x^2 = 4^2 + 5^2$$
$$= 16 + 25$$
$$= 41$$
So, $x = \sqrt{41} = 6.4$ km (1 dp)

Exercise 4B

In this exercise, give your answers to a suitable degree of accuracy.

1 An aircraft flies 80 km due north. It then flies 72 km due west. Calculate how far the aircraft would have travelled had it taken the direct route.

2 A flagpole is 10 m high. It is held in position by two ropes which are fixed to the ground, 4 m away from the foot of the flagpole. Calculate the length of each rope.

3 An 8 m ladder is placed against a wall so that the foot of the ladder is 2 m away from the bottom of the wall. Calculate how far the ladder reaches up the wall.

4 The diagram shows the side wall of a shed. Calculate the length of the sloping roof.

2.6 m

3.5 m

2.4 m

5 The diagram shows a walkway leading from the dock on to a ferry. Calculate the vertical height of the walkway above the dock.

8 m

7.8 m

6 Two sides of a right-angled triangle are 20 cm and 30 cm. Calculate the length of the third side in each of the following cases.

a It is the hypotenuse.

b It is not the hypotenuse.

7 ABC is an isosceles triangle.

a Calculate the perpendicular height, h.

b Hence calculate the area of the triangle.

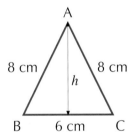

A

8 cm   8 cm

h

B   6 cm   C

8 The diagram shows three towns X, Y and Z connected by straight roads. Calculate the shortest distance from X to the road connecting Y and Z.

X

6 km   6 km

Y   8 km   Z

9 The triangle PQR is drawn on a coordinate grid, as shown on the right.

a The length of PQ is 3 units. Write down the length of QR.

b Calculate the length of PR.

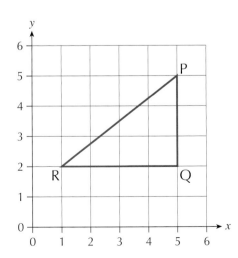

10 Calculate the length between each of the following pairs of coordinate points.

    a   A(2, 3) and B(4, 7)   **b**   C(1, 5) and D(4, 3)

    c   E(–1, 0) and F(2, –3)   **d**   G(–5, 1) and H(4, –3)

Extension Work

Pythagorean triples

Each set of the three numbers in the table on the right obey Pythagoras' theorem, $c^2 = a^2 + b^2$, where a, b and c are whole numbers. Each set of numbers is called a **Pythagorean triple**, named after Pythagoras, who first discovered a formula for finding them.

a	b	c
3	4	5
5	12	13
7	24	25

a   Continue the table to find other Pythagorean triples. You may wish to use a spreadsheet to help you.

b   Can you find the formula which Pythagoras discovered, giving b and c when the value of a is known?

c   Do multiples of any Pythagorean triple still give another Pythagorean triple?

Loci

A **locus** (plural 'loci') is the movement of a point according to a given set of conditions or a rule.

In Year 8, you met two important constructions, which can now be stated to be loci.

Example 4.4

- The locus of a point which is always equidistant from each of two fixed points, A and B, is the perpendicular bisector of the line joining the two points.

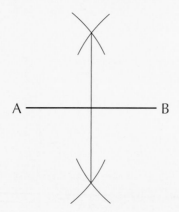

- The locus of a point which is equidistant from two fixed lines AB and BC, which meet at B, is the bisector of the angle ABC.

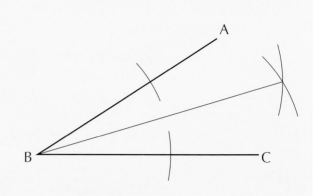

A locus can sometimes be a region.

Example 4.5

- A point which moves so that it is always 5 cm from a fixed point X has a locus which is a circle of radius 5 cm, with its centre at X.

- The locus of a set of points which are 5 cm or less from a fixed point X is a region inside a circle of radius 5 cm, with its centre at X.

  Note that the region is usually shaded.

- The locus of a set of points which are less than 5 cm from a fixed point X is a region inside a circle of radius 5 cm, with its centre at X.

  Note that the boundary usually is drawn as a dashed line to show that the points which are exactly 5 cm from X are *not* to be included.

Exercise 4C

(1) Using a ruler and compasses, construct the perpendicular bisector of each of the following lines.

a

A ——— B
6 cm

b

C
4.5 cm
D

(2) Using a ruler and compasses, construct the bisector of each of the following angles.

a

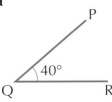
P
40°
Q   R

b

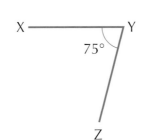
X ——— Y
75°
Z

c

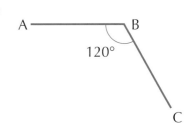
A ——— B
120°
C

(3) X is a fixed point. Draw diagrams to show the following.

a The locus of a point which is always 3 cm from X.
b The locus of a point which is always 3 cm or less from X.
c The locus of a point which is always less than 3 cm from X.

(4) A and B are two points, 6 cm apart. Draw a diagram to show the region which is 4 cm or less from A and 3 cm or less from B.

5 Make a copy of Treasure Island, as shown on the right. The treasure is buried at a point X on the island.

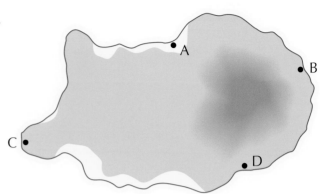

X is equidistant from A and D and is also equidistant from B and C. Mark the position of the treasure on your map.

 6 The diagram shows two perpendicular fences, PQ and QR. Bob wants to plant a tree so that it is equidistant from both fences and equidistant from P and R.

On a copy of the diagram, mark, with a cross, the position where Bob plants the tree.

 7 A radar station at X has a range of 100 km, and a radar station at Y has a range of 80 km. The direct distance from X to Y is 140 km.

Using a scale of 1 cm to 20 km, make a scale drawing to show the region where an aircraft can be picked up by both radar stations.

 8 A and B are two barns which are 120 m apart. A farmer wants to fence off an area of land that is nearer to barn A than barn B and is within 80 m of barn B. Using a scale of 1 cm to 20 m, make a scale drawing to show the area of land enclosed by the fence.

A   B

120 m

9 P is a fixed point and a point Q moves in space so that the length of PQ is always 10 cm. Describe the locus of Q.

 10 A fly moves around a strip light such that it is always 5 cm from the light. Describe the locus of the fly.

1 X is a point on the circumference of a circle. Draw the locus of X as the circle rolls along the line AB.

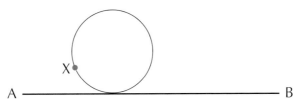

To help you draw the locus, use a coin and a ruler. Put a mark on the coin and as it rolls along the edge of the ruler, make marks on your paper for different positions of the coin, as on the diagram below. Join the marks with a curve to show the locus of X.

2 The diagram on the right shows a 6 m ladder leaning against the wall of a house. The ground is slippery and the ladder slides down the wall until it lies flat on the ground.

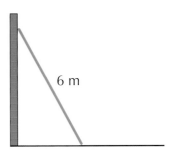

Make a scale drawing to show the locus of the middle point of the ladder as the ladder slides down the wall. Use a scale of 1 cm to 1m.

3 If you have access to ICT facilities, find how to draw the locus for more complex rules.

4 A builder wants to make a straight path from House A to the road, and another straight path from House B to the same point on the road.

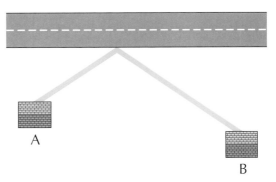

Draw a sketch to show where the paths should go in order to make the lengths of the paths as short as possible.

Congruent triangles

You already know how to construct triangles from given dimensions, as summarised below.

Three sides (SSS)

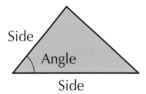

Two sides and the included angle (SAS)

Two angles and the included side (ASA)

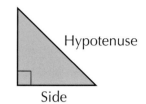

Right angle, hypotenuse and side (RHS)

You can use these conditions to show that two triangles are congruent, as Example 4.6 shows.

Example 4.6 Show that △ABC is congruent to △XYZ.

The diagram shows the following:
∠B = ∠X
∠C = ∠Y
BC = XY

So, △ABC is congruent to △XYZ (ASA).

This can be written as:
△ABC ≡ △XYZ

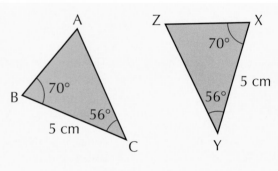

Exercise 4D

1 Show that each of the following pairs of triangles are congruent. Give reasons for each answer and state which condition of congruency you are using: SSS, SAS, ASA or RHS.

a

b

c

d

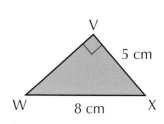

2 Explain why △ABC is congruent to △XYZ.

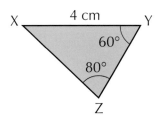

3 **a** Explain why △PQR is not necessarily congruent to △XYZ.

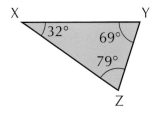

b Check your answer by trying to draw one of the triangles.

4 ABC is an isosceles triangle with AB = AC.
The perpendicular from A meets BC at D.

Show that △ABD is congruent to △ACD.

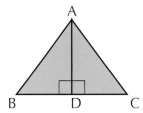

5 Draw a rectangle ABCD. Draw in the diagonals AC and BD to intersect at X. State the different sets of congruent triangles in your diagram.

Extension **Work**

1 Show that the opposite angles in a parallelogram are equal by using congruent triangles.

2 Draw a kite and label its vertices ABCD with AB = AD. Now draw the diagonals and label their intersection E.

a Show that △ABC is congruent to △ADC.

b State all other pairs of congruent triangles.

3 Construct as many different triangles as possible by choosing any three measurements from the following: 4 cm, 5 cm, 40° and 30°.

4 Show what happens when you try to construct a triangle for which the given angle is not included between the two given sides (SSA). There are three cases to consider.

Circle theorems

The following terms for parts of a circle were met in Year 8.

A circle is a set of points equidistant from a **centre**, O.

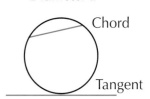

Circumference The distance around a circle.

Radius The distance from the centre of a circle to its circumference.

Diameter The distance from one side of a circle to the other, passing through the centre.

Chord A line which cuts a circle into two parts.

Tangent A line which touches a circle at a single point on its circumference.

Exercise 4E introduces two important circle theorems.

Exercise 4E

1 **The angle between a tangent and a radius**

- Draw a circle, centre O, with a radius of 3 cm.
- Draw a tangent to the circle with the point of contact at A.
- Draw the radius OA.
- Measure the angle between the tangent and the radius.
- Write down what you notice.
- Repeat for circles with different radii.

You have just completed a practical demonstration to show an important circle theorem:

A radius is perpendicular to a tangent at the point of contact.

Draw a diagram in your book to explain this theorem.

2 **The perpendicular bisector of a chord**

- Draw a circle, centre O, with a radius of 3 cm.
- Draw a chord anywhere inside the circle.
- Construct the perpendicular bisector of the chord.
- Write down what you notice.
- Repeat for circles with different radii.

You have just completed a practical demonstration to show another important circle theorem:

The perpendicular bisector of a chord passes through the centre of a circle.

Draw a diagram in your book to explain this theorem.

3 Calculate the size of the lettered angle in each of the following diagrams.

a

b

c

d

e

f

g

h

i

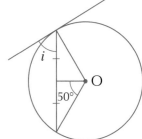

4 Use Pythagoras' theorem to calculate the length x in each of the following diagrams. Give your answers to one decimal place.

a

b

c

d

⑤ The lines AB and CD below are tangents to a circle. The circle touches the tangents at the points E and F. On a copy of the diagram, construct the circle, using a ruler and compasses.

Hint: Construct two lines to find the centre of the circle.

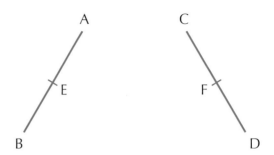

⑥ XY and XZ are two chords of the same circle. On a copy of the diagram, construct the circle, using a ruler and compasses.

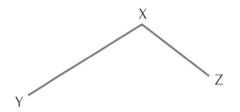

Extension Work

1   **The angle in a semicircle**

● Draw a circle, centre O, with a radius of 3 cm.

● Draw a diameter and label it AB.

● Mark a point P anywhere on the circumference.

● Complete the triangle APB in the semicircle.

● Measure ∠APB.

● Write down what you notice.

● Repeat for different points on the circumference.

You have just completed a practical demonstration to show yet another important circle theorem:

The angle formed in a semicircle equals 90°.

Draw a diagram in your book to explain this theorem.

Use this theorem to calculate the size of the lettered angles in each of the following diagrams.

a   b   c   d   e

2　The diagram on the right shows two circles intersecting at B. O is the centre of the small circle and AO is the diameter of the large circle with its centre at P.

Prove that AB is a tangent to the small circle.

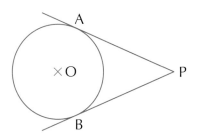

3　AP and BP are tangents to a circle with centre O. By using congruent triangles, prove that AP = BP.

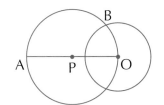

Tessellations and regular polygons

A **tessellation** is a repeating pattern made on a plane (flat) surface with identical shapes which fit together exactly, leaving no gaps.

This section will show you how some of the regular polygons tessellate.

Remember: To show how a shape tessellates, draw up to about ten repeating shapes.

Example 4.7 ▷　The diagrams below show how equilateral triangles and squares tessellate.

Exercise 4F

①　On an isometric grid, show how a regular hexagon tessellates.

②　Trace this regular pentagon onto card and cut it out to make a template.

　　a　Use your template to show that a regular pentagon does not tessellate.

　　b　Explain why a regular pentagon does not tessellate.

3 Trace this regular octagon onto card and cut it out to make a template.

    a Use your template to show that a regular octagon does not tessellate.

    b Explain why a regular octagon does not tessellate.

4 **a** Copy and complete the table below for regular polygons.

Regular polygon	Size of each interior angle	Does this polygon tessellate?
Equilateral triangle		
Square		
Regular pentagon		
Regular hexagon		
Regular octagon		

    b Use the table to explain why only some of the regular polygons tessellate.

    c Do you think that a regular nonagon tessellates? Explain your reasoning.

Extension Work

Polygons can be combined together to form a **semi-tessellation**. Two examples are shown below.

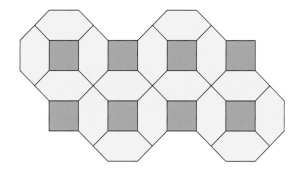

Rectangles and isosceles triangles   **Squares and hexagons**

Invent your own semi-tessellations and make a poster to display in your classroom.

Practical Pythagoras

This activity is a practical demonstration to show Pythagoras' theorem. You will need a sheet of thin card and a pair of scissors.

- In your book, draw the right-angled triangle X, as on the right.

- On the card, draw eight more triangles identical to X. Cut them out and place them to one side.

- On your original triangle, X, draw squares on each of the three sides of the triangle. Label them A, B and C, as below.

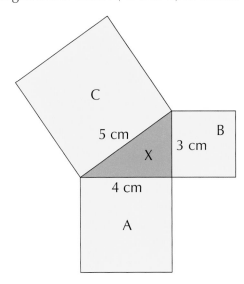

- On the card, draw another diagram identical to this. Cut out the squares A, B and C.

- Arrange the cut-outs of the eight triangles and three squares as in the two diagrams below.

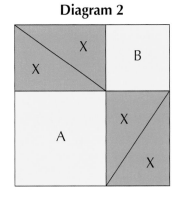

- What can you say about the total area of Diagram 1 and of Diagram 2?

- Now remove the four triangles from each diagram.

- What can you say about the areas of squares A, B and C?

- Show how this demonstrates Pythagoras' theorem.

Extension **Work**

The activity on page 75 showed a practical demonstration of Pythagoras' theorem. You can also prove Pythagoras' theorem by using algebra.

Copy the proof below into your book and make sure you can follow each step.

To prove Pythagoras' theorem

A right-angled triangle has sides a, b and c.

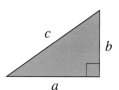

Draw the following diagram using four of these triangles.

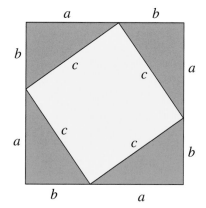

The area of each triangle $= \frac{1}{2}ab$

So, the area of the four triangles $= 2ab$

The area of the large square $= (a + b)^2$

The area of the large square can also be given as $c^2 + 2ab$

Therefore: $(a + b)^2 = c^2 + 2ab$

$$a^2 + 2ab + b^2 = c^2 + 2ab$$

which gives $a^2 + b^2 = c^2$

This is Pythagoras' theorem.

LEVEL BOOSTER

5 I know how to tessellate shapes.

6 I can find and use interior and exterior angles of polygons.

7 I can use and apply Pythagoras' theorem.
I know how to find the locus of a set of points.
I can recognise congruent triangles.

8 I know the difference between a practical demonstration and a proof.
I can solve problems using circle theorems.

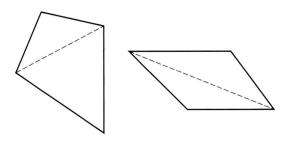

1 *2000 Paper 2*

a Any quadrilateral can be split into two triangles.

Explain how you know that the angles inside a quadrilateral add up to 360°.

b What do the angles inside a pentagon add up to?

c What do the angles inside a heptagon (seven-sided shape) add up to?

Show your working.

2 *2001 Paper 2*

a Calculate the length of the unknown side of this right-angled triangle.

Show your working.

12 cm

17 cm

Not drawn accurately

b Calculate the length of the unknown side of this right-angled triangle.

Show your working.

5 cm

11 cm

Not drawn accurately

3 *2001 Paper 2*

The diagram shows five triangles. All lengths are in centimetres.

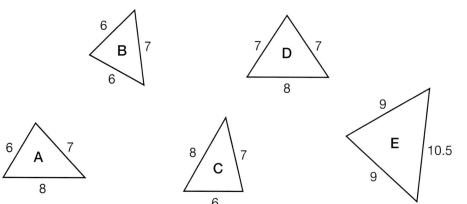

Write the letters of two triangles that are congruent to each other.

Explain how you know they are congruent.

FM **4** *2006 Paper 2*

In a wildlife park in Africa, wardens want to know the position of an elephant in a certain area.

They place one microphone at each corner of a **4 km by 4 km** square.

Each microphone has a range of $3\frac{1}{2}$ km.

The elephant is **out of range** of microphones **A** and **B**.

Where in the square could the elephant be?

Show the region **accurately** on a copy of the diagram, and **label** the region **R**.

Scale: 2 cm to 1 km

5 *2003 Paper 2*

Two right-angled triangles are joined together to make a larger triangle ACD.

a Show that the perimeter of triangle ACD is 78 cm.

b Show that triangle ACD is also a right-angled triangle.

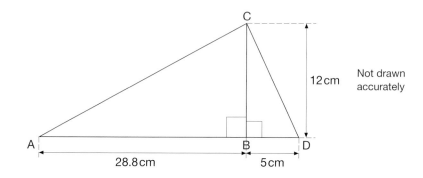

12 cm

Not drawn accurately

28.8 cm

5 cm

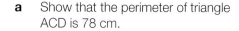

8

6 *2003 Paper 1*

The diagram shows three points, A, B and C, on a circle, centre O. AC is the diameter of the circle.

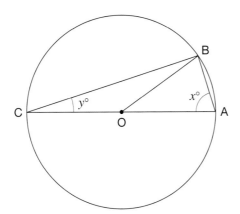

a Angle BAO is $x°$ and angle BCO is $y°$. Explain why angle ABO must be $x°$ and CBO must be $y°$.

b Use algebra to show that angle ABC must be 90°.

FM Garden design

Greg has just moved house and is designing his new garden.

To work out the questions related to Greg's garden, you will need a copy of the Activity Worksheet on page 271.

1 At the end of the garden there is going to be a chicken run.

A piece of netting will be fixed from the long south fence to the east fence, as shown on the activity worksheet.

Calculate the length of netting that is needed.

Round your answer up to the nearest 0.1 m.

2 Instead of 7 m wide, Greg considers making the run 2.5 m wide.

If the same length of netting from Question 1 is used to make the triangular chicken run, how far along the east fence would the netting reach?

Round your answer down to the nearest 0.1 m.

3 The hexagonal seat that goes around the tree is to be made from planks of wood. Each of the six sections are identical.

Work out the angles, (shown in the diagram), that each section needs to be cut at.

4 A large semi-circular table will be placed in front of the BBQ area, as shown here.

Draw the table accurately on the activity worksheet.

5 There is going to be a circular pond of radius 1 m at the end of the garden. The centre of the pond will be 4 m from the corner where the short south fence meets the northwest fence. The pond will be equidistant from the two fences.

Draw the pond accurately on the activity worksheet.

Leave in your construction lines.

6 A rotary washing line is to be placed 3 m from the corner where the long south fence meets the west fence. The washing line will be equidistant from the two fences.

Show the position of the rotary washing line on the activity worksheet with a cross (X).

Leave in your construction lines.

7 Paving slabs are going to be put underneath the rotary washing line.

a Which of the following slabs tessellate? Explain how you know. Draw a sketch if it will help you explain more fully.

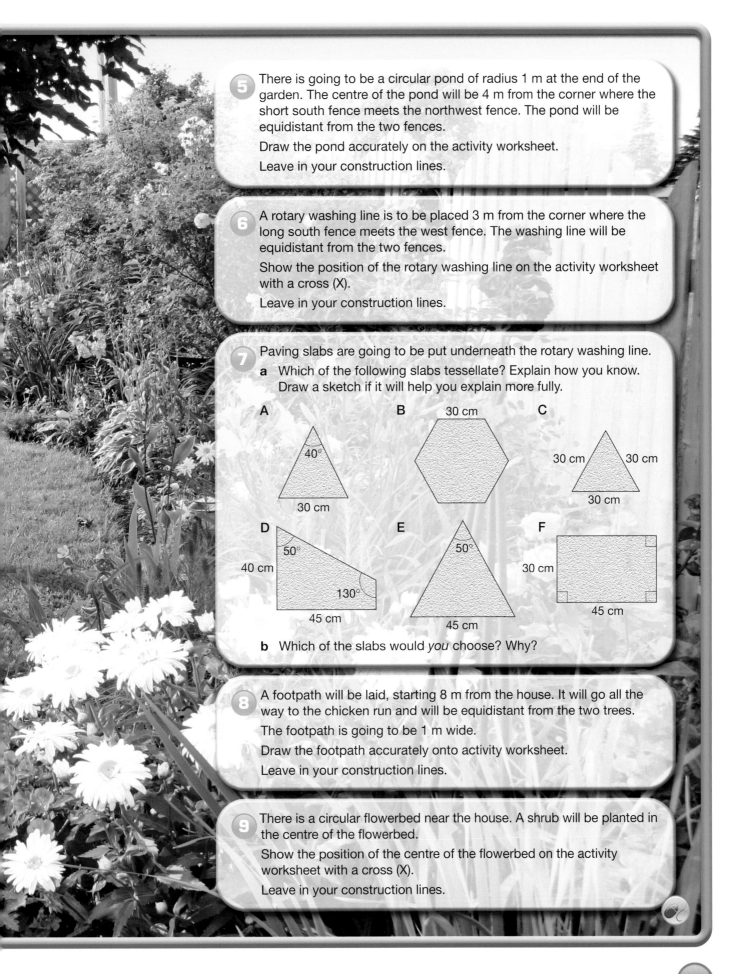

A

40°

30 cm

B

30 cm

C

30 cm   30 cm

30 cm

D

50°

40 cm

130°

45 cm

E

50°

45 cm

F

30 cm

45 cm

b Which of the slabs would *you* choose? Why?

8 A footpath will be laid, starting 8 m from the house. It will go all the way to the chicken run and will be equidistant from the two trees.

The footpath is going to be 1 m wide.

Draw the footpath accurately onto activity worksheet.

Leave in your construction lines.

9 There is a circular flowerbed near the house. A shrub will be planted in the centre of the flowerbed.

Show the position of the centre of the flowerbed on the activity worksheet with a cross (X).

Leave in your construction lines.

This chapter is going to show you

- How to plan a statistical investigation
- How to interpret correlation from two scatter graphs
- How to draw and use lines of best fit on a scatter graph
- How to interpret time series graphs
- How to draw a cumulative frequency graph and use it to estimate median and interquartile range
- How to estimate a mean from a large set of data

What you should already know

- How to calculate statistics
- How to collect data using a suitable method
- How to draw and interpret graphs for discrete data
- How to compare two sets of data using mode, median, mean or range

Scatter graphs and correlation

The maximum temperature, rainfall and hours of sunshine were recorded each day in a town on the south coast of England.

Look at the two scatter graphs below, which were plotted from this data. Is it possible to work out the relationship between rainfall and hours of sunshine?

The graph on the left shows **negative correlation**. In this case, it means that the higher the temperature, the less rainfall there is.

The graph on the right shows **positive correlation**. In this case, it means that the higher the temperature, the more hours of sunshine there are.

Looking at both graphs together, what do they tell you about the effects of changes in temperature?

From the graph on the left, high rainfall means low temperature. From the graph on the right, low temperature means little sunshine. So, you can deduce that high rainfall means little sunshine. That is, rainfall and sunshine are negatively correlated. The graph opposite illustrates this.

The graph on the right shows **no correlation** between the temperature and the number of fish caught daily off Rhyl – as you might expect.

Here is a table which gives you the rules for combining two scatter graphs, which have a common axis, to obtain the resulting correlation.

	Positive correlation	**No correlation**	**Negative correlation**
Positive correlation	Positive	No correlation	Negative
No correlation	No correlation	*Cannot tell*	No correlation
Negative correlation	Negative	No correlation	Positive

As you may see from the table, the new graph can have its axes in either order, as this does not affect the correlation.

To remember these rules, think of the rules for multiplying together positive and negative numbers. See below.

Multiply (×)	**+**	**0**	**−**
+	+	0	−
0	0	*The exception*	0
−	−	0	+

1 A competition has three different games.

	Game A	Game B	Game C
Score	62	53	

a   Ryan plays two games.

To win, Ryan needs a mean score of 60.

How many points does he need to score in Game C? Show your working.

b   Ian and Nina play the three games.

Ian's scores		40	
Nina's scores	35	40	45

Their scores have the same mean.

The range of Ian's scores is twice the range of Nina's scores. Copy the table above and fill in the missing scores.

The scatter diagrams show the scores of everyone who plays all three games.

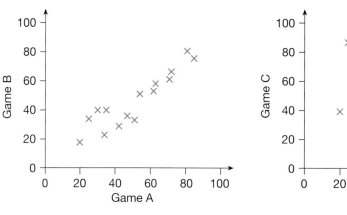

c   Look at the scatter diagrams and read the statements below:

  • Positive relationship
  • No relationship

Which statement most closely describes the relationship between these games?

  i   Game A and Game B

  ii Game A and Game C

  iii Game B and Game C

2 A post office compares the cost of postage with the weight of each parcel and also the cost of postage with the size of each parcel. The results are shown on the scatter graphs below.

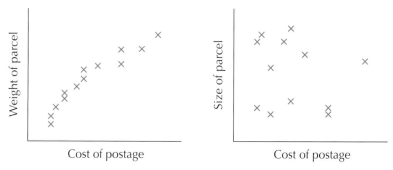

a   Describe the type of correlation between the weight of parcels and the cost of postage.

b   Describe the type of correlation between the size of parcels and the cost of postage.

c   Describe the relationship between the weight of parcels and the size of parcels.

d   Draw a scatter graph to show the correlation between the weight of parcels and the size of parcels. (Plot about 10 points for your graph.)

(3) A pupil compared the ages of a group of men with the length of their hair and also with their weights. His results are shown on the two scatter graphs.

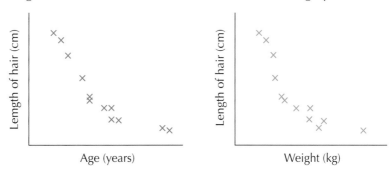

a Describe the type of correlation between the length of hair and age.

b Describe the type of correlation between the length of hair and weight.

c Describe the relationship between age and weight.

d Draw a scatter graph to show the correlation between age and weight. (Plot about 10 points for your graph.)

Extension Work

Collect test marks for ten pupils in three different subjects: for example, mathematics, science and art. Draw the scatter graphs for mathematics/science, mathematics/art and science/art. Comment on your results. You may wish to use a table to show the test marks.

	Pupil 1	Pupil 2	Pupil 3	Pupil 4	Pupil 5	Pupil 6	Pupil 7	Pupil 8	Pupil 9	Pupil 10
Maths										
Science										
Art										

Scatter graphs and lines of best fit

Look at the two scatter graphs below. One shows a positive correlation and one shows a negative correlation, which you met in the previous lesson.

A **line of best fit** shows a trend on a scatter graph. Predictions, or estimates, can then be made using the line of best fit to show what might happen in certain circumstances.

To draw a line of best fit, first look at the correlation to decide which direction to draw the line. Then, using a ruler, draw a straight line between all the plotted points, passing as close as possible to all of them. Each line should have approximately equal numbers of points on each side.

All the lines of best fit which you will meet will be straight, ruled lines to show positive or negative correlation.

0–60 time against engine size

Weight against engine size

Example 5.1 ▷ The table shows the marks obtained by 10 pupils in their maths and science tests.

a Draw a scatter graph to show the results. **b** Draw a line of best fit.

c Sarah scored 70 in her maths test but was absent for the science test. Use the line of best fit to estimate the result she would have obtained in science.

Pupil	1	2	3	4	5	6	7	8	9	10
Maths	32	75	53	76	25	62	85	48	39	50
Science	41	80	44	60	30	57	63	48	47	56

a

Maths and science test results for 10 pupils

b

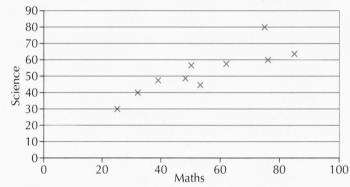

Maths and science test results for 10 pupils

c The estimate of Sarah's science mark is 62.

1 The table shows the scores of some pupils in a mental test and in a written test.

Pupil	Andy	Betty	Chris	Darren	Eve	Frank	Gina	Harry	Ingrid	Jack
Mental	12	16	21	25	20	11	17	14	13	19
Written	24	29	33	12	35	18	45	25	28	36

a Plot the data on a scatter graph. Use the x-axis for the mental test from 0 to 30, and the y-axis for the written test from 0 to 50.

b Draw a line of best fit.

c One person did not do as well as expected on the written test. Who do you think it was? Give a reason.

2 The table shows the age of a group of home-owners and the distance that they live from their local shops.

Name	Kylie	Liam	Mick	Norris	Ollie	Philip	Qaysar	Richard	Steven	Trevor
Age (years)	18	22	28	34	40	42	50	56	65	72
Distance from shops (miles)	2.5	2	3	1.8	2.4	1.9	2.5	0.5	0.3	0.2

a Plot the data on a scatter graph. Use the x-axis for the age (years) from 0 to 80, and the y-axis for the distance from the shops from 0 to 5 miles.

b Draw a line of best fit.

c State what you think your line of best fit tells you about this group of people.

3 A survey is carried out to compare pupils' ages with the amount of money that they spend each week.

Age (years)	10	10	11	11	12	12	12	14	14	15
Amount spent each week (£)	5	8	7	9.50	10	12	6	14	15	13

a Plot the data on a scatter graph. Use the x-axis for age from 8 years to 20 years, and the y-axis for amount spent from £0 to £15.

b Draw a line of best fit.

c Use your line of best fit to estimate how much a 13-year-old would spend each week.

Extension Work

Look again at Questions **2** and **3**.

1 For Question **2**, explain why it might not be sensible to use your line of best fit to estimate the distance from the shops for a young child.

2 For Question **3**, explain why it would not be sensible to use your line of best fit to estimate the amount spent each week for a 20-year-old.

Time series graphs

A time series graph is any graph which has a time scale.

Look at the graphs below to see whether you can match each graph to one of the statements listed after graph 5.

Graph 1: Mean temperature difference from normal for UK in 2002

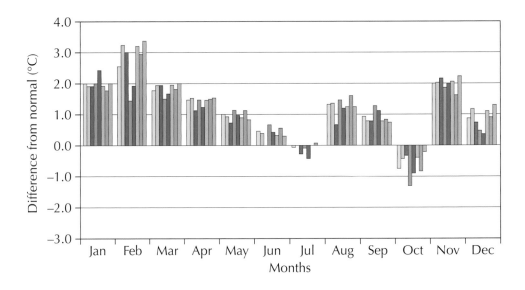

Graph 2: Average annual temperatures of Central England 1659–2001

Graph 3: Monthly rainfall data for Perth, Australia

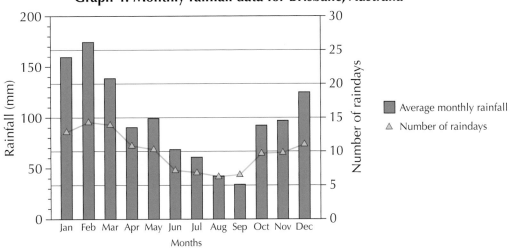

Graph 4: Monthly rainfall data for Brisbane, Australia

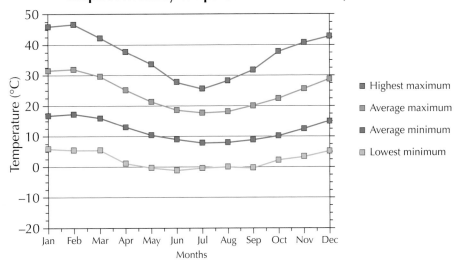

Graph 5: Monthly temperature data for Perth, Australia

Statement A: February is the hottest month here.

Statement B: October was colder than normal.

Statement C: September is a fairly dry month in Australia.

Statement D: This country is gradually getting warmer.

Statement E: The difference between the lowest and highest temperatures is least in July.

Exercise 5C

 1 The time series graph shows the height to which a ball bounces against the time taken to reach that height.

(a) Write a comment stating what happens to the length of time for which the ball is in the air after each bounce.

(b) This ball always bounces to a fixed fraction of its previous height. What fraction is this?

(c) After how many bounces does this ball bounce to less than half of the greatest height?

(d) In theory, how many bounces does the ball make before it comes to rest?

 2 Look again at the graph showing the mean temperature changes in the UK for 2002.

(a) Use the graph to support an argument that global warming is taking place.

(b) Tammy says: 'The graph shows that global warming is taking place'. Give a reason why Tammy could be wrong.

 3 Look again at the graphs showing the rainfall for Perth and Brisbane.

(a) Which month has the greatest rainfall in Perth?

(b) Which month has the least rainfall in Brisbane?

(c) Explain how you can tell that Perth and Brisbane are not in the same region.

(d) Which place, Perth or Brisbane, has more days of rainfall over the year? Show how you work it out.

Extension Work

Use an atlas, encyclopaedia or the Internet to find a graph on whose coordinates, shape and trend you would be able to comment.

Two-way tables

An Internet company charges delivery for goods based on the type of delivery – normal delivery (taking 3 to 5 days) or next-day delivery – and also on the cost of the order. The table shows how it is calculated.

Cost of order	Normal delivery (3 to 5 days)	Next-day delivery
0–£10	£1.95	£4.95
£10.01–£30	£2.95	£4.95
£30.01–£50	£3.95	£6.95
£50.01–£75	£2.95	£4.95
Over £75	Free	£3.00

This is called a two-way table.

Example 5.2 ▷ Use the two-way table above to answer the questions about delivery costs.

a Comment on the difference in delivery charges for normal and next-day delivery.

b Two items cost £5 and £29. How much would you save by ordering them together: **i** using normal delivery? **ii** using next-day delivery?

a It always costs more using next-day delivery but for goods costing between £10.01 and £30, or between £50.01 and £75, it is only £2 more. It is £3 more for all other orders.

b Using normal delivery and ordering the items separately, it would cost £1.95 + £2.95 = £4.90, but ordering them together would cost £3.95. The saving would be £4.90 – £3.95 = 95p

Using next-day delivery and ordering the items separately, it would cost £4.95 + £4.95 = £9.90, but ordering them together would cost £6.95. The saving would be £9.90 – £6.95 = £2.95

Exercise 5D

 1 The table shows the percentage of boys and girls by age group who have a mobile phone.

a Comment on any differences between boys and girls.

b Comment on any other trends that you notice.

Age	Boys	Girls
10	18%	14%
11	21%	18%
12	42%	39%
13	53%	56%
14	56%	59%
15	62%	64%

2 The cost of a set of old toys depends on whether the toys are still in the original boxes and also on the condition of the toys. The table shows the percentage value of a toy compared with its value if it is in perfect condition and boxed.

Condition	Boxed	Not boxed
Excellent	100%	60%
Very good	80%	50%
Good	60%	40%
Average	40%	25%
Poor	20%	10%

a Copy and complete the table.

Condition	Difference between boxed and not boxed
Excellent	100% − 60% = 40%
Very good	
Good	
Average	
Poor	

b Explain the effect of the set being boxed compared with the condition of the toys.

3 A school analyses the information on the month of birth for 1000 pupils. The results are shown in the table.

Month	Jan	Feb	Mar	Apr	May	Jun	Jul	Aug	Sep	Oct	Nov	Dec
Boys	34	36	43	39	47	50	44	39	55	53	42	35
Girls	37	31	36	35	44	43	36	40	52	49	43	37

a On the same grid, plot both sets of values to give a time series graph for the boys and another for the girls.

b Use the graphs to examine the claim that more children are born in the summer than in the winter.

4 The heights of 70 Year 9 pupils are recorded. Here are the results given to the nearest centimetre.

Height (cm)	Boys	Girls
130–139	3	3
140–149	2	4
150–159	10	12
160–169	14	11
170–179	6	5

Use the results to examine the claim that boys are taller than girls in Year 9. You may use a frequency diagram to help you.

Look at the two-way table showing the number of different colours of the 80 cars in the school car park. If a car is chosen at random, what is the probability that it is one of the following?

		Colour of cars				
		Red	White	Blue	Black	Other
	Peugeot	8	1	4	1	4
	Ford	11	2	4	2	6
Make of cars	**Vauxhall**	5	4	0	0	2
	Citroen	1	2	2	0	3
	Other	6	3	3	4	2

a   Peugeot

b   Red

c   Red Peugeot

d   Not blue

e   Not a Ford

Cumulative frequency diagrams

In this section, you will learn how to draw cumulative frequency diagrams for large sets of grouped data. You will also find out how to use these to obtain estimates of the median and the interquartile range.

'Cumulative' means to build up or to accumulate.

Example 5.3   The table shows the waiting times of 100 people in a bus station.

Time waiting, T (min)	Number of passengers
$0 < T \le 5$	14
$5 < T \le 10$	35
$10 < T \le 15$	26
$15 < T \le 20$	18
$20 < T \le 25$	7

a   Draw a cumulative frequency diagram.

b   Estimate the median and the interquartile range.

Example **5.3**
continued

a First, you need to change the table from a **frequency** table into a **cumulative frequency** table. This is sometimes called a less than or less than or equal to cumulative frequency table.

There are 14 passengers with a waiting time of less than or equal to 5 minutes.

There are 14 + 35 = 49 passengers with a waiting time of less than or equal to 10 minutes.

Continue to build up until the table is complete for 100 passengers:

Time waiting, T (min)	Cumulative frequency
$T \leq 5$	14
$T \leq 10$	14 + 35 = 49
$T \leq 15$	49 + 26 = 75
$T \leq 20$	75 + 18 = 93
$T \leq 25$	93 + 7 = 100

Now plot this information onto a cumulative frequency graph, starting with (0, 0), (5, 14), (10, 49) and so on.

The points can be joined up with straight lines or a curve.

To estimate the median, read off from the graph at the mid-value of the cumulative frequency. In this case, read off at 50.

This gives the median as 10.2 minutes.

To estimate the interquartile range, first obtain the values of the lower quartile and the upper quartile.

To estimate the lower quartile, read off from the graph at the one-quarter value of the cumulative frequency, which is 25. This gives the lower quartile as 6.6 minutes.

To estimate the upper quartile, read off from the graph at the three-quarter value of the cumulative frequency, which is 75. This gives the upper quartile as 15 minutes.

To work out the interquartile range:

Interquartile range = Upper quartile – Lower quartile
= 15 – 6.6
= 8.4 minutes

Exercise 5E

For each table of data, do the following.

a   Copy and complete the cumulative frequency table.

b   Draw the cumulative frequency graph.

c   Use your graph to estimate the median and interquartile range.

1 The temperature over 100 days

Temperature, T (°C)	Number of days
$0 < T \le 5$	8
$5 < T \le 10$	15
$10 < T \le 15$	42
$15 < T \le 20$	25
$20 < T \le 25$	10

Temperature, T (°C)	Cumulative frequency
$T \le 5$	
$T \le 10$	
$T \le 15$	
$T \le 20$	
$T \le 25$	

2 The time taken to walk to school by 40 pupils

Time, t (min)	Number of pupils
$0 < t \le 5$	5
$5 < t \le 10$	12
$10 < t \le 15$	9
$15 < t \le 20$	7
$20 < t \le 25$	4
$25 < t \le 30$	3

Time, t (min)	Cumulative frequency
$t \le 5$	
$t \le 10$	
$t \le 15$	
$t \le 20$	
$t \le 25$	
$t \le 30$	

3 The mass of 80 sacks of potatoes

Mass, M (kg)	Number of sacks
$23 < M \le 24$	0
$24 < M \le 25$	15
$25 < M \le 26$	31
$26 < M \le 27$	22
$27 < M \le 28$	12

Mass, M (kg)	Cumulative frequency
$M \le 24$	
$M \le 25$	
$M \le 26$	
$M \le 27$	
$M \le 28$	

Estimation of a mean from grouped data

You are now going to learn how to estimate a **mean** from a table of **grouped data**.

When data is grouped, it is not possible to calculate an exact value for the mean, as you do not have the exact value of each piece of data.

Example 5.4 ▷

The times for 100 cyclists to complete a 200 m time trial are grouped in the table.

Obtain an estimate for the mean time.

Time, t (seconds)	Frequency, f
$13 < T \leq 14$	12
$14 < T \leq 15$	21
$15 < T \leq 16$	39
$16 < T \leq 17$	20
$17 < T \leq 18$	8

Because the data is grouped, you have to assume that in each class the data is centred on the mid-class value.

This means, for example, that in the first class $13 < T \leq 14$, you assume that there are 12 cyclists with times around 13.5 seconds (the mid-value of the class).

Add an extra column to the table to give:

Time, t (seconds)	Frequency, f	Mid-value, x, of time (seconds)
$13 < T \leq 14$	12	13.5
$14 < T \leq 15$	21	14.5
$15 < T \leq 16$	39	15.5
$16 < T \leq 17$	20	16.5
$17 < T \leq 18$	8	17.5

To calculate the mean time, you need to estimate the total time taken for each class.

For example, in the first class, you have 12 cyclists taking approximately 13.5 seconds. That is: $12 \times 13.5 = 162$ seconds

Add a fourth column to show the total times for each class. Then add up these times to obtain:

Time, t (seconds)	Frequency, f	Mid-value, x, of time (seconds)	$f \times x$ (seconds)
$13 < T \leq 14$	12	13.5	162
$14 < T \leq 15$	21	14.5	304.5
$15 < T \leq 16$	39	15.5	604.5
$16 < T \leq 17$	20	16.5	330
$17 < T \leq 18$	8	17.5	140
Total = 100			**Total = 1541**

Estimate of the total time taken by the 100 cyclists = 1541 seconds

Estimate of the mean time = $\dfrac{1541}{100}$ = 15.41 seconds

7

1 For each table of values given, do the following.

a Rewrite the table with four columns, as shown in Example 5.4.

b Complete the table including the totals, as shown in Example 5.4.

c Obtain an estimate of the mean.

i

Mass, M (kg)	Frequency, f
$0 < M \le 2$	8
$2 < M \le 4$	11
$4 < M \le 6$	10
$6 < M \le 8$	5
$8 < M \le 10$	6

ii

Length, L (cm)	Frequency, f
$20 < L \le 24$	13
$24 < L \le 28$	35
$28 < L \le 32$	24
$32 < L \le 36$	8

2 The temperature of a school swimming pool was recorded every day over a period of 100 days. The results are summarised in the table below.

Temperature, T (°C)	Frequency, f
$0 < T \le 10$	17
$10 < T \le 20$	23
$20 < T \le 30$	56
$30 < T \le 40$	3
$40 < T \le 50$	1

Obtain an estimate of the mean temperature.

3 The times taken by 40 pupils to complete an obstacle course are below.

Time, t (min)	Frequency, f
$5 < t \le 6$	8
$6 < t \le 7$	10
$7 < t \le 9$	11
$9 < t \le 13$	5
$13 < t \le 15$	6

Hint: Be careful, these classes are different widths.

For each of the questions above, find the class which contains the median.

8

Statistical investigations

Investigating a problem will involve several steps. Three examples will be studied from different subjects alongside an overall plan.

Step	Example 1 PE	Example 2 Science	Example 3 Geography
1 Decide which general topic to study	How to improve pupil performance in sport	Effect of engine size on a car's acceleration	Life expectancy versus cost of housing
2 Specify in more detail	A throwing event	A particular make of car	Compare house prices in Yorkshire with those in South-east England
3 Consider questions which you could investigate	How much further do pupils throw using a run up? Is a Year 9 pupil able to throw as far as a Year 11 pupil of the same height?	Does a bigger engine always mean that a car can accelerate faster?	Do people who live in expensive housing tend to live longer?
4 State your hypotheses (your guesses at what could happen)	Distance thrown will improve using a run up. Year 11 pupils of the same height may be physically stronger and would therefore throw further	In general, more powerful engines produce the greater acceleration. More powerful engines tend to be in heavier cars and therefore the acceleration will not be affected. Larger engines in the same model of car will improve acceleration	People in expensive housing have greater incomes and also may have a longer life expectancy
5 Sources of information required	Survey of distance thrown with different lengths of run-up	Magazines and/or books with information on engine sizes and acceleration times for 0–60 mph	Library or the Internet for census data for each area

Step	Example 1 PE	Example 2 Science	Example 3 Geography
6 Relevant data	Choose pupils from different age groups with a range of heights Make sure that there is an equal number of boys and girls Choose pupils from the full range of ability	Make of car, engine size and acceleration **Note:** The government requires car manufacturers to publish the time taken to accelerate from 0–60 mph	Average cost of housing for each area Data about life expectancy for each area
7 Possible problems	Avoid bias when choosing your sample or carrying out your survey	Petrol engines must be compared with other petrol engines not with diesel engines	
8 Data collection	Make sure that you can record all the factors which may affect the distance thrown: for example, age or height	Make sure that you can record all the information which you need, such as engine size and weight of car. Remember to quote sources of data	Extract relevant data from sources. Remember to quote sources of data
9 Decide on the level of accuracy required	Decide how accurate your data needs to be: for example, nearest 10 cm	Round any published engine sizes to the nearest 100 cm^3 (usually given as 'cc' in the car trade), which is 0.1 litre For example, a 1905 cc engine has a capacity of approximately 1.9 litres	
10 Determine sample size	Remember that collecting too much information may slow down the experiment		
11 Construct tables for large sets of raw data in order to make work manageable	Group distances thrown into intervals of 5 metres Use two-way tables to highlight differences between boys' and girls' data		Group population data in age groups of, for example, 10 year intervals
12 Decide which statistics are most suitable	When the distances thrown are close together, use the mean. When there are a few extreme values, use the median		Sample should be sufficiently large to be able to use the mean

Exercise 5G

 Look at the three examples presented in the preceding table and investigate either one of the problems given or a problem of your own choice. You should follow the steps given there, including your own ideas.

Extension Work

Think of a problem related to a piece of work, such as a foreign language essay or a history project. See whether you can use the step-by-step plan to carry out a statistical investigation.

For example, you may wish to compare the word length of an English and a French piece of writing, or you may wish to compare data about two wars.

LEVEL BOOSTER

6
I can draw conclusions from scatter graphs.
I have a basic understanding of correlation.

7
I can draw a line of best fit on a scatter diagram by inspection.
I can estimate the mean from a grouped frequency.

8
I can interpret and construct cumulative frequency diagrams using the upper boundary of a class interval.
I can estimate the median and the interquartile range, and use these to compare distributions and make inferences.

1 *2002 Paper 2*

A newspaper wrote an article about public libraries in England and Wales. It published this diagram.

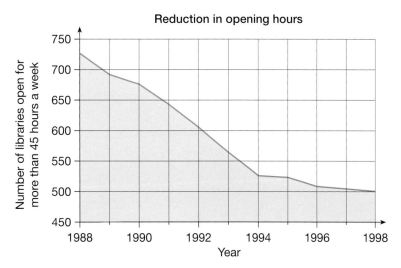

Reduction in opening hours

Use the diagram to decide whether each statement below is true or false, or whether you cannot be certain.

a The number of libraries open for more than 45 hours per week fell by more than half from 1988 to 1998.

☐ True   ☐ False   ☐ Cannot be certain

Explain your answer.

b In 2004 there will be about 450 libraries open in England and Wales for more than 45 hours a week.

☐ True   ☐ False   ☐ Cannot be certain

Explain your answer.

2 *2006 Paper 1*

The scatter graph shows 15 pupils' coursework and test marks.

To find a pupil's **total** mark, you add the coursework mark to the test mark.

a Which pupil had the highest **total** mark?

b Look at the statement below. State whether it is True or False.

> The range of coursework marks was greater than the range of test marks.

Explain your answer.

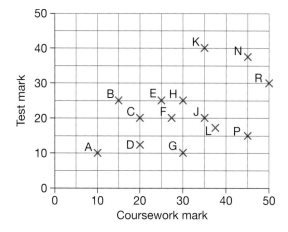

c Pupils with total marks in the shaded region on the graph win a prize.

What is the **smallest total mark** needed to win a prize?

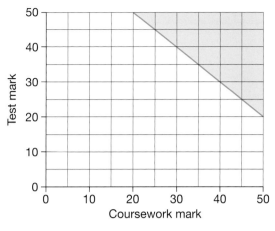

d Another school has a different rule for pupils to win a prize.

Rule: The coursework mark must be 25 or more, and
the test mark must be 25 or more, and
the total mark must be 65 or more.

On a copy of the graph to the right, shade the region of total marks for which pupils would win a prize.

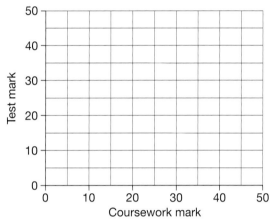

3 *2003 Paper 1*

The scatter graph shows information about trees called poplars.

a What does the scatter graph show about the relationship between the diameter of the tree trunk and the height of the tree?

b The height of a different tree is 3 m. The diameter of its trunk is 5 cm. Use the graph to explain why this tree is not likely to be a poplar.

c Another tree is a poplar. The diameter of its trunk is 3.2 cm. Estimate the height of this tree.

d Below are some statements about drawing lines of best fit on scatter graphs. Copy each statement, and then tick it to show whether the statement is True or False.

Lines of best fit must always …

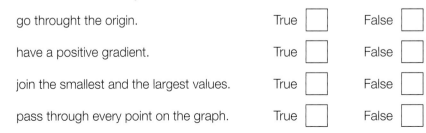

go throught the origin.	True ☐	False ☐
have a positive gradient.	True ☐	False ☐
join the smallest and the largest values.	True ☐	False ☐
pass through every point on the graph.	True ☐	False ☐

4 *2001 Paper 2*

The goldcrest is Britain's smallest species of bird.

On winter days, a goldcrest must eat enough food to keep it warm at night.
During the day, the mass of the bird increases.

The scatter diagram shows the mass of goldcrests at different times during winter days.
It also shows the line of best fit.

a Estimate the mass of a goldcrest at 11:30 am.

b Estimate how many grams, on average, the mass of a goldcrest increases during one hour.

c Which goldcrest represented on the scatter diagram is least likely to survive the night if it is cold?

Give your coordinates of the correct point on the scatter diagram.
Then explain why you chose that point.

5 *2006 Paper 1*

A pupil investigated whether pupils who study more watch less
television.

The scatter graph shows his results. The line of best fit is
also shown.

a What type of correlation does the graph show?

b The pupil says the equation of the line of best fit is
$y = x + 40$

Explain how you can tell that this equation is **wrong**.

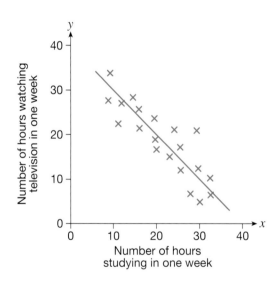

6 *2001 Paper 1*

The first 'Thomas the Tank Engine' stories were written in 1945. In the 1980s, the stories were rewritten.

The cumulative frequency graph shows the number of words per sentence for one of the stories.

There are 58 sentences in the old version.

There are 68 sentences in the new version.

a Estimate the median number of words per sentence in the old version and in the new version.

Show your method on a copy of the graph.

b What can you tell from the data about the number of words per sentence in the old version and in the new version?

c Estimate the percentage of sentences in the old version that had more than 12 words per sentence. Show your working.

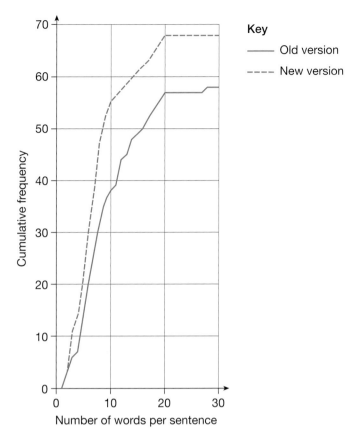

7 *2007 Paper 1*

5000 pupils took part in a test. Pupils took two papers, paper 1 and paper 2.

The graph shows the cumulative frequencies of their marks for each paper.

Use the graph to answer these questions.

For each question state True, or False, or Not enough information.

a The median mark for **paper 1** was about 38.

True   False   Not enough information

Explain your answer.

b The interquartile range of the marks for **paper 1** was about 23.

True   False   Not enough information

Explain your answer.

c Paper 1 was easier than paper 2.

True   False   Not enough information

Explain your answer.

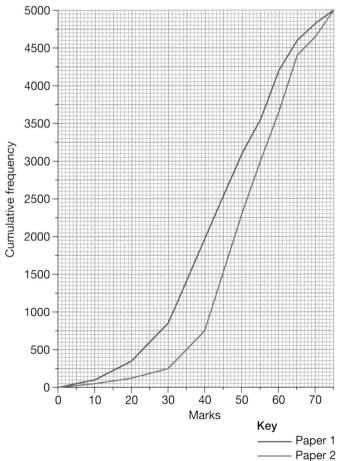

8 *2003 Paper 1*

Tom did a survey of the age distribution of people at a theme park. He asked 160 people. The cumulative frequency graph shows his results.

a Use the graph to estimate the median age of people at the theme park.

b Use the graph to estimate the interquartile range of the age of people at the theme park. Show your method on the graph.

c Tom did a similar survey at a flower show. Results:

  The median age was 47 years.

  The interquartile range was 29 years.

Compare the age distribution of the people at the flower show with that of the people at the theme park.

FM Rainforest deforestation

Since 1970, over 600 000 km² of Amazon rainforest have been destroyed. This is an area larger than Spain.

Between the years 2000 and 2005, Brazil lost over 132 000 km² of forest – an area about the same size as Greece.

The table below shows how much of the rainforests in Brazil have been lost each year since 1988.

Deforestation figure

Year	Deforestation (sq km)
1988	21 000
1989	18 000
1990	14 000
1991	11 000
1992	14 000
1993	15 000
1994	15 000
1995	29 000
1996	18 000
1997	13 000
1998	17 000
1999	17 000
2000	18 000
2001	18 000
2002	21 000
2003	25 000
2004	27 000
2005	19 000
2006	14 000
2007	10 000

Use the information on the left to answer these questions.

1 From 1988 to 1991, Brazil had an economic slowdown. From 1992 to 1995, Brazil had economic growth.

   a What does the chart and the information above suggest about a link between deforestation and the economy in Brazil.

   b What do think was happening to Brazil's economy:

     i from 1998 to 2004?

     ii from 2005-7?

2 Draw a cumulative graph, showing the total deforestation since 1988, year by year.

3 If the rate of deforestation from 2005–7 continued at the same rate, estimate when the deforestation would be 4000 km^2.

The pie chart below shows the three main reasons for deforestation in the Amazon from 2000–5.

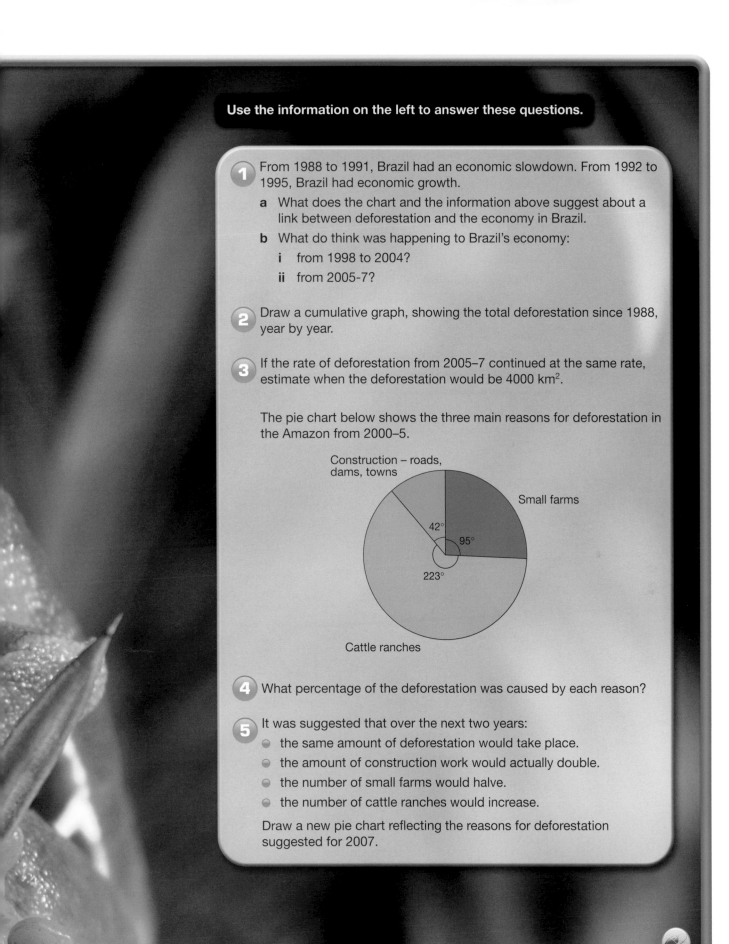

Construction – roads, dams, towns

Small farms

42°

95°

223°

Cattle ranches

4 What percentage of the deforestation was caused by each reason?

5 It was suggested that over the next two years:
- the same amount of deforestation would take place.
- the amount of construction work would actually double.
- the number of small farms would halve.
- the number of cattle ranches would increase.

Draw a new pie chart reflecting the reasons for deforestation suggested for 2007.

This chapter is going to show you

- How to solve problems using similar triangles
- How to convert from one metric unit to another for area and volume
- How to calculate the length of arcs and the area of sectors
- How to calculate the volume of a cylinder
- How to solve problems involving speed

What you should already know

- How to use ratio
- How to find alternate and corresponding angles in parallel lines
- The metric units for area and volume
- The formulae for the circumference and the area of a circle
- How to calculate the volume of a prism

Similar triangles

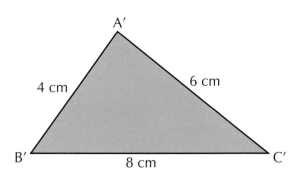

Triangle ABC has been mapped onto triangle A'B'C' by an enlargement of scale factor 2.

Under an enlargement, all of the angles are the same size, and the corresponding sides are in the same ratio.

So in this example, AB : A'B' = AC : A'C' = BC : B'C' = 1 : 2

This can also be written as $\dfrac{A'B'}{AB} = \dfrac{A'C'}{AC} = \dfrac{B'C'}{BC} = 2$

The two triangles are said to be **similar**.

Two triangles are similar if their angles are the same size, or if their corresponding sides are in the same ratio. If one of these conditions is true, then so is the other.

Example 6.1 ▷ Show that the two triangles below are similar.

In triangle ABC, ∠C = 80°

In triangle XYZ, ∠X = 48°

(The sum of the angles in a triangle = 180°)

Since the angles in both triangles are the same, triangle ABC is similar to triangle XYZ.

Example 6.2 ▷ Triangle ABC is similar to triangle DEF. Calculate the length of the side DF.

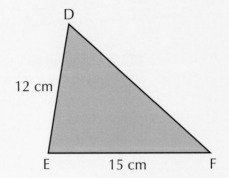

Let the side DF = x

Since the triangles are similar, corresponding sides are in the same ratio.

So, $\dfrac{DE}{AB} = \dfrac{EF}{BC} = \dfrac{DF}{AC} = 3$

Therefore, since $\dfrac{DF}{AC} = 3$, $\dfrac{x}{6} = 3$

So, $x = 18$ cm

Example 6.3 ▷ In the triangle below, EB is parallel to DC. Calculate the length of DC.

∠AEB = ∠ADC (corresponding angles in parallel lines)
∠ABE = ∠ACD (corresponding angles in parallel lines)

So, triangle AEB is similar to triangle ADC since the angles are the same size (∠A is common to both triangles).

Let the side DC = x

Since triangle AEB is similar to triangle ADC, corresponding sides are in the same ratio.

So, $\dfrac{DC}{EB} = \dfrac{AC}{AB}$

Therefore, $\dfrac{x}{3} = \dfrac{8}{4} = 2$

So, $x = 2 \times 3 = 6$ cm

Exercise 6A

1 State whether each of the pairs of triangles below are similar.

a

b

c

d

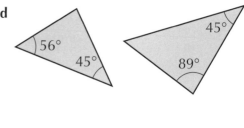

2 a Explain why triangle ABC is similar to triangle XYZ.

b Find the length of XY.

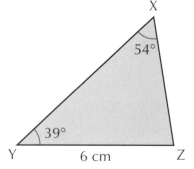

3 a Explain why triangle ABC is similar to triangle PQR.

b Find the length of the side QR.

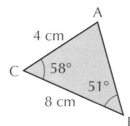

4 In the diagram on the right, ST is parallel to QR.

a Explain why triangle PST is similar to triangle PQR.

b Find the length of the side ST.

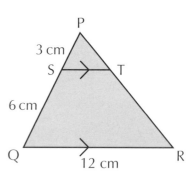

5 In the diagram on the right, AB is parallel to DE.

a Explain why triangle ABC is similar to triangle CDE.

b Find the length of the side DE.

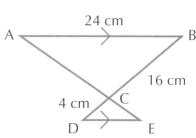

6 In the diagram on the right, LM is parallel to PQ.
Given that OL = 15 cm, OQ = 10 cm and
PQ = 8 cm, find the length of LM.

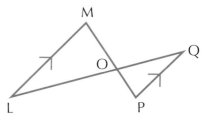

7 Use similar triangles to find the height of the tower in the diagram below.

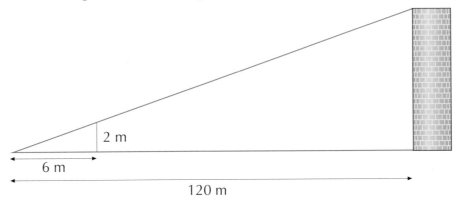

2 m

6 m

120 m

8 The rope on the pair of stepladders, shown on the right,
stops the steps from opening too far. Use similar triangles
to find the length of the rope.

150 cm

50 cm

120 cm

Extension Work

1 In each of the following, write down the pair of similar triangles and find
the length marked *x*.

a

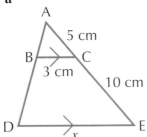

A

5 cm

B   C

3 cm

10 cm

D   E

x

b

P

S

15 cm

10 cm

Q   *x*   T   12 cm   R

c

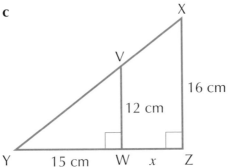

X

V

16 cm

12 cm

Y   15 cm   W   *x*   Z

d

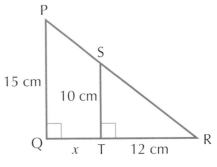

J

x

K   L

3 cm

10 cm

M   N

9 cm

2 This question will show you how to divide a line in a given ratio.

Divide the line AB in the ratio 1 : 4

- Firstly, draw a line XB 5 cm in length in the ratio
  XY : YB = 1 cm : 4 cm
- Next, draw a line joining X and A.
- Now, draw a line parallel to XA from the point Y to meet AB at C.
- Point C divides the line AB in the ratio 1 : 4

Use this method to divide four lines of any length in the following ratios.

   a 1 : 3   **b** 1 : 5   **c** 2 : 3   **d** 3 : 5

Metric units for area and volume

The following are the metric units for area, volume and capacity which you need to know. Also given are the conversions between these units.

Area	Volume	Capacity
$10\,000 \text{ m}^2 = 1$ hectare (ha) $10\,000 \text{ cm}^2 = 1 \text{ m}^2$ $1 \text{ m}^2 = 1\,000\,000 \text{ mm}^2$ $100 \text{ mm}^2 = 1 \text{ cm}^2$	$1\,000\,000 \text{ cm}^3 = 1 \text{ m}^3$ $1000 \text{ mm}^3 = 1 \text{ cm}^3$	$1 \text{ m}^3 = 1000$ litres (l) $1000 \text{ cm}^3 = 1$ litre $1 \text{ cm}^3 = 1$ millilitre (ml) 10 millilitres $= 1$ centilitre (cl) 1000 millilitres $= 100$ centilitres $= 1$ litre

The unit symbol for litres is the letter l. To avoid confusion with the digit 1 (one), the full unit name may be used instead of the symbol.

Remember:

To change **large** units to **smaller** units, **always multiply** by the conversion factor.

To change **small** units to **larger** units, **always divide** by the conversion factor.

Example 6.4 ▷

Convert each of the following as indicated.

  a $72\,000 \text{ cm}^2$ to m^2 **b** 0.3 cm^3 to mm^3 **c** 4500 cm^3 to litres

  a $72\,000 \text{ cm}^2 = 72\,000 \div 10\,000 = 7.2 \text{ m}^2$

  b $0.3 \text{ cm}^3 = 0.3 \times 1000 = 300 \text{ mm}^3$

  c $4500 \text{ cm}^3 = 4500 \div 1000 = 4.5$ litres

Exercise **6B**

1 Express each of the following in cm².

    a   4 m²   **b**   7 m²   **c**   20 m²   **d**   3.5 m²   **e**   0.8 m²

2 Express each of the following in mm².

    a   2 cm²   **b**   5 cm²   **c**   8.5 cm²   **d**   36 cm²   **e**   0.4 cm²

3 Express each of the following in cm².

    a   800 mm²   **b**   2500 mm²   **c**   7830 mm²   **d**   540 mm²   **e**   60 mm²

4 Express each of the following in m².

    a   20 000 cm²   **b**   85 000 cm²   **c**   270 000 cm²

    d   18 600 cm²   **e**   3480 cm²

5 Express each of the following in mm³.

    a   3 cm³   **b**   10 cm³   **c**   6.8 cm³   **d**   0.3 cm³   **e**   0.48 cm³

6 Express each of the following in m³.

    a   5 000 000 cm³   **b**   7 500 000 cm³   **c**   12 000 000 cm³

    d   650 000 cm³   **e**   2000 cm³

7 Express each of the following in litres.

    a   8000 cm³   **b**   17 000 cm³   **c**   500 cm³   **d**   3 m³   **e**   7.2 m³

8 Express each of the following as indicated.

    a   85 ml in cl   **b**   1.2 litres in cl   **c**   8.4 cl in ml

    d   4500 ml in litres   **e**   2.4 litres in ml

9 How many square paving slabs, each of side 50 cm, are needed to cover a rectangular yard measuring 8 m by 5 m?

10 A football pitch measures 120 m by 90 m. Find the area of the pitch in the following units.

    a   m²   **b**   Hectares

11 A fish tank is 1.5 m long, 40 cm wide and 25 cm high. How many litres of water will it hold if it is filled to the top?

12 The volume of the cough medicine bottle is 240 cm³. How many days will the cough medicine last?

13 How many lead cubes of side 2 cm can be cast from 4 litres of molten lead?

COUGH
MEDICINE

Two 5 ml spoonfuls to be
taken four times a day

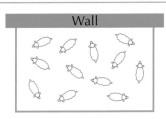

Extension Work

FM

1   A farmer has 100 m of fencing to enclose his sheep. He uses the wall for one side of the rectangular sheep-pen. If each sheep requires 5 m² of grass inside the pen, what is the greatest number of sheep that the pen can hold?

Wall

2
| 12 inches = 1 foot |
| 3 feet = 1 yard |

Use this information to find:

a   the number of square inches in one square yard.

b   the number of cubic inches in one cubic yard.

3   What is an acre? Use reference books or the Internet to find out.

Length of an arc and area of a sector

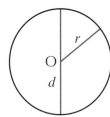

In Year 8, you found how to calculate the circumference and the area of a circle using the formulae:

$$C = \pi d = 2\pi r$$
$$A = \pi r^2$$

where $\pi = 3.142$, or use the $\boxed{\pi}$ key on your calculator.

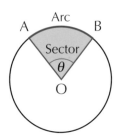

The arc, AB, is part of the circumference. The sector AOB is a slice of the circle enclosed by the arc AB, and the radii OA and OB.

∠AOB is the angle of the sector, and is usually denoted by the Greek letter θ (pronounced *theta*).

The length of the arc AB, as a fraction of the circumference, is $\dfrac{\theta}{360}$

So, the length of the arc AB $= \dfrac{\theta}{360} \times \pi d$

Similarly, the area of the sector AOB $= \dfrac{\theta}{360} \times \pi r^2$

Example 6.5 ▷

Calculate:

a   The length of the arc AB.

b   The area of the sector AOB.

Give your answers correct to three significant figures (sf).

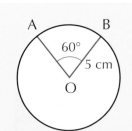

a   Length of the arc AB $= \dfrac{60}{360} \times \pi \times 10 = 5.24$ cm (3 sf)

b   Area of the sector AOB $= \dfrac{60}{360} \times \pi \times 5^2 = 13.1$ cm² (3 sf)

Exercise 6C

In this exercise, let π = 3.142 or use the π key on your calculator.

1 For each of the circles below, calculate:

  i the length of the arc.

  ii the area of the sector.

   Give your answers correct to three significant figures.

a

b

c

d

e

f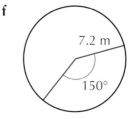

2 A flowerbed in a park is in the shape of a sector of a circle.

  a Calculate the total perimeter of the flowerbed.

  b Calculate the area of the flowerbed.

   Give your answers correct to three significant figures.

3 Calculate the total perimeter of the 'Pacman' shape on the right. Give your answer to the nearest millimetre.

4 Calculate the area of the shaded segment on the right. Give your answer to the nearest square centimetre.

Extension Work

For the following circles, calculate: **i** the length of the arc. **ii** the area of the sector.

Give your answers in terms of π.

a

b

c

d

e

Volume of a cylinder

In Year 8 you found how to calculate the volume of a prism.

The volume V of a prism is found by multiplying the area A of its cross-section by its length l:

$$V = Al$$

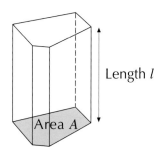

Length l

Area A

The cross-section of a cylinder is a circle with radius r.

The area of the cross-section is $A = \pi r^2$

If the height of the cylinder is h, then the volume V for the cylinder is given by the formula:

$$V = \pi r^2 \times h = \pi r^2 h$$

h

r

Example 6.6 ▷

Calculate the volume of the cylinder, giving the answer correct to three significant figures.

$$V = \pi \times 5^2 \times 8 = 628 \text{ cm}^3 \text{ (3 sf)}$$

5 cm

8 cm

Exercise 6D

In this exercise take $\pi = 3.142$ or use the $\boxed{\pi}$ key on your calculator.

① Calculate the volume of each of the following cylinders. Give your answers correct to three significant figures.

a   6 cm
10 cm

b   3 cm
8 cm

c   4 m
1.5 m

d   2 m
12 m

e   5 cm
0.5 cm

② The diameter of a 2p coin is 2.6 cm and its thickness is 2 mm. Calculate the volume of the coin, giving your answer to the nearest cubic millimetre.

3 Three different shaped cake tins are shown below.

a

7 cm
24 cm
14 cm

b

25 cm
13 cm
8 cm
10 cm

c

20 cm
7.5 cm

Which cake tin has the greatest volume?

4 The diagram on the right shows a tea urn.

30 cm
50 cm

a Calculate the volume of the urn, giving your answer in litres, correct to one decimal place.

b A mug holds 25 cl of tea. How many mugs of tea can be served from the urn?

5 The diagram on the right shows a cylindrical paddling pool.

2 m
48 cm

a Calculate the volume of the pool, giving your answer in cubic metres, correct to three significant figures.

b How many litres of water are in the pool when it is three quarters full? Give your answer to the nearest litre.

6 The canister on the right has a capacity of 10 litres.

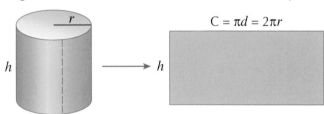

40 cm
Capacity
10 l

a Write down the volume of the canister in cubic centimetres.

b Calculate the area of the base of the canister.

c Calculate the radius of the base of the canister, giving your answer correct to one decimal place.

7

8

Extension Work

In this exercise, take π = 3.142 or use the π key on your calculator.

1 Surface area of a cylinder

When an open cylinder is cut and opened out, a rectangle is formed with the same length as the circumference of the base of the cylinder.

r

h

$C = \pi d = 2\pi r$

h

The curved surface area of the cylinder is the same as the area of the rectangle.

The area of the rectangle is $2\pi rh$.

The total surface area of the cylinder is the curved surface area plus the area of the circles at each end.

The formula for the total surface area of a cylinder is $A = 2\pi rh + 2\pi r^2$

Use this formula to calculate the total surface area of the following cylinders. Give your answers correct to three significant figures.

a   3 cm
    8 cm

b   5 m
    2 m

2   The volume of a can is to be 1000 cm³. The area of the metal used to make the can is to be kept to a minimum. What should the height and the radius of the can be?

A spreadsheet could be used to complete this question.

Rate of change

A **rate of change** is a way of comparing how one quantity changes with another. Examples of rates of change are:

Speed with units in miles per hour (mph), kilometres per hour (km/h) or metres per second (m/s).

Density with units in grams per cubic centimetre (g/cm³).

Fuel consumption with units in miles per gallon (mpg) or kilometres per litre (km/l).

Speed, distance and time

Speed is the distance travelled per unit of time. The relationships between speed, distance and time can be expressed by the following three formulae.

$$\text{Speed} = \frac{\text{Distance}}{\text{Time}} \qquad \text{Distance} = \text{Speed} \times \text{Time} \qquad \text{Time} = \frac{\text{Distance}}{\text{Speed}}$$

When we refer to speed, we usually mean **average speed**, as it is unusual to maintain the same exact speed in one journey.

The relationships between distance, D, time, T, and speed, S, can be remembered by using the triangle:

Covering up the quantity you want to find gives the three formulae you need:

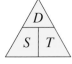

$$S = \frac{D}{T} \qquad\qquad D = ST \qquad\qquad T = \frac{D}{S}$$

Example 6.7 ▷

A plane travels at an average speed of 500 mph. Find the distance travelled by the plane in $3\frac{1}{2}$ hours.

Using the formula $D = ST$, the distance travelled $= 500 \times 3\frac{1}{2} = 1750$ miles

Example 6.8

A coach travels 180 km on a motorway at an average speed of 80 km/h. Find the time taken for the journey.

Using the formula $T = \dfrac{D}{S}$, the time taken $= \dfrac{180}{80} = 2.25$ hours $= 2\frac{1}{4}$ hours

or 2 hours 15 minutes

Density

Density is the mass of a substance per unit of volume.

1 cm³ of gold has a mass of 19.3 g. We say that the density of gold is 19.3 g per cm³, written briefly as 19.3 g/cm³.

$$\text{Density} = \frac{\text{Mass}}{\text{Volume}}$$

The relationships between density, D, mass, M, and volume, V, can be remembered by using this triangle:

Covering up the quantity you want to find gives the three formulae you need:

$$D = \frac{M}{V} \qquad\qquad M = DV \qquad\qquad V = \frac{M}{D}$$

Example 6.9

The volume of a metal rod is 4 cm³ and its mass is 32 g. Find the density of the metal.

Using the formula $D = \dfrac{M}{V}$, the density of the metal is $\dfrac{32}{4} = 8$ g/cm³

Example 6.10

Find the mass of a stone, which has a volume of 40 cm³ and a density of 2.25 g/cm³.

Using the formula $M = DV$, the mass of the stone $= 2.25 \times 40 = 90$ g

Exercise 6E

1. An Intercity train has an average speed of 120 mph. Find the distance the train travels during the following times.

   a 2 hours b $1\frac{1}{2}$ hours c 15 minutes d 20 minutes

2. The road distance between Leeds and London is 210 miles. Find the average speed of a car for each of the following journey times between the two cities.

   a 4 hours b 5 hours
   c $3\frac{1}{2}$ hours d 3 hours 20 minutes

3. John's average cycling speed is 12 mph. Find the time it takes him to cycle the following distances.

   a 36 miles b 30 miles c 40 miles d 21 miles

4 Copy and complete the following table.

	Distance travelled	Time taken	Average speed
a	150 miles	2 hours	
b	540 kilometres	$4\frac{1}{2}$ hours	
c		5 hours	25 mph
d		2 hours 15 minutes	100 km/h
e	250 metres		20 m/s
f	200 miles		60 mph

5 A gamekeeper fires his gun and the bullet travels at 120 m/s. Find the distance covered by the bullet in 1.8 seconds.

6 The distance between New York and San Francisco is 2550 miles. A plane takes off from New York at 7 am and lands at San Francisco at 11.15 am. Find the average speed of the plane.

7 Change each of the following speeds, given in kilometres per hour, to metres per second.

    a 36 km/h   **b** 90 km/h   **c** 120 km/h

8 If the density of a marble is 2.8 g/cm³, find the mass of a marble that has a volume of 56 cm³.

9 Find the volume of a liquid that has a mass of 6 kg and a density of 1.2 g/cm³. Give your answer in litres.

10 A 1 kg bag of sugar has a volume of 625 cm³. Find the density of the sugar in g/cm³.

SUGAR
1 kg

Extension Work

1 Frank travels 105 miles on a motorway. The first 30 miles of his journey are completed at an average speed of 60 mph. He then stops for 30 minutes at a service station before completing the final stage of his journey at an average speed of 50 mph.

Find the average speed for the whole of his journey.

2 A train travels at an average speed of 50 mph for 2 hours. It then slows down to complete the final 30 minutes of the journey at an average speed of 40 mph.

Find the average speed of the train for the whole journey.

3 Sue cycles to visit a friend who lives 30 km from her home. She cycles to her friend's house travelling at an average speed of 20 km/h and returns home travelling at an average speed of 15 km/h.

Find her average speed over the whole journey.

4 The density of kitchen foil is 2.5 g/cm³. A roll of kitchen foil is 10 m long, 30 cm wide and is 0.06 mm thick. Calculate the mass of the roll of foil.

Kitchen Foil   10 m

5 A car uses petrol at a rate of 30 mpg.
- **a** How far can the car travel on 3 gallons of petrol?
- **b** How many gallons of petrol are required for a journey of 600 miles?

6 In Science, other measures for rates of change are used. Use reference books or the Internet to find the formulae and the units used for acceleration, pressure and power.

LEVEL BOOSTER

5
I know the metric units for area, volume and capacity.

6
I can use the formulae to calculate the circumference and the area of a circle.
I can use metric units for area, volume and capacity when solving problems.

7
I can calculate the volume of a cylinder.
I can solve problems involving speed.

8
I know how to use similar triangles.
I can calculate the length of an arc and the area of a sector.

National Test questions

6

1   *2001 Paper 2*

   a   A coach travels 300 miles at an average speed of 40 mph. For how many hours does the coach travel?

   b   An aeroplane flies 1860 miles in 4 hours. What is its average speed?

   c   A bus travels for $2\frac{1}{2}$ hours at an average speed of 24 mph. How far does the bus travel?

7

2   *2003 Paper 1*

   The diagram shows the distance between my home, H, and the towns, A and B. It also shows information about journey times.

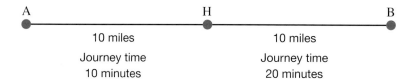

   a   What is the average speed of the journey from my home to town A?

   b   What is the average speed of the journey from my home to town B?

   c   I drive from town A to my home and then to town B. The journey time is 30 minutes. What is my average speed?

   Show your working.

3   *2005 5–7 Paper 2*

   The diagram shows two circles and a square, ABCD.

   A and B are the centres of the circles.

   The radius of each circle is **5 cm**.

   Calculate the area of the **shaded part** of the square.

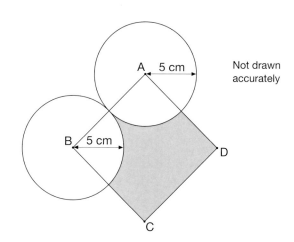

8

4   *2000 Paper 1*

   a   The triangles below are similar.

      What is the value of *p*? Show your working.

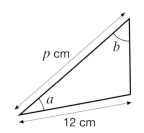

b Triangles ABC and BDC are similar.

What is the length of CD?

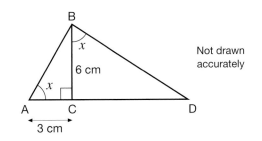

Not drawn accurately

c Look at the triangles on the right.

Are they similar? Show working to explain how you know.

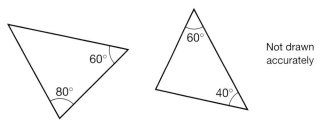

Not drawn accurately

5 *2001 Paper 2*

The diagram shows parts of two circles, sector A and sector B.

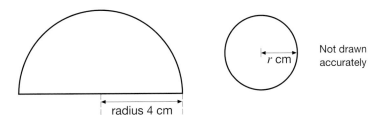

a Which sector has the bigger area?
Show working to explain your answer.

b The perimeter of a sector is made from two straight lines and an arc. Which sector has the bigger perimeter?

Show working to explain your answer.

c A semi-circle of radius 4 cm, has the same area as a complete circle of radius *r* cm.

Not drawn accurately

What is the radius of the complete circle? Show your working.

6 *2003 Paper 2*

A cylinder has a radius of 2.5 cm. The volume of the cylinder, in cm³, is 4.5π.

What is the height of the cylinder? Show your working.

Athletics stadium

An athletics stadium is having a 'face-lift'.

1 The shot-put circle is going to be resurfaced.

  a What is the area of the circle?

  b The circle is resurfaced with a sand and cement mix which is 25 mm thick.

    What is the volume of the sand and cement mix that is needed to resurface the shot-put circle?

2.135 m

2 The high jump zone is also going to be resurfaced.

  a What is the area of the high jump zone?

  b Resurfacing costs £57.50 per square metre.

    What is the cost to resurface the high jump zone?

30 m

3 The running track is going to be repainted.

The diagram shows the dimensions of the inside line of the track.

  a What is the total distance of the inside line?

  b The track has eight lanes. Each lane is 1 m wide.

    What is the total distance of all the lines?

  c One litre of paint is needed for 4 m of line.

    How many litres of paint are needed for all eight lanes?

  d A large tin of paint holds 20 litres. How many tins are needed?

  e One tin of paint costs £52.70. What is the total cost of the paint?

73 m

85 m

4 A new winners' podium is going to be built.

This sketch shows the dimensions.

What is the total volume of the podium?

20 cm   3rd   1st   2nd   40 cm   60 cm

90 cm   90 cm   90 cm

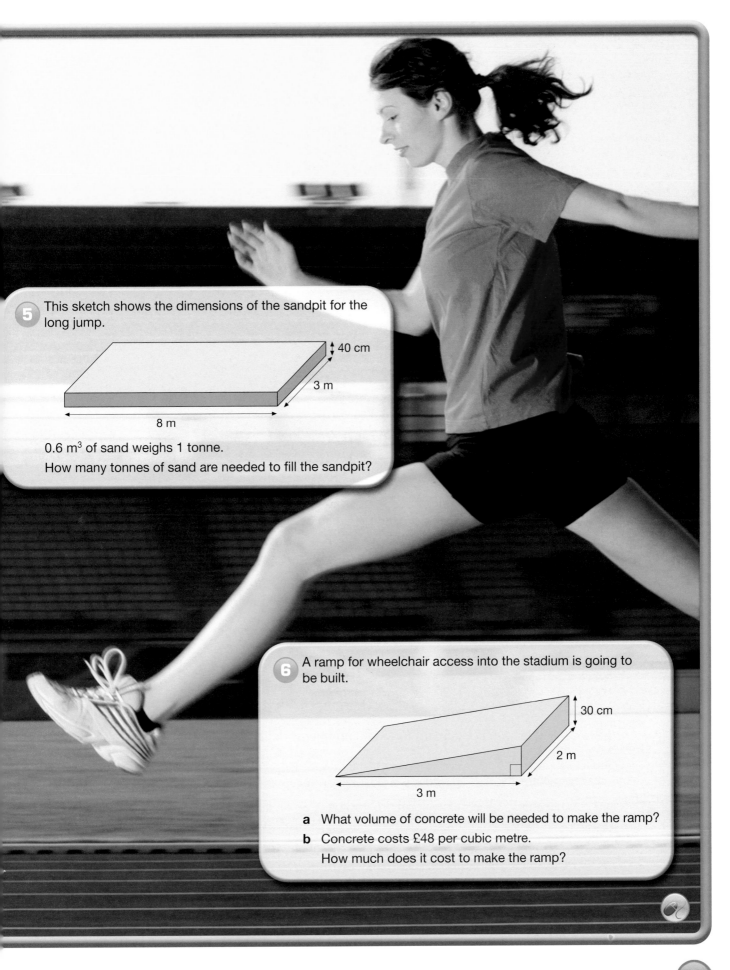

5 This sketch shows the dimensions of the sandpit for the long jump.

40 cm
3 m
8 m

0.6 m³ of sand weighs 1 tonne.

How many tonnes of sand are needed to fill the sandpit?

6 A ramp for wheelchair access into the stadium is going to be built.

30 cm
2 m
3 m

a What volume of concrete will be needed to make the ramp?

b Concrete costs £48 per cubic metre.

How much does it cost to make the ramp?

This chapter is going to show you

- How to write numbers in standard form and how to calculate with them
- How to calculate with numbers given to different degrees of accuracy
- How to write recurring decimals as fractions

What you should already know

- How to multiply and divide by 10, 100, 0.1 and 0.01
- How to round numbers to various degrees of accuracy

Standard form

Standard form is a way of writing concisely very large and very small numbers such as those that occur in physics and astronomy. For example, $53\,000\,000\,000\,000$ can be written as 5.3×10^{13}.

There are three things to remember about a number expressed in standard form. These are explained on the typical example given below.

Rule 1

The first part is a number between 1 and 10

Rule 2

The first part is always multiplied by a power of 10

Rule 3

The power of 10 is either a positive or negative integer (whole number)

$$5.3 \times 10^{13}$$

In general, the standard form of a number is defined as:

$A \times 10^n$

where $1 \le A < 10$ and n is a positive or negative integer.

Examples of standard form are: radius of an electron, 2.82×10^{-15} m; mean radius of the earth, 6.4×10^6 m; speed of light, 2.998×10^8 m/s.

You have already met the way that calculators display numbers in standard form. For example, the number above may be displayed as:

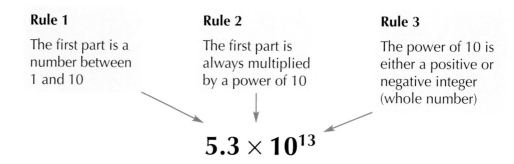

5.3×10^{13}

Example 7.1 ▷ Express each of the following numbers in standard form.

    a   760 000   **b** 0.000 005 42   **c** 36×10^7 **d** 0.24×10^{-2}

    a   Count how many places the digits have to be moved to the right to get the number between 1 and 10:

$$760\,000 = 7.6 \times 10^5$$

    b   Moving the digits to the left makes the power negative.

$$0.000\,005\,42 = 5.42 \times 10^{-6}$$

    c 36×10^7 is not in standard form, as the first part is not a number between 1 and 10. So proceed as follows:

$$36 \times 10^7 = 3.6 \times 10 \times 10^7 = 3.6 \times 10^8$$

    d   Proceed as in part **b**:

$$0.24 \times 10^{-2} = 2.4 \times 10^{-1} \times 10^{-2} = 2.4 \times 10^{-3}$$

Example 7.2 ▷ Write each of the following standard form numbers as an ordinary number.

    a 3.45×10^6 **b** 8.9×10^{-2} **c** 7.632×10^4

    a   Move the digits to the left the same number of places as the power of 10:

$$3.45 \times 10^6 = 3.45 \times 1\,000\,000 = 3\,450\,000$$

    b   A negative power of 10 means move the digits to the right:

$$8.9 \times 10^{-2} = 8.9 \times 0.01 = 0.089$$

    c   Proceed as in part **a**:

$$7.632 \times 10^4 = 7.632 \times 10\,000 = 76\,320$$

Exercise 7A

1 Write each of the following numbers in standard form. (All have positive powers of 10.)

    a   5 690   **b**   1 200 000   **c**   938 000   **d**   77 800

    e   396 500 000 **f**   561   **g**   73   **h**   4 300 000 000

2 Write each of the following numbers in standard form. (All have negative powers of 10.)

    a   0.0034   **b**   0.056   **c**   0.000 0371   **d**   0.000 0092

    e   0.76   **f**   0.0005   **g**   0.000 0072   **h**   0.0004

3 Write each of the following numbers in standard form. (These have a mixture of positive and negative powers of 10.)

    a   8 900 000   **b**   0.0053   **c**   18 000   **d**   33 300 000

    e   0.000 0067   **f**   8923   **g**   0.735   **h**   0.000 09

4 Write each of the following standard form numbers as an ordinary number.

    a 2.3×10^6 **b** 4.56×10^2 **c** 6.7×10^5 **d** 3.59×10^3

    e 9×10^6 **f** 2.01×10^6 **g** 3.478×10^4 **h** 8.73×10^7

5 Write each of the following standard form numbers as an ordinary number.

a	6.7×10^{-5}	**b**	3.85×10^{-2}	**c**	7.8×10^{-4}	**d**	5.39×10^{-3}
e	8×10^{-6}	**f**	1.67×10^{-1}	**g**	3.21×10^{-3}	**h**	6.6×10^{-7}

6 Write each of the following standard form numbers as an ordinary number.

a	4.6×10^{3}	**b**	5.766×10^{-2}	**c**	9.3×10^{2}	**d**	1.22×10^{-3}
e	5×10^{4}	**f**	3.05×10^{-1}	**g**	4.82×10^{6}	**h**	5.43×10^{-2}

7 Write each of the following numbers in standard form.

a	43×10^{5}	**b**	56.8×10^{2}	**c**	0.78×10^{4}	**d**	0.58×10^{3}
e	94×10^{-5}	**f**	20.1×10^{-5}	**g**	0.8×10^{-3}	**h**	80×10^{-3}
i	25×10^{-4}	**j**	0.56×10^{-2}	**k**	0.67×10^{5}	**l**	35.9×10^{3}

Extension Work

Calculate, or use the Internet, to find out the following and write the answers in standard form.

1 Average distance of the Sun from the Earth in kilometres

2 Width of a red blood cell

3 Number of seconds that are in 70 years

4 The mass of an electron

5 The mass of a cubic metre of uranium in grams at 4°C

Multiplying with numbers in standard form

Example 7.3 ▷ Calculate each of the following. Give your answer in standard form. Do not use a calculator.

a $(3 \times 10^3) \times (2 \times 10^4)$ **b** $(4 \times 10^2) \times (5 \times 10^3)$ **c** $(2.5 \times 10^{-3}) \times (6 \times 10^5)$

a Rewrite the problem as $3 \times 2 \times 10^3 \times 10^4$. Then multiply the numbers and add the powers of 10:
$$3 \times 2 \times 10^3 \times 10^4 = 6 \times 10^7$$

b After multiplying 4 by 5, this is not in standard form, so it needs to be converted:
$$4 \times 5 \times 10^2 \times 10^3 = 20 \times 10^5$$
$$20 \times 10^5 = 2 \times 10 \times 10^5 = 2 \times 10^6$$

c After multiplying 2.5 by 6, this is also not in standard form, so proceed as in part **b**:
$$2.5 \times 6 \times 10^{-3} \times 10^5 = 15 \times 10^2$$
$$= 1.5 \times 10 \times 10^2$$
$$= 1.5 \times 10^3$$

Example 7.4 ▷

Light from the sun takes about 8 minutes to reach the earth. Light travels at 299 792 kilometres per second. How far is the sun from the earth? Give your answer in standard form.

First, convert 8 minutes to seconds:

8 minutes = 8×60 = 480 seconds

Then multiply speed of light by number of seconds to get distance of the sun from the earth:

$480 \times 299\,792 = 144\,000\,000 = 1.44 \times 10^8$ km (rounded to 3 sf)

Example 7.5 ▷

Use a calculator to work out each of the following. Give your answer in standard form to 3 sf.

a $(3.74 \times 10^4) \times (2.49 \times 10^3)$ **b** $(1.255 \times 10^{-3}) \times (5.875 \times 10^{-2})$

The key on a calculator with which to enter standard form is usually $\boxed{\times 10^x}$.

Remember that a negative power will need the negative key $\boxed{(-)}$.

So, to enter 3.74×10^4 press these keys: $\boxed{3}$ $\boxed{.}$ $\boxed{7}$ $\boxed{4}$ $\boxed{\times 10^x}$ $\boxed{4}$

Note the × sign is *not* pressed. If this key is pressed the wrong value is entered.

a Enter the following:

$\boxed{3}$ $\boxed{.}$ $\boxed{7}$ $\boxed{4}$ $\boxed{\times 10^x}$ $\boxed{4}$ $\boxed{\times}$ $\boxed{2}$ $\boxed{.}$ $\boxed{4}$ $\boxed{9}$ $\boxed{\times 10^x}$ $\boxed{3}$ $\boxed{=}$

The display will be 93126000 or 9.3126×10^7.

When rounded to 3 sf, the answer is 9.31×10^7.

b Enter the following:

$\boxed{1}$ $\boxed{.}$ $\boxed{2}$ $\boxed{5}$ $\boxed{5}$ $\boxed{\times 10^x}$ $\boxed{(-)}$ $\boxed{3}$ $\boxed{\times}$ $\boxed{5}$ $\boxed{.}$ $\boxed{8}$ $\boxed{7}$ $\boxed{5}$ $\boxed{\times 10^x}$ $\boxed{(-)}$ $\boxed{2}$ $\boxed{=}$

The display will be:

0.000073731 or 7.3731×10^{-5}

When rounded to 3 sf, the answer is 7.37×10^{-5}.

Exercise 7B

1 Do not use a calculator for this question. Work out each of the following and give your answers in standard form.

a $(2 \times 10^3) \times (4 \times 10^2)$ **b** $(3 \times 10^2) \times (4 \times 10^5)$ **c** $(4 \times 10^3) \times (2 \times 10^4)$

d $(3 \times 10^{-2}) \times (3 \times 10^{-3})$ **e** $(4 \times 10^{-5}) \times (8 \times 10^{-3})$ **f** $(6 \times 10^3) \times (7 \times 10^{-6})$

g $(4.2 \times 10^{-4}) \times (5 \times 10^2)$ **h** $(6.5 \times 10^4) \times (4 \times 10^{-2})$ **i** $(7 \times 10^6) \times (8 \times 10^{-4})$

j $(2.5 \times 10^6) \times (9 \times 10^{-2})$ **k** $(2.8 \times 10^5) \times (4 \times 10^{-3})$ **l** $(6 \times 10^3)^2$

2 You may use a calculator for this question. Work out each of the following and give your answers in standard form. Do not round off your answers.

a $(4.3 \times 10^4) \times (2.2 \times 10^5)$ **b** $(6.4 \times 10^2) \times (1.8 \times 10^5)$

c $(2.8 \times 10^2) \times (4.6 \times 10^7)$ **d** $(1.9 \times 10^{-3}) \times (2.9 \times 10^{-2})$

e $(7.3 \times 10^{-2}) \times (6.4 \times 10^6)$ **f** $(9.3 \times 10^4) \times (1.8 \times 10^{-6})$

g $(3.25 \times 10^4) \times (9.2 \times 10^{-1})$ **h** $(2.85 \times 10^4) \times (4.6 \times 10^{-2})$

i $(3.6 \times 10^2)^3$

8

3 You may use a calculator for this question. Work out each of the following and give your answers in standard form. Round your answers to three significant figures.

a	$(2.35 \times 10^5) \times (4.18 \times 10^5)$	**b**	$(1.78 \times 10^5) \times (4.09 \times 10^2)$
c	$(9.821 \times 10^2) \times (7.402 \times 10^6)$	**d**	$(2.64 \times 10^{-2}) \times (8.905 \times 10^{-5})$
e	$(4.922 \times 10^4) \times (8.23 \times 10^{-8})$	**f**	$(7.92 \times 10^3) \times (7.38 \times 10^{-6})$
g	$(4.27 \times 10^{-3}) \times (6.92 \times 10^8)$	**h**	$(2.65 \times 10^{-5}) \times (5.87 \times 10^{-2})$
i	$(7.83 \times 10^6)^2$	**j**	$(2.534 \times 10^{-2})^3$

4 Zip discs are used to store large amounts of information. One megabyte (Mb) is 1 million bytes.

How many bytes are there in a pack of five 250 Mb zip discs? Answer in standard form.

5 There are approximately 120 000 hairs on a human head. Each hair is about 1×10^{-5} metres in diameter.

If all the hairs on a head were laid side by side, what would the total width be?

Extension **Work**

1 Use the Internet to find out about very large numbers. Look up 'googol' on a search engine.

Note: The name of the well-known search engine is google, which is pronounced in the same way.

2 Can you find the meaning of 'googolplex'?

3 What is the largest number of any practical use?

Dividing with numbers in standard form

Example 7.6 Calculate each of the following. Give your answer in standard form. Do not use a calculator.

a $(3 \times 10^6) \div (2 \times 10^2)$ **b** $(4 \times 10^{-6}) \div (5 \times 10^{-3})$ **c** $(1.2 \times 10^5) \div (4 \times 10^{-2})$

a Rewrite the problem as $(3 \div 2) \times (10^6 \div 10^2)$. Note that the numbers and the powers have been separated but there is still a multiplication sign between them. This is because standard form numbers are always expressed in this way.

Divide the numbers and subtract the powers of 10, which gives:
$$(3 \div 2) \times (10^6 \div 10^2) = 1.5 \times 10^4$$

b $(4 \div 5) \times (10^{-6} \div 10^{-3}) = 0.8 \times 10^{-3}$. After dividing 4 by 5, this is not in standard form, so it needs to be converted:
$$0.8 \times 10^{-3} = 8 \times 10^{-1} \times 10^{-3} = 8 \times 10^{-4}$$

c After dividing 1.2 by 4, this is also not in standard form, so proceed as in part **b**:
$$(1.2 \div 4) \times (10^5 \div 10^{-2}) = 0.3 \times 10^7$$
$$= 3 \times 10^{-1} \times 10^7$$
$$= 3 \times 10^6$$

Example 7.7 ▷ A nanometre is a billionth of a metre, or about $\frac{1}{25\,400\,000}$ inch. Write $1 \div 25\,400\,000$ as a number in standard form to three significant figures.

Doing the calculation on a calculator, the display may say:

3.937×10^{-8} or 0.00000003937

When rounded and put into standard form, the answer is 3.94×10^{-8}.

Exercise 7C

① Do not use a calculator for this question. Work out each of the following and give your answers in standard form.

a $(6 \times 10^6) \div (2 \times 10^2)$ b $(3 \times 10^6) \div (4 \times 10^3)$ c $(4 \times 10^3) \div (2 \times 10^4)$

d $(9 \times 10^{-2}) \div (3 \times 10^{-7})$ e $(4 \times 10^8) \div (8 \times 10^2)$ f $(6 \times 10^3) \div (5 \times 10^{-6})$

g $(4.5 \times 10^{-4}) \div (5 \times 10^2)$ h $(1.6 \times 10^6) \div (4 \times 10^{-3})$ i $(8 \times 10^9) \div (5 \times 10^4)$

j $(2.5 \times 10^{-3}) \div (5 \times 10^{-6})$ k $(2.8 \times 10^5) \div (4 \times 10^{-3})$ l $\sqrt{(9 \times 10^6)}$

② You may use a calculator for this question. Work out each of the following and give your answers in standard form. Do not round off your answers.

a $(8.1 \times 10^9) \div (1.8 \times 10^5)$ b $(6.48 \times 10^5) \div (1.6 \times 10^3)$

c $(3.78 \times 10^2) \div (1.35 \times 10^7)$ d $(9.86 \times 10^{-3}) \div (2.9 \times 10^{-5})$

e $(5.12 \times 10^{-2}) \div (6.4 \times 10^6)$ f $(2.88 \times 10^4) \div (4.8 \times 10^{-6})$

g $(6.44 \times 10^4) \div (9.2 \times 10^{-1})$ h $(3.68 \times 10^4) \div (4.6 \times 10^{-2})$

i $\sqrt[3]{(8 \times 10^6)}$

③ You may use a calculator for this question. Work out the following and give your answers in standard form. Round your answers to three significant figures.

a $(2.3 \times 10^8) \div (4.1 \times 10^3)$ b $(6.7 \times 10^5) \div (4.9 \times 10^2)$

c $(9.8 \times 10^2) \div (7.4 \times 10^6)$ d $(2.6 \times 10^{-2}) \div (8.9 \times 10^{-5})$

e $(4.9 \times 10^4) \div (8.2 \times 10^{-8})$ f $(6.9 \times 10^3) \div (2.4 \times 10^{-6})$

g $(4.3 \times 10^{-3}) \div (6.9 \times 10^8)$ h $(2.6 \times 10^{-5}) \div (5.8 \times 10^{-2})$

i $\sqrt{(6.25 \times 10^6)}$ j $\sqrt[3]{(1.728 \times 10^9)}$

④ The circumference of the earth at the equator is 4×10^4 km. Calculate the radius of the earth. Give your answer in standard form.

⑤ A virus is 3×10^{-5} m wide. How many would fit across the head of a pin which is 1 mm wide?

Extension Work

Use the Internet to find out about very small numbers. Look up 'centi' on a search engine.

Can you find out the meaning of these prefixes: milli, micro, nano, pico, femto, atto, zepto and yocto?

Upper and lower bounds 1

Form 7Q are making invitations to their Christmas party. They cut pieces of card 10 cm wide on which to write the invitations. They make envelopes 10.5 cm wide in which to put them.

INVITATION

10 cm   10.5 cm

The invitations are accurate to the nearest centimetre and the envelopes are accurate to the nearest half centimetre. Will all of the invitations fit into all of the envelopes?

Example 7.8 ▷ Give the possible range of values for each of the following.

a A football crowd which is 3400 to the nearest hundred

b A piece of wood which is 32 cm long to the nearest centimetre

c The mass of a marble which is 12 g to two significant figures

a The smallest value is 3350 and the greatest is 3449.

b The smallest value is 31.5 cm and the greatest is 32.4$\dot{9}$. But to make the range easier, the **upper bound** is given as 32.5 cm. Strictly speaking, the ranges should be expressed as:

$$31.5 \leq \text{Actual length} < 32.5$$

(Note the 'strict' inequality for the upper bound.)

c The actual values must be within three significant figure limits:
$$11.5 \leq \text{Mass} < 12.5$$

Example 7.9 ▷ A rectangle is measured as 15 cm by 10 cm. Both measurements are given to the nearest centimetre. What are the greatest and least possible values of the perimeter?

The length is $14.5 \leq \text{Length} < 15.5$ and the width is $9.5 \leq \text{Width} < 10.5$

Least perimeter is given by:
$$14.5 + 9.5 + 14.5 + 9.5 = 48 \text{ cm}$$

Greatest perimeter is given by:
$$15.5 + 10.5 + 15.5 + 10.5 = 52 \text{ cm}$$

So, $48 \leq \text{Perimeter} < 52$

Note: It is easier to calculate with upper bounds if recurring decimals are not used.

Exercise 7D

① Find the upper and lower bounds between which each of the following quantities lie.

a The number of toffees in a tin which is 30 to the nearest 10

b The amount of rice in a bag which is 20 g to the nearest 10 g

c The speed of a car which is 70 mph to the nearest 10 mph

d The speed of a car which is 70 mph to the nearest unit

e The length of a piece of string which is 20 cm to one significant figure

f The length of a piece of string which is 20 cm to two significant figures

g The mass of a cake which is 500 g to the nearest 10 g

h The mass of a donut which is 50 g to the nearest gram

i The capacity of a jug which holds 1 litre to the nearest cubic centimetre

j The storage capacity of a hard drive which is 40 Gb to two significant figures

2 A lawn is 4 m by 3 m, each measurement accurate to the nearest 10 cm.

a What are the upper and lower bounds for the length of the lawn?

b What are the upper and lower bounds for the width of the lawn?

c What are the upper and lower bounds for the perimeter of the lawn?

3 A tile is 10 cm by 10 cm, measured to the nearest centimetre.

a What are the smallest possible dimensions of the tile?

b What are the largest possible dimensions of the tile?

c If ten of the tiles are placed side by side will they be guaranteed to cover a length of 98 cm?

d John wants to tile a wall which is 3 m long by 2 m high. Will he have enough tiles if he has 700 tiles?

4 Woodville United had crowds of 1200, 1300, 1600, 1000 and 1400 for the first five matches of the season. Each of these values was recorded to the nearest 100.

a What was the least possible total for the five matches?

b What was the greatest possible total for the five matches?

5 There are 200 sweets in a jar, measured to the nearest 10. They weigh 200 g to the nearest 10 g.

a Between what bounds does the number of sweets lie?

b Between what bounds does the mass of the sweets lie?

c Why are the answers to parts **a** and **b** different?

6 A petri dish contains 24 000 bacteria, measured to the nearest thousand.

a What is the least number of bacteria in the dish?

b What is the most number of bacteria in 10 similar dishes?

7 A bat colony has 230 bats, measured to the nearest 10.

a What is the least number of bats there could be?

b What is the greatest number of bats there could be?

8 Mr Ahmed wants to lay a path of slabs 20 m long. He buys 50 slabs which are 40 cm square to the nearest centimetre. Can he be sure he has enough slabs to cover 20 m?

9 A mug holds 200 ml of a drink to the nearest 10 ml. A jug holds 1900 ml to the nearest 100 ml. Can you be sure that nine mugfuls can be poured into a jug without spilling?

10 An exam has five modules. The mark for each module is given to the nearest 5%. Melanie scores 45, 50, 65, 40 and 55 on the five modules. The final grade is based on the actual total of the marks. To get a pass a pupil needs a total of 250 marks (50%). Can Melanie be sure of passing?

1   A piece of wood is 1.2 m long to the nearest centimetre. A piece is cut off, which is 85 cm to the nearest cm. Assuming that there is no loss of length due to the cutting, explain why the largest possible length left is 36 cm and the smallest possible length left is 34 cm.

2   A rectangle has an area of 45 cm², measured to the nearest 5 cm². The width is 2 cm measured to the nearest cm. Explain why the largest possible length is 31.67 cm and the smallest possible length is 17 cm.

Upper and lower bounds 2

Form 7Q are making biscuits for their Christmas party. They take lumps of mixture, which weigh 25 g to the nearest 5 g, from a bowl of mixture containing 3 kg to the nearest 100 g. Can they be sure to make enough biscuits to give each member of the form of 30, four biscuits?

Example 7.10 ▷   A rectangle has a length of 20 cm and a width of 12 cm, both measured to the nearest centimetre. What are the upper and lower bounds of the area of the rectangle?

The upper and lower bounds of the length are 19.5 ≤ Length < 20.5

The upper and lower bounds of the width are 11.5 ≤ Width < 12.5

The upper bound of the area is:
    20.5 × 12.5 = 256.25 cm²

The lower bound of the area is:
    19.5 × 11.5 = 224.25 cm²

The upper and lower bounds of the area are 224.25 ≤ Area < 256.25 cm²

Example 7.11 ▷   A briefcase containing a laptop has a mass of 3.5 kg, measured to the nearest 100 g. The laptop is taken out and the briefcase now has a mass of 0.5 kg, measured to the nearest 100 g. What are the upper and lower bounds of the mass of the laptop?

The upper and lower bounds of the briefcase plus laptop are 3450 ≤ Mass < 3550

The upper and lower bounds of the briefcase without laptop are 450 ≤ Mass < 550

The greatest difference is:
    3550 – 450 = 3100 = 3.1 kg

The least difference is:
    3450 – 550 = 2900 = 2.9 kg

The upper and lower bounds of the laptop are 2.9 ≤ Mass < 3.1 kg

Example 7.12 ▷ | $a = 7.2$ to one decimal place; $b = 4.52$ to two decimal places. What are the upper and lower bounds of $a \div b$?

The upper and lower bounds of a are $7.15 \leq a < 7.25$

The upper and lower bounds of b are $4.515 \leq b < 4.525$

The greatest value from the division is:

$7.25 \div 4.515 = 1.606$ (3 dp)

The least value from the division is:

$7.15 \div 4.525 = 1.580$ (3 dp)

The upper and lower bounds for $\frac{a}{b}$ are $1.580 \leq \frac{a}{b} < 1.606$

Exercise 7E

(1) Find the limits (upper and lower bounds) of the area of each of the following rectangles. All measurements are to the nearest centimetre.

a 3 cm 6 cm

b 2 cm 8 cm

c 9 cm 12 cm

(2) $a = 12$, $b = 18$ and $c = 24$. All the values are to the nearest whole number.

a Write down the upper and lower bounds of a, b and c.

b Work out the upper and lower bounds of each of these.

   i $a \times b$ **ii** $b \div a$ **iii** $(a + b) \times c$ **iv** c^2

(3) Speed = Distance ÷ Time

A car travels for 40 miles, measured to the nearest mile, in a time of 30 minutes, measured to the nearest minute.

a What is the greatest possible speed of the car?

b What is the least possible speed of the car?

(4) Distance = Speed × Time

A plane travels at 550 mph, to the nearest 10 mph, for 2 hours, measured to the nearest tenth of an hour.

a What is the greatest possible distance travelled?

b What is the least possible distance travelled?

(5) There are 200 sweets in a jar, measured to the nearest 10. They weigh 600 g to the nearest 10 g.

a What is the least possible mass of each sweet?

b What is the greatest possible mass of each sweet?

(6) A square has an area of 100 cm^2 measured to the nearest 10 cm^2. What are the upper and lower bounds of the side of the square?

7 $a = 3.2$, $b = 4.5$ and $c = 6.8$, all values being accurate to one decimal place. Work out the greatest and least possible values of the following.

a $a \times b \times c$ **b** $\dfrac{(a + b)}{c}$ **c** $a + b - c$ **d** $(b - a)^2$

8 A rectangle has an area of 250 cm², measured to the nearest 10 cm². The length is 25 cm, measured to the nearest centimetre. What are the upper and lower bounds of the width of the rectangle?

9 On his bathroom scales, which measure to the nearest kilogram, Mr Wilson's case had a mass of 22 kg. On the way to the airport, he took out a coat. On the airport scales, which measure to the nearest tenth of a kilogram, the case weighed 19.8 kg. What are the upper and lower bounds for the weight of the coat?

10 Holes are drilled which have a radius of 4 cm measured to one significant figure. Cylindrical rods are made with a radius of 4.0 cm, measured to two significant figures. Will every rod fit in every hole?

> ## Extension Work
>
> **1** A cube has a volume of 500 cm³, measured to the nearest 100 cm³. What are the upper and lower bounds for the surface area of the cube? Write your answer to 4 sf.
>
> **2** A sphere has a volume of 300 cm³, measured to the nearest 10 cm³. What are the upper and lower bounds for the surface area of the sphere? Write your answer to 4 sf. (Volume of a sphere = $\frac{4}{3}\pi r^3$; surface area = $4\pi r^2$)

Recurring decimals

$$\tfrac{3}{8} = 0.375 \qquad \tfrac{2}{3} = 0.666\,666\ldots \qquad \pi = 3.141\,59\ldots$$

The decimals shown above are, from left to right, a **terminating decimal**, a **recurring decimal** and a **decimal** which never terminates nor recurs. This is called an **irrational number**.

Every recurring decimal can be written as a fraction.

To show a recurring decimal, a small dot is placed over the first and last of the recurring digits. For example:

$$\tfrac{5}{18} = 0.2\dot{7} \qquad \tfrac{4}{11} = 0.\dot{3}\dot{6} \qquad \tfrac{2}{7} = 0.\dot{2}85\,71\dot{4}$$

Example 7.13 ▷   Write each of the following fractions as a recurring decimal.

a $\frac{5}{9}$ **b** $\frac{4}{7}$ **c** $\frac{7}{11}$

Use a calculator to divide each numerator by its denominator.

a $\frac{5}{9} = 5 \div 9 = 0.555\,555\ldots = 0.\dot{5}$

b $\frac{4}{7} = 4 \div 7 = 0.571\,428\,5714\ldots = 0.\dot{5}71\,42\dot{8}$

c $\frac{7}{11} = 7 \div 11 = 0.636\,363\ldots = 0.\dot{6}\dot{3}$

Example 7.14 ▷ Write each of the following recurring decimals as a fraction in its simplest form.

   a $0.\overset{\cdot}{4}\overset{\cdot}{8}$ **b** $0.\overset{\cdot}{3}4\overset{\cdot}{2}$ **c** $3.\overset{\cdot}{4}$

   a Because there are two recurring digits, the denominator is 99 (see table below).

Fraction	$\frac{1}{9}$	$\frac{1}{99}$	$\frac{1}{999}$
Decimal	0.111 111	0.010 101	0.001 001
Dot form	$0.\overset{\cdot}{1}$	$0.\overset{\cdot}{0}\overset{\cdot}{1}$	$0.\overset{\cdot}{0}0\overset{\cdot}{1}$

      So, you have:

$$0.\overset{\cdot}{4}\overset{\cdot}{8} = \frac{48}{99} = \frac{16}{33} \quad \text{(Cancel by 3)}$$

   b Because there are three recurring digits, the denominator is 999. So you have:

$$0.\overset{\cdot}{3}4\overset{\cdot}{2} = \frac{342}{999} = \frac{38}{111} \quad \text{(Cancel by 9)}$$

   c Ignore the whole number. Hence, you have:

$$0.\overset{\cdot}{4} = \frac{4}{9}$$

      This does not cancel, so $3.\overset{\cdot}{4} = 3\frac{4}{9}$

Example 7.15 ▷ Write each of the following recurring decimals as a fraction in its simplest form.

   a $0.\overset{\cdot}{6}\overset{\cdot}{3}$ **b** $0.2\overset{\cdot}{3}\overset{\cdot}{8}$ **c** $2.0\overset{\cdot}{4}1\overset{\cdot}{2}$

In these examples (apart from **a**), the method used in Example 7.14 cannot be used because the recurring decimals do not occur immediately after the decimal point.

   a Because there are two recurring digits, multiply the original number, x, by 100. This gives:

$$x = 0.63636363\ldots \quad (1)$$
$$100x = 63.636363\ldots \quad (2)$$

      Subtract equation 1 from equation 2, to obtain:

$$99x = 63$$
$$x = \frac{63}{99} = \frac{7}{11}$$

   b Because there are two recurring digits, multiply the original number, x, by 100. This gives:

$$x = 0.23838383\ldots \quad (1)$$
$$100x = 23.8383838\ldots \quad (2)$$

      Subtract equation 1 from equation 2, to obtain:

$$99x = 23.6$$
$$x = \frac{23.6}{99} = \frac{236}{990} = \frac{118}{495}$$

Example 7.15

continued

c Because there are three recurring digits, multiply the original fraction, x, by 1000 (ignoring the whole number, 2). This gives:

$$x = 0.0412412412 \quad (1)$$
$$1000x = 41.2412412... \quad (2)$$
$$999x = 41.2$$
$$x = \frac{41.2}{999} = \frac{412}{9990} = \frac{206}{4995}$$

Replace the 2, which gives $2\frac{206}{4995}$

8

Exercise 7F

1 Write each of the following fractions as a recurring decimal.

   a $\frac{4}{7}$ **b** $\frac{76}{101}$ **c** $\frac{23}{33}$ **d** $\frac{1}{3}$ **e** $\frac{2}{9}$

2 Write down the ninths as recurring decimals: for example, $\frac{1}{9} = 0.\dot{1}$. Describe any patterns you see.

3 Write down the elevenths as recurring decimals: for example, $\frac{1}{11} = 0.\dot{0}\dot{9}$, $\frac{2}{11} = 0.\dot{1}\dot{8}...$. Describe any patterns you see.

4 Write down the sevenths as recurring decimals: for example, $\frac{1}{7} = 0.\dot{1}42\,85\dot{7}$, $\frac{2}{7} = 0.\dot{2}85\,71\dot{4}...$. Describe any patterns you see.

5 Write each of the following recurring decimals as a fraction in its simplest form.

   a $0.\dot{4}\dot{5}$ **b** $0.3\dot{2}\dot{1}$ **c** $0.\dot{8}$ **d** $0.\dot{7}2\dot{9}$ **e** $0.\dot{1}\dot{2}$
   f $0.8\dot{1}$ **g** $0.110\dot{7}$ **h** $0.7\dot{8}$ **i** $0.80\dot{1}$ **j** $0.\dot{9}$

6 Write each of the following recurring decimals as a fraction. Write each fraction in its simplest form.

   a $0.0\dot{4}$ **b** $0.0\dot{5}\dot{6}$ **c** $0.5\dot{7}\dot{8}$ **d** $0.0\dot{7}0\dot{4}$ **e** $0.03\dot{4}\dot{5}$

7 Write each of the following recurring decimals as a mixed number.

   a $2.3\dot{9}\dot{2}$ **b** $1.0\dot{5}$ **c** $5.2\dot{1}0\dot{8}$ **d** $2.40\dot{8}\dot{2}$

Extension Work

The thirteenths are recurring decimals. They always have six recurring digits which fit into one of two cycles. These are shown right.

For example: $\frac{1}{13} = 0.\dot{0}769\dot{23}$ and $\frac{2}{13} = 0.\dot{1}538\dot{46}$

Without using a calculator, and by working out the first one or two digits, write down all the thirteenths as recurring decimals.

For example:

$$\frac{1}{13} = \frac{0.07...}{13\sqrt{1.000000}}$$

So, the recurring decimal must be $0.\dot{0}7692\dot{3}$.

Efficient use of a calculator

You have previously used the keys which control brackets, memory, sign change and fractions. This section will remind you how to use these keys and a few others which can be found on most scientific calculators.

Example 7.16 ▷

Use a calculator to evaluate each of the following.

a $[3.5^2 + (5.2 - 2.34)]^2$ **b** $\dfrac{36.7 \times 18.32}{3.7(5.6 - 2.91)}$ **c** $\dfrac{13}{15} - \dfrac{11}{18}$

a Key in as follows:

[( ] [3] [.] [5] [x^2] [+] [( ] [5] [.] [2] [−] [2] [.] [3] [4] [ )] [ )] [x^2] [=]

The answer is 228.3121.

b Key in as follows:

[( ] [3] [6] [.] [7] [×] [1] [8] [.] [3] [2] [ )] [÷] [( ] [3] [.] [7] [×]
[( ] [5] [.] [6] [−] [2] [.] [9] [1] [ )] [ )] [=]

The answer is 67.551 8939..., which can be rounded to 67.6.

c Key in as follows:

[▤] [1] [3] [▼] [1] [5] [▶] [−] [▤] [1] [1] [▼] [1] [8] [▶] [=]

The answer is $\frac{23}{90}$.

Example 7.17 ▷

Use the power key to evaluate: **a** 5.9^4 and **b** $81^{\frac{3}{4}}$

The power key may be marked $x^{\blacksquare}$, or be an inverse or shift function.

a Key in the following:

[5] [.] [9] [$x^{\blacksquare}$] [4] [=]

The answer is 1211.7361.

b Key in the following:

[8] [1] [$x^{\blacksquare}$] [▤] [3] [▼] [4] [▶] [=]

The answer is 27.

Exercise 7G

1 Using the π key on your calculator, work out each of the following. Round each answer to a suitable degree of accuracy.

a $\pi \times 7^2$ **b** $\sqrt{\pi} \div 8$ **c** $2 \times \pi \times 10 \times 9 + \pi \times 9^2$

2 Using the power key on your calculator, work out each of the following. Round your answers to a suitable degree of accuracy if necessary.

a 3.7^2 **b** 8^5 **c** 1.25^3 **d** 0.074^5

3 Using the power key and the fraction key, calculate each of the following.

a $9^{\frac{1}{2}}$ b $64^{\frac{1}{2}}$ c $121^{\frac{1}{2}}$ d $2.25^{\frac{1}{2}}$

4 Using the power key and the fraction key, calculate each of the following.

a $8^{\frac{1}{3}}$ b $64^{\frac{1}{3}}$ c $125^{\frac{1}{3}}$ d $0.216^{\frac{1}{3}}$

5 Use your calculator to work out each of the following. Round your answers to a suitable degree of accuracy.

a $\sqrt{16.5^2 - 4.7^2}$ b $\dfrac{5.65 \times 56.8}{3.04(3.4 - 1.9)}$ c $[4.6^2 + (3.2 - 1.73)]^2$

d $3.8 - [2.9 - (12.3 \times 8.4)]$ e $\dfrac{6\sqrt{5.2^2 + 4^2}}{5}$

6 Use the fraction key to work out each of these.

a $\frac{11}{18} + \frac{17}{22}$ b $\left(\frac{7}{8} - \frac{5}{6}\right) \times \left(\frac{5}{7} - \frac{3}{5}\right)$ c $\left(\frac{2}{3} + \frac{5}{8}\right) \div \left(\frac{4}{9} - \frac{1}{6}\right)$

Extension Work

Choose a number between 1 and 2, say 1.5. Key it into the calculator display.

Perform the following sequence of key presses: $+$ 1 $=$ x^{-1} $=$

Note: The x^{-1} key is called the **reciprocal** key.

After the sequence has been performed, the display should show $\frac{2}{5}$ or 0.4.

Repeat the above sequence of key presses. The display should now show 0.714 … .

Keep repeating the above sequence of key presses until the first three decimal places of the number in the display start to repeat.

LEVEL BOOSTER

6
I can round numbers to two or more decimal places.
I can use the power and root buttons on my calculator.

7
I can use my calculator efficiently to solve more complex calculations.
I can round numbers to one significant figure.
I can write down upper and lower bounds for a quantity.

8
I can convert from ordinary numbers to standard form and vice versa.
I can multiply and divide using numbers in standard form.
I can calculate limits using upper and lower bounds.
I can convert recurring decimals to fractions.

1 *2002 Paper 2*

A company sells and processes films of two different sizes. The tables show how much the company charges.

I want to take 360 photos. I need to buy the film, pay for the film to be printed and pay for the postage.

a Is it cheaper to use all films of 24 photos or all films of 36 photos?

b How much cheaper is it?

Film size: 24 photos	
Cost of each film	£2.15
Postage	Free
Cost to print film	£0.99
Postage of each film	60p

Film size: 36 photos	
Cost of each film	£2.65
Postage	Free
Cost to print film	£2.89
Postage of each film	60p

2 *2007 Paper 2*

The value of π correct to 7 decimal places is:

3.1415927

a Write the value of π correct to 4 decimal places.

b Which value below is closest to the value of π?

$\frac{179}{57}$ $\qquad$ $3\frac{1}{7}$ $\qquad$ $\left(\frac{16}{9}\right)^2$ $\qquad$ $\frac{355}{113}$

3 *2006 Paper 1*

a Put these values in order of size with the smallest first.

5^2 $\qquad$ 3^2 $\qquad$ 3^3 $\qquad$ 2^4

b Look at this information.

5^5 is 3125

What is 5^7?

4 *2007 Paper 1*

Here is the rule to find the geometric mean of two numbers.

Multiply the two numbers together, then find the **square root** of the result.

Example: geometric mean of 4 and 9 $= \sqrt{4 \times 9}$

$\qquad\qquad\qquad\qquad\qquad = \sqrt{36}$

$\qquad\qquad\qquad\qquad\qquad = 6$

a For the two numbers **10** and x, the geometric mean is **30**.

What is the value of x?

b Reena says:

'For the two numbers **–2** and **8**, it is **impossible** to find the geometric mean.'

Is Reena correct?

Explain your answer.

5 *2006 Paper 1*

Copy these multiplication grids and write in the missing numbers.

×	8	
9	72	
–6		30

×	0.2	
3		1.2
		6

6 *2001 Paper 1*

$\dfrac{1}{2500}$ is equal to 0.0004.

a Write 0.0004 in standard form.

b Write $\dfrac{1}{2500}$ in standard form.

c Work out

$$\frac{1}{2500} + \frac{1}{2500}$$

Show your working, and write your answer in standard form.

7 *2002 Paper 2*

The star nearest the Earth (other than the Sun) is Proxima Centauri. Proxima Centauri is 4.22 light-years away. (One light-year is 9.46×10^{12} kilometres.)

Suppose a spaceship could travel at 40 000 km per hour.

a Copy the following calculations. Then state what each one represents. The first one is done for you.

   i $4.22 \times 9.46 \times 10^{12}$ Number of km from Earth to Proxima Centauri

   ii $\dfrac{4.22 \times 9.46 \times 10^{12}}{40\,000}$ ……

   iii $\dfrac{4.22 \times 9.46 \times 10^{12}}{40\,000 \times 24 \times 365.25}$ ……

b Work out

$$\frac{4.22 \times 9.46 \times 10^{12}}{40\,000 \times 24 \times 365.25}$$

Give your answer to the nearest thousand.

8 *2007 Paper 2*

a One light year is approximately 9 430 000 000 000 kilometres.

Write this distance in standard form.

b A star called Wolf 359 is approximately **7.8 light years** from Earth.

About how many kilometres is this?

Write your answer in standard form.

9 *2006 Paper 1*

    a   Look at the number.

        8.679×10^4

        Round it to the nearest thousand.

        Give your answer in **standard form.**

    b   Now look at this number.

        8.679×10^{-4}

        Round it to the nearest **thousandth**.

        Give your answer in **standard form.**

10 *2005 Paper 1*

    a   Show that $(4 \times 10^8) \times (8 \times 10^4) = 3.2 \times 10^{13}$

    b   What is $(4 \times 10^8) \div (8 \times 10^4)$?

        Write your answer in standard form.

Paper

Paper sizes

Standard paper sizes are called A0, A1, A2 and so on.
A0 is approximately 1188 mm by 840 mm.
The next size A1 is found by cutting A0 in half.

Here is a diagram of a piece of paper of size A0.

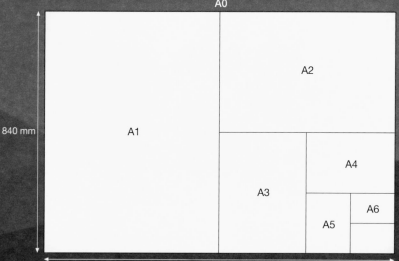

Paper for sale

1 ream = 500 sheets

Reams of Paper – Special offer

Grade of paper	Prices		
	1 ream	5–9 reams	10+ reams
Standard	£2.10		
Special	£1.80	SAVE $\frac{1}{3}$ per ream	EXTRA 10% discount
Quality	£3.00		
Photo	£3.60		

Example for Standard paper:

1 ream costs £2.10
5 reams at full price = 5 × £2.10 = £10.50
Saving = $\frac{1}{3}$ of £10.50 = £3.50
Cost of 5 reams = £7.00
10 reams with $\frac{1}{3}$ off = 2 × £7.00 = £14.00
Extra 10% discount = £1.40
Cost of 10 reams = £12.60

Buy 5 reams
You save
£3.50

Buy 10 reams
You save
£8.40

1 How many sheets of paper are there in 400 reams of paper?

2 The thickness of a piece of paper is 1.2×10^{-1} mm.
How high would 4 reams (2000 sheets) of this paper be?
Give your answer as an ordinary number in centimetres.

3 Here is a table of paper sizes.

Paper size	A0	A1	A2	A3	A4	A5
Length (mm)	1188	840	594			
Width (mm)	840	594				

Copy and complete the table.
Check your result for A4 paper by measuring.

4 How many pieces of A5 paper would be needed to make a piece of A1 paper?

5 Look at the special offers.
  a Work out the cost of 3 reams of Special grade paper.
  b Work out the cost of 5 reams of Quality grade paper.
  c Work out the difference between the cost of 9 reams of Photo grade pagper and 10 reams of Photo grade paper.

6 Work out the saving if you buy 20 reams of Quality paper using the offers.

145

This chapter is going to show you	What you should already know
• How to interpret negative powers • How to interpret powers given as fractions, including square roots and cube roots • How to construct quadratic and cubic graphs	• How to find square roots and cube roots • What a factor is

Index notation with algebra – negative powers

You met two rules of algebra regarding indices in Year 8.

When multiplying powers of the same variable, *add the indices*:

$$x^A \times x^B = x^{A+B}$$

Example 8.1 ▷ Simplify each of these.

    a $g^4 \times g$ **b** $3t^2 \times 5t^4$

    a $g^4 \times g = g^{4+1} = g^5$

    b $3t^2 \times 5t^4 = (3 \times 5)t^{2+4} = 15t^6$

When dividing powers of the same variable, *subtract the indices*:

$$x^A \div x^B = x^{A-B}$$

Example 8.2 ▷ Simplify each of these.

    a $m^6 \div m^3$ **b** $6w^5 \div 2w$

    a $m^6 \div m^3 = m^{6-3} = m^3$

    b $6w^5 \div 2w = (6 \div 2)w^{5-1} = 3w^4$

As you have already seen, powers of numbers and variables can be negative, as in 4^{-1}, x^{-3} and 10^{-5}. This section will show you that negative powers obey the same rules as positive powers stated above. Follow through Example 8.3 to see how the rules work for negative powers.

Example 8.3 ▶ Simplify each of the following.

a $6x^4 \div 2x^{-1}$ **b** $2m^{-1} \times 4m^{-2}$

a $6x^4 \div 2x^{-1} = (6 \div 2)x^{4--1} = 3x^5$

b $2m^{-1} \times 4m^{-2} = (2 \times 4)m^{-1+-2} = 8m^{-3}$

Investigation ▶ Work through each of the following. Write your answer:

i using a negative power.   **ii** in fraction form.

The answers to the first two questions have been completed for you.

a **i** $4 \div 4^2 = 4^{1-2} = 4^{-1}$ **ii** $4 \div 4^2 = 4 \div 16 = \dfrac{1}{4}$ That is: $4^{-1} = \dfrac{1}{4^1}$

b **i** $4 \div 4^3 = 4^{1-3} = 4^{-2}$ **ii** $4 \div 4^3 = 4 \div 64 = \dfrac{1}{16} = \dfrac{1}{4^2}$ That is: $4^{-2} = \dfrac{1}{4^2}$

c **i** $4 \div 4^4 =$ **ii**   That is:

d **i** $4 \div 4^5 =$ **ii**   That is:

Write down a generalisation from the investigation of x^{-n}.

Exercise 8A

① Simplify each of the following.

a $4x^2 \times x^3$	**b** $m^3 \times 7m$	**c** $n^5 \div n^3$	**d** $x^6 \div x$
e $8m^5 \div 2m$	**f** $3x \times 2x^3$	**g** $5t^3 \times 3t$	**h** $10m^6 \div 2m^3$
i $g^5 \times g^4$	**j** $5m^6 \div 5m^2$	**k** $8t^5 \div 2t^3$	**l** $5m^3 \times 3m^5$
m $12q^4 \times 4q^2$	**n** $am^2 \times bm^3$	**o** $cy \times dy^3$	

② Simplify each of the following. Your answers should not contain fractions.

a $4x \div x^3$	**b** $7m^3 \div m^5$	**c** $n^2 \div n^5$
d $8x^6 \div 2x^9$	**e** $8m^2 \div 2m^7$	**f** $3x \div 2x^3$
g $5t^3 \times 3t^{-5}$	**h** $10m \div 2m^3$	**i** $g^{-5} \times g^4$

③ Simplify each of the following.

a $x^3 \div x^{-4}$	**b** $m^4 \div m^{-3}$	**c** $n^{-2} \div n^{-4}$
d $4x^5 \div 2x^{-3}$	**e** $9m^{-4} \div 3m^{-1}$	**f** $6x \div 2x^{-2}$
g $4t^{-2} \times 3t^{-5}$	**h** $12m \div 2m^{-4}$	**i** $3g^{-4} \times 2g^{-1}$

④ Write each of the following in fraction form.

a m^{-1}	**b** k^{-2}	**c** x^{-3}	**d** n^{-4}
e $5m^{-2}$	**f** $4y^{-1}$	**g** $8x^{-3}$	**h** ab^{-1}

⑤ Write each of the following using a negative power.

a $\dfrac{1}{5}$	**b** $\dfrac{1}{4}$	**c** $\dfrac{3}{x}$	**d** $\dfrac{1}{x^2}$
e $\dfrac{1}{m^6}$	**f** $\dfrac{1}{9}$	**g** $\dfrac{5}{x^4}$	**h** $\dfrac{A}{m^3}$

6 Simplify each of the following.

a	$3x^4 \times x^{-3} \times x$	**b**	$2m^3 \times 5m^{-4} \times 3m^2$	**c**	$4n^3 \div 2n^3 \times 3n$
d	$8x^5 \div 2x^{-2} \times 3x^3$	**e**	$10m^3 \div 5m \times 3m^{-4}$	**f**	$4x^2 \times 3x^{-3} \times 2x^{-1}$
g	$4t^5 \times 5t^{-1} \times 3t^{-1}$	**h**	$12m^5 \div 3m^2 \times 2m^{-4}$	**i**	$3g^6 \times g^{-4} \times 3g^{-1}$
j	$7m^7 \div 7m^5 \times 4m^{-3}$	**k**	$18t^6 \div 3t^{-4} \times 5t^{-3}$	**l**	$6m^2 \times 4m^3 \div m^{-2}$
m	$3q^5 \times 2q^3 \div q^{-4}$	**n**	$km^2 \times pm^3 \div m^{-1}$	**o**	$dy^3 \times ey \div y^{-4}$

Extension Work

1 Find some values of x which meet each of the following conditions.
  a x^2 is always larger than x.
  b x^2 is always smaller than x.
  c $x^2 = x$

2 Find some values of x which meet each of the following conditions.
  a x^2 is always larger than $5x$.
  b x^2 is always smaller than $5x$.
  c $x^2 = 5x$

Square roots, cube roots and other fractional powers

The **square root** of a given number is that number which, when multiplied by itself, produces the given number.

For example, the square root of 36 is 6, since $6 \times 6 = 36$. A square root is represented by the symbol $\sqrt{}$. For example, $\sqrt{36} = 6$

Example 8.4

Solve: **a** $x^2 = 49$ **b** $(x + 3)^2 = 25$

a Taking the square root of both sides gives $x = 7$ and -7

The negative value of x is also a solution, because $-7 \times -7 = 49$

Note that all square roots have two solutions: a positive value and its negative.

b Taking square roots of both sides gives $x + 3 = \pm 5$

If $x + 3 = +5 \Rightarrow x = 2$ and if $x + 3 = -5 \Rightarrow x = -8$

The **cube root** of a given number is that number which, when multiplied by itself twice, produces the given number.

For example, the cube root of 64 is 4, since $4 \times 4 \times 4 = 64$. A cube root is represented by the symbol $\sqrt[3]{}$. For example, $\sqrt[3]{64} = 4$

Example 8.5

Solve $y^3 = 216$

Taking the cube root of both sides gives $y = 6$

Note that the sign (+ or –) of the value is the *same* as the sign of the original number, because here $+ \times + \times + = +$. If the original number had been –216, the solution would have been –6 (because $- \times - \times - = -$).

You should be familiar with the following square roots and cube roots.

$\sqrt{1}$	$\sqrt{4}$	$\sqrt{9}$	$\sqrt{16}$	$\sqrt{25}$	$\sqrt{36}$	$\sqrt{49}$	$\sqrt{64}$	$\sqrt{81}$	$\sqrt{100}$	$\sqrt{121}$	$\sqrt{144}$	$\sqrt{169}$	$\sqrt{196}$	$\sqrt{225}$
±1	±2	±3	±4	±5	±6	±7	±8	±9	±10	±11	±12	±13	±14	±15

$\sqrt[3]{1}$	$\sqrt[3]{8}$	$\sqrt[3]{27}$	$\sqrt[3]{64}$	$\sqrt[3]{125}$	$\sqrt[3]{216}$	$\sqrt[3]{343}$	$\sqrt[3]{512}$	$\sqrt[3]{729}$	$\sqrt[3]{1000}$
1	2	3	4	5	6	7	8	9	10

Often a calculator will be needed to find a square root or a cube root. So, do make sure you know how to use the power key and root key on your calculator.

When decimal numbers are involved, solutions are usually rounded to one decimal place. For example: $\sqrt[3]{250} = 6.3$, $\sqrt{153} = 12.4$

Expressions of the form $x^{\frac{1}{n}}$

The investigation below demonstrates how to interpret powers given as fractions.

Investigation ▷

This investigation looks at the values of expressions which are given in the form $x^{\frac{1}{n}}$. The index $\frac{1}{n}$ shows that the nth root of x is to be taken, as shown below.

You know that $\sqrt{3} \times \sqrt{3} = 3$

$3^{\frac{1}{2}} \times 3^{\frac{1}{2}}$ can be simplified to $3^{\frac{1}{2}+\frac{1}{2}}$

So, $3^{\frac{1}{2}} \times 3^{\frac{1}{2}} = 3^{\frac{1}{2}+\frac{1}{2}} = 3^1 = 3$

This means that $3^{\frac{1}{2}}$ is the same as $\sqrt{3}$.

a Simplify $5^{\frac{1}{3}} \times 5^{\frac{1}{3}} \times 5^{\frac{1}{3}}$

b What does $5^{\frac{1}{3}}$ mean?

c What meaning can be given to these expressions? **i** $x^{\frac{1}{4}}$ **ii** $x^{\frac{1}{5}}$

d Write down what you can say about the expression $x^{\frac{1}{n}}$.

Example 8.6 ▷

Find $3^{\frac{1}{4}}$ using a calculator.

Press the following keys:

[3] [SHIFT] [$x^{\blacksquare}$] [4]

which gives the answer 1.316, correct to three decimal places.

On some makes of calculator the root key is [$x^{\frac{1}{y}}$] or [$\sqrt[y]{x}$]

Exercise 8B

1 Jack has done his homework incorrectly. Find out on which line he has gone wrong and correct the homework from there.

a Solve the equation $2x^2 = 50$

$x^2 = 2 \times 50 = 100$

$x = 10$ and -10

b Solve the equation $4x^2 = 36$

$4x = \sqrt{36} = 6$ and -6

$x = \frac{6}{4}$ and $-\frac{6}{4}$

$x = 1\frac{1}{2}$ and $-1\frac{1}{2}$

2 Use a calculator to find the positive root of each of the following to one decimal place.

a $\sqrt{26}$ **b** $\sqrt{55}$ **c** $\sqrt{94}$ **d** $\sqrt{109}$ **e** $\sqrt{275}$

3 Without using a calculator, state the cube root of each of the following numbers.

    a 8   **b** 1   **c** 125   **d** 27   **e** 1000

    f −64   **g** −1   **h** −1000   **i** 0.001   **j** 0.008

4 Use a calculator to find the cube root of each of the following to one decimal place.

    a 86   **b** 100   **c** 45   **d** 267   **e** 2000

5 State which of each pair of numbers is larger.

    a $\sqrt{10}, \sqrt[3]{50}$ **b** $\sqrt{30}, \sqrt[3]{150}$ **c** $\sqrt{20}, \sqrt[3]{60}$

    d $\sqrt{35}, \sqrt[3]{200}$ **e** $\sqrt{15}, \sqrt[3]{55}$ **f** $\sqrt{40}, \sqrt[3]{220}$

6 Write down two solutions to each of the following equations.

    a $x^2 = 9$ **b** $x^2 = 36$ **c** $x^2 = 49$ **d** $x^2 = 121$

7 Solve each of these equations. Each has two solutions.

    a $x^2 + 4 = 40$ **b** $x^2 + 8 = 33$ **c** $m^2 + 13 = 62$

    d $t^2 + 23 = 104$ **e** $t^2 - 6 = 10$ **f** $x^2 - 12 = 52$

    g $8 + k^2 = 152$ **h** $12 + g^2 = 133$ **i** $21 + h^2 = 70$

    j $150 - t^2 = 101$ **k** $210 - n^2 = 146$ **l** $175 - y^2 = 94$

8 Solve each of these equations. Each has two solutions.

    a $(x + 3)^2 = 16$ **b** $(x + 5)^2 = 64$ **c** $(m + 1)^2 = 49$

    d $(t + 7)^2 = 900$ **e** $(t + 5)^2 = 400$ **f** $(k + 8)^2 = 144$

    g $(x - 2)^2 = 9$ **h** $(h - 4)^2 = 36$ **i** $(n - 7)^2 = 121$

9 I square a number, add 18 to the outcome and get 67. What are the two possible numbers I have squared?

10 I think of a number, subtract 5, square it and get the answer 169. What are the two possible numbers I am thinking of?

11 Write down the value of each of the following without using a power. Use a calculator to help you.

    a $16^{\frac{1}{2}}$ **b** $25^{\frac{1}{2}}$ **c** $81^{\frac{1}{2}}$ **d** $100^{\frac{1}{2}}$

    e $8^{\frac{1}{3}}$ **f** $1000^{\frac{1}{3}}$ **g** $(-64)^{\frac{1}{3}}$ **h** $(-125)^{\frac{1}{3}}$

    i $625^{\frac{1}{4}}$ **j** $81^{\frac{1}{4}}$ **k** $1296^{\frac{1}{4}}$ **l** $32^{\frac{1}{5}}$

    m $729^{\frac{1}{6}}$ **n** $3125^{\frac{1}{5}}$ **o** $1024^{\frac{1}{10}}$ **p** $729^{\frac{1}{3}}$

Extension   **Work**

Investigate each of the following statements to see which are:

i always true.   **ii** sometimes true.

For those which are sometimes true, state when they are true.

    a $\sqrt{A} + \sqrt{B} = \sqrt{(A + B)}$ **b** $\sqrt[3]{A} \times \sqrt[3]{B} = \sqrt[3]{(A \times B)}$

    c $\sqrt{A} - \sqrt{B} = \sqrt{(A - B)}$ **d** $\sqrt{A} \div \sqrt{B} = \sqrt{(A \div B)}$

Quadratic graphs

A quadratic equation has the form $y = ax^2 + bx + c$. That is, it is an equation which has a square as its highest power.

Follow through Example 8.7 in which a graph is drawn from a quadratic equation. This example demonstrates that the graph of a quadratic equation is a curved line.

Example 8.7 ▶

Draw a graph of the equation $y = x^2 - 4x + 3$ between $x = -1$ and $x = 4$.

Start by constructing a table of coordinates for values of x from -1 to 4. To do this, calculate each part of the quadratic equation, then add the parts together.

x	**−1**	**0**	**1**	**2**	**3**	**4**
x^2	1	0	1	4	9	16
$-4x$	4	0	−4	−8	−12	−16
3	3	3	3	3	3	3
$y = x^2 - 4x + 3$	8	3	0	−1	0	3

Plot these points and join them with a smooth curve. The outcome is shown on the right.

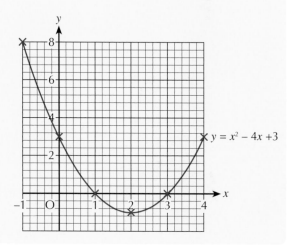

Notice that the graph has a smooth U-shape. All quadratic graphs have a similar shape, although some will be upside down.

When drawing quadratic graphs, remember the following important points.

- They have curved bottoms (or tops).
- There are *no* straight sections in the graph.
- There are *no* kinks, bulges or sharp points.

Exercise 8C

(1) Copy and complete each table and use the suggested scale to draw a smooth graph of each equation.

a $y = x^2$

x	**−3**	**−2**	**−1**	**0**	**1**	**2**	**3**
x^2	9						9
$y = x^2$	9						9

- x on the horizontal axis, scale 2 cm to 1 unit, from −3 to 3
- y on the vertical axis, scale 2 cm to 1 unit, from 0 to 9

b $y = x^2 + 4$

x	–3	–2	–1	0	1	2	3
x^2	9						9
4	4	4	4	4	4		4
$y = x^2 + 4$	13						13

- x on the horizontal axis, scale 2 cm to 1 unit, from –3 to 3
- y on the vertical axis, scale 2 cm to 1 unit, from 0 to 13

c $y = x^2 + x$

x	–4	–3	–2	–1	0	1	2
x^2	16						
x	–4	–3					2
$y = x^2 + x$	12						

- x on the horizontal axis, scale 2 cm to 1 unit, from –4 to 2
- y on the vertical axis, scale 2 cm to 1 unit, from –1 to 12

d $y = x^2 + 3x - 1$

x	–4	–3	–2	–1	0	1	2
x^2	16						
$3x$	–12						
–1	–1						
$y = x^2 + 3x - 1$	3						

- x on the horizontal axis, scale 2 cm to 1 unit, from –4 to 2
- y on the vertical axis, scale 2 cm to 1 unit, from –3 to 9

2 Construct a table of values for each of the following equations. Then, using a suitable scale, draw its graph.

a $y = 2x^2$ from $x = -3$ to 3
b $y = x^2 + 2x$ from $x = -4$ to 2
c $y = x^2 + 2x - 3$ from $x = -4$ to 2
d $y = x^2 + x - 2$ from $x = -3$ to 3

3 Investigation

a Construct a table of values for each equation below. Then plot the graph of each equation on the same pair of axes, $x = -2$ to 2. Use a scale of 4 cm to 1 unit on the horizontal axis and 1 cm to 1 unit on the vertical axis.

i $y = x^2$　　**ii** $y = 2x^2$　　**iii** $y = 3x^2$　　**iv** $y = 4x^2$

b Comment on your graphs.

c Sketch on your diagram the graphs with these equations.

i $y = \frac{1}{2}x^2$　　**ii** $y = 2\frac{1}{2}x^2$　　**iii** $y = 5x^2$

4 Investigation

a Construct a table of values for each equation below. Then plot the graphs of each equation on the same pair of axes, $x = -3$ to 3. Use a scale of 2 cm to 1 unit on both the horizontal and vertical axes.

i $y = x^2$　　**ii** $y = x^2 + 1$　　**iii** $y = x^2 - 1$
iv $y = x^2 + 2$　　**v** $y = x^2 - 2$

b Comment on your graphs.

c Sketch on your diagram the graphs with these equations.

  i $y = x^2 + 3$ **ii** $y = x^2 - \frac{1}{2}$ **iii** $y = x^2 + 3\frac{1}{2}$

Extension Work

1 **a** Construct a suitable table of values and draw the graph of the equation $y = 1 - x^2$.

  b Comment on the shape of the graph.

2 **a** Draw the graph of $y = x^2$.

  b Draw the reflection on the x-axis of the graph of $y = x^2$ on the same grid.

  c What is the equation of this reflection?

Cubic graphs

A cubic equation is one which has a cube as its highest power. For example: $y = x^3$, $y = 4x^3 + 5$ and $y = 3x^3 + x^2$.

Example 8.8 ▷ Draw a graph of the equation $y = x^3 + 4x^2$ between $x = -5$ and $x = 2$.

Start by constructing a table of coordinates for values of x from -5 to 2. To do this, calculate each part of the cubic equation, then add the parts together.

x	-5	-4	-3	-2	-1	0	1	2
x^3	-125	-64	-27	-8	-1	0	1	8
$4x^2$	100	64	36	16	4	0	4	16
$y = x^3 + 4x^2$	-25	0	9	8	3	0	5	24

Plot these points and join them with a smooth curve. The outcome is shown on the right.

Notice that the graph is a smooth curve with two bends or turning points. All cubic graphs have a similar shape. Sometimes the two bends coincide, giving the graph a single twist instead. (One example of such a graph is given above by $y = x^3 + 3x^2 + 3x + 1$.)

Also notice that this graph starts in the third quadrant (bottom left-hand corner) and finishes in the first quadrant (top right-hand corner). Others start in the second quadrant (top left-hand corner) and finish in the fourth (bottom right-hand corner).

Exercise 8D

1. Plot the graph of the equation $y = x^3$ for values of x from -2 to 2.

2. Plot the graph of the equation $y = x^3 - 9x$ for values of x from -3 to 3.

3. Plot the graph of the equation $y = x^3 - x + 3$ for values of x from -2 to 2. You will need to include $x = -0.5$ and $x = 0.5$ in your table.

4. Plot the graph of the equation $y = x^3 - 5x^2 - 4$ for values of x from -2 to 3.

5. By drawing suitable graphs, solve the following pair of simultaneous equations.
   $$x + y = 4$$
   $$y = x^3 + 1$$

   There is only one solution.

6. The velocity, v metres per second, of a particle moving along a straight line is given by $v = 1 + t^3$, where t is the time in seconds.

   Draw the velocity–time graph for the first 3 seconds.

Extension Work

Investigate the shapes of each of the following graphs.

a $y = x^{-1}$ b $y = x^{-2}$ c $y = x^{-3}$

LEVEL BOOSTER

5
I know the squares of the first 15 integers and the corresponding square roots.
I know the cubes of 1, 2, 3, 4, 5 and 10 and the corresponding cube roots.
I can calculate powers and simplify algebraic expressions using index form.

6
I can solve quadratic equations by taking square roots, giving two possible solutions.

7
I can use the index laws of addition and subtraction to simplify expressions.
I can draw and interpret graphs of quadratic functions.

8
I know that a negative power is the reciprocal of the positive power.
I know that fractional powers represent roots.
I can draw and interpret graphs of cubic functions.

1 *2007 Paper 2*

Write the missing numbers.

$6x + 2 = 10$ $1 - 2y = 10$

so $6x + 1 = \ldots$ so $(1 - 2y)^2 = \ldots$

2 *2007 Paper 1*

Look at this information.

$y^2 = 10$

Copy and complete the following equations, using the information to find the missing numbers.

$y^4 =$

$y^{\square} = 1000$

3 *2007 Paper 1*

  a Is 3^{100} even or odd?

     Explain your answer.

  b Write down the number below that is the same as $3^{100} \times 3^{100}$

     3^{200} 6^{100} 9^{200} $3^{10\,000}$ $9^{10\,000}$

4 *2006 Paper 1*

Look at this equation.

$$y = \frac{60}{\pm\sqrt{x} - 10}$$

  a Find y when $x = 19$.

     There are two answers. Write them both down.

  b You cannot find a value for y when $x = 10$.

     Explain why not.

  c There are other values of x for which you cannot find a value for y.

     Give one such value of x.

FM Packages

Maximum package dimensions

The Post Office will only accept packages that follow the following rules.

Regular cuboidal packages

The length (greatest dimension) cannot be longer than 1.5 m.

The girth is the distance around the package (2 × width + 2 × height).

The girth and the length put together must not exceed 3 m in total.

Height

Length   Width

Irregular packages

Greatest dimension cannot exceed 1.5 m.

Girth is measured around the thickest part of package.

The girth plus the length must not exceed 3 m in total.

Girth measured around thickest part

Length measured as greatest dimension

Prices

Up to and including 10 kg:	£14.99
Every kg or part thereof:	Add 80p
Maximum weight:	30 kg

Use the information above to answer these questions.

1 For each of the cuboidal packages in the following table say whether it is acceptable to the Post Office. If it is not, give a reason why.

Package	Weight	Length	Width	Height
A	15 kg	1.2 m	70 cm	20 cm
B	22 kg	160 cm	30 cm	20 cm
C	10 kg	110 cm	80 cm	10 cm
D	40 kg	90 cm	50 cm	20 cm
E	16 kg	80 cm	60 cm	30 cm
F	20 kg	90 cm	70 cm	40 cm
G	32 kg	1 m	60 cm	60 cm
H	3000 g	1.8 m	20 cm	20 cm
I	4 kg	50 cm	50 cm	50 cm
J	18 kg	140 cm	50 cm	30 cm

2 For each of the acceptable packages in Question 1, work out the cost of postage.

3 Each of the following cuboidal packages is at the limit of acceptability. Work out the missing dimension.

a
? cm
100 cm   40 cm

b
50 cm
150 cm   ? cm

c
? cm
120 cm   60 cm

d
20 cm
? cm   40 cm

e
50 cm
80 cm   ? cm

f
x cm
100 cm   x cm

4 The following irregular packages are just acceptable. Work out the missing dimension.

a
60 cm
75 cm
? cm   45 cm

b
70 cm
70 cm
120 cm   ? cm

c
30 cm
50 cm
20 cm   60 cm
? cm   60 cm

d
? cm
? cm
150 cm   ? cm

5 Tubes are often used to send things through the post.
Calculate the maximum diameter, d, for tubes with the following lengths, l.
Give your answers to the nearest centimetre.

a 150 cm   **b** 100 cm   **c** 80 cm

6 Calculate the maximum possible length, l, for tubes with the following diameters, d.
Give your answers to the nearest centimetre.

a 10 cm   **b** 60 cm   **c** 70 cm

7 What is the largest possible acceptable dimension, in centimetres, of a cubical package?
Give your answers to the nearest centimetre.
?
?   ?

Probability statements

You have already studied many probability situations. Check, using the tables below, that you remember how each of the probabilities is worked out.

Also, make sure that you know and understand all the **probability** terms which are used in this chapter.

Single event	Outcome	Probability
Roll a dice	5	$\frac{1}{6}$
Toss a coin	Head	$\frac{1}{2}$
Two blue counters and three green counters in a bag	Blue	$\frac{2}{5}$

Two events	Outcome	Probability
Roll two dice	Double 6	$\frac{1}{36}$
Toss two coins	Two heads	$\frac{1}{4}$
Toss a coin and roll a dice	Head and 5	$\frac{1}{12}$

Most of the combined events you have dealt with so far have been **independent events**. Two events are said to be independent when the outcome of one of them does not affect the outcome of the other event. Example 9.1 illustrates this situation.

Example 9.1 ▷ A Glaswegian girl was late for school on Friday, the day before the world record for throwing the javelin was broken in Sydney by a Korean athlete. Were these events connected in any way?

The pupil's late arrival at school clearly could have no effect on the Korean's performance on the Saturday. So, the two events are independent.

Now look closely at the statements in Examples 9.2 and 9.3, and the comments on them. In Exercise 9A, you will have to decide which given statements are sensible.

Example 9.2 ▷ Daniel says: 'There is a 50–50 chance that the next person to walk through the door of a supermarket will be someone I know because I will either know them or I won't.'

The next person that walks through the door may be someone whom he knows, but there are far more people whom he does not know. So, there is more chance of she/he being someone whom he does not know. Hence, the statement is incorrect.

Example 9.3 ▷ Clare says: 'If I buy a lottery ticket every week, I am bound to win sometime.'

Each week, the chance of winning is very small (1 chance in 13 983 816), so it is highly unlikely that Clare would win in any week. Losing one week does not increase your chances of winning the following week.

Exercise 9A

1 Write a comment on each of the following statements, explaining why the statement is incorrect.

   a A game for two players is started by rolling a six on a dice. Ashad says: 'I never start first because I'm unlucky.'

   b It will rain tomorrow because it rained today.

   c There is a 50% chance of snow tomorrow because it will either snow or it won't.

   d There are mint, chocolate and plain sweets in the packet, so the probability of picking out a chocolate sweet is $\frac{1}{3}$.

2 Decide whether each of the following statements is correct or incorrect.

   a I fell down yesterday. I don't fall down very often, so it could not possibly happen again today.

   b I have just tossed a coin to get a Head three times in succession. The next time I throw the coin, the probability that I will get a Head is still $\frac{1}{2}$.

   c My bus is always on time. It will be on time tomorrow.

   d There is an equal number of red and blue counters in a bag. My friend picked a counter out and it was blue. She then put it back. It is more likely that I will get red when I pick one out.

3 Here are three coloured grids. The squares have either a winning symbol or a losing symbol hidden.

   a If you pick a square from each grid, is it possible to know on which you have the greatest chance of winning?

Grid 1 Grid 2 Grid 3

b You are now told that on Grid 1 there are three winning squares, on Grid 2 there are five winning squares and on Grid 3 there are four winning squares. Which grid gives you the least chance of winning?

c Helen says that there are more winning squares on Grid 2, which means that there is more chance of winning using Grid 2. Explain why she is wrong.

4 Here are three events, *A*, *B*, and *C*.

A Jonathan writes computer programs on Monday evenings.
B Jonathan watches television on Monday evenings.
C Jonathan wears a blue shirt on Mondays.

Which of these events are independent?

a *A* and *B*   **b** *A* and *C*   **c** *B* and *C*

Extension Work

Draw each of the following different-sized grids.
- 5 by 5 grid with seven winning squares
- 6 by 6 grid with ten winning squares
- 10 by 10 grid with 27 winning squares

Work out which grid gives you the best chance of finding a winning square. Explain your reasoning.

Mutually exclusive events and exhaustive events

In Year 8, you looked at **mutually exclusive events**. Remember that these are events which do *not* overlap.

Example 9.4 ▷ | Which of these three types of number are mutually exclusive: odd, even and prime?

Odd and even numbers are mutually exclusive. Odd and prime numbers, and even and prime numbers are not: for example, 11 and 2.

Example 9.5 ▷ | There are red, green and blue counters in a bag.
- Event A: Pick a red counter.
- Event B: Pick a blue counter.
- Event C: Pick a counter that is not green.

Which pairs of events are mutually exclusive?

Events A and B are mutually exclusive because there is no overlap. A red counter and a blue counter are different.

Events A and C are *not* mutually exclusive because they overlap. A red counter and a counter which is not green could be the same colour.

Events B and C are *not* mutually exclusive because they overlap. A blue counter and a counter which is not green could be the same colour.

Example 9.6 ▷ The eight counters shown are contained in a bag.
A counter is chosen at random.

a What is the probability of picking a red counter?
b What is the probability of not picking a red counter?
c What is the probability of picking a green counter?
d What is the probability of picking a blue counter?
e What is the sum of the three probabilities in **a**, **c** and **d**?

a There are three red counters out of a total of eight. This gives:

$$P(\text{red}) = \tfrac{3}{8}$$

b Since there are five outcomes which are not red counters, this means:

$$P(\text{not red}) = \tfrac{5}{8}$$

Notice that

$$P(\text{red}) + P(\text{not red}) = \tfrac{3}{8} + \tfrac{5}{8} = 1$$

So, if you know P(Event happening), then

P(Event not happening) = 1 – P(Event happening)

c There is one green counter, which means:

$$P(\text{green}) = \tfrac{1}{8}$$

d There are four blue counters, which means:

$$P(\text{blue}) = \tfrac{4}{8} = \tfrac{1}{2}$$

e The sum of the probabilities is
P(red) + P(green) + P(blue)

$$= \tfrac{3}{8} + \tfrac{1}{8} + \tfrac{4}{8} = 1$$

All these events are mutually exclusive because only one counter is taken out at a time.

Also, because they cover all possibilities, they are called **exhaustive events**.

Note that the probabilities of exhaustive events which are also mutually exclusive **add up to 1**.

Exercise 9B

1 Discs lettered A, B, C, D and E, and the probability of choosing each, are shown.

P(A) = 0.3   P(B) = 0.1   P(C) = ?   P(D) = 0.25   P(E) = 0.05

a What is the probability of choosing a disc with either A or B on it?
b What is the probability of choosing a disc with C on it?
c What is the probability of choosing a disc which does not have E on it?

2 A set of 25 cards is shown.

a What is the probability of choosing a card with a fish on it?

b What is the probability of choosing a card with a fish or a cow on it?

c What is the probability of choosing a card with a sheep or a pig on it?

d What is the probability of choosing a card *without* a fish on it?

3 A spinner is shown with the probabilities of its landing on red, green or blue.

What is the probability of the spinner landing on one of the following?

a Red or green   **b** Blue or green

c Blue, green or red   **d** Yellow

4 The discs shown right are placed in a bag. One of them is chosen at random. Here are four events.

    A   A red disc is chosen.

    B   A blue disc is chosen.

    C   A green disc is chosen.

    D   A green or blue disc is chosen.

State which events are mutually exclusive, exhaustive, both or neither.

a *A* and *B*   **b** *A* and *C*   **c** *A* and *D*   **d** *B* and *D*

Extension Work

You can work out how many times that you expect something to happen over a number of trials using this formula:

  Expected number of successes = Probability of success in each trial × Number of trials

For example, the probability of the spinner in Question **3** landing on green is 0.25. If the spinner is spun 20 times, you have:

    Expected number of times it lands on green = 0.25 × 20 = 5 times

Copy and complete the table of the expected number of successes in each case.

Probability of success	Number of trials	Expected number of successes
$\frac{1}{2}$	10	
$\frac{1}{4}$	80	
$\frac{2}{3}$	60	
0.24	100	
0.4	150	
0.75	120	

6

Combining probabilities and tree diagrams

There are four pets in a vet's waiting room, a white dog, a white cat, a black dog and a black cat. Two of these pets are owned by David. He has a dog and a cat. How many different possibilities are there?

Sometimes tree diagrams are used to help to calculate probabilities when there are two or more events.

Example 9.7 ▷ Dawn makes candles. The probability that a candle is damaged is 0.1. Each candle is made independently.

Dawn makes two candles. Calculate the probability that:

a both candles are damaged.

b only one candle is damaged.

The probabilities can be written on a tree diagram as shown.

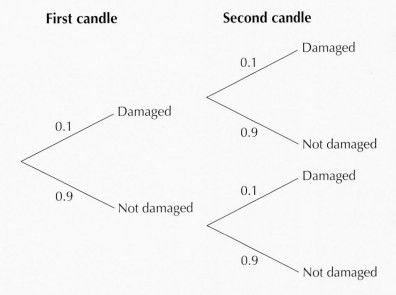

To work out the probability of one event happening and then another event happening independently, the probabilities must be multiplied together.

a The probability that the first candle is damaged and the second candle is damaged = 0.1 × 0.1 = 0.01

b There are two ways that *only one* candle could be damaged.

The first candle could be damaged and the second candle not damaged. Or the first candle could be not damaged and the second candle damaged.

The probability that the first candle is damaged and the second candle is not damaged = 0.1 × 0.9 = 0.09

The probability that the first candle is not damaged and the second candle is damaged = 0.9 × 0.1 = 0.09

This gives a total probability of 0.09 + 0.09 = 0.18

Often, probability questions use fractions which need to be simplified.

Example 9.8 ▷ A cube is chosen from each bag. What is the probability of choosing two red cubes?

The probability of choosing a red cube from the first bag is $\frac{4}{5}$.

The probability of choosing a red cube from the second bag is $\frac{3}{4}$.

The probability of choosing red *and* red $= \frac{4}{5} \times \frac{3}{4} = \frac{3}{5}$

Here is a two-way table showing all the different combinations.

		Second bag	
		Red $\frac{3}{4}$	**Blue** $\frac{1}{4}$
First bag	**Red** $\frac{4}{5}$	$\frac{4}{5} \times \frac{3}{4} = \frac{3}{5}$	$\frac{4}{5} \times \frac{1}{4} = \frac{1}{5}$
	Blue $\frac{1}{5}$	$\frac{1}{5} \times \frac{3}{4} = \frac{3}{20}$	$\frac{1}{5} \times \frac{1}{4} = \frac{1}{20}$

8

Exercise 9C

1 Two fair, six-sided dice are rolled. Copy and complete the tree diagram and use it to calculate the probability that the first dice lands on 5 or 6, and the second dice lands on an even number.

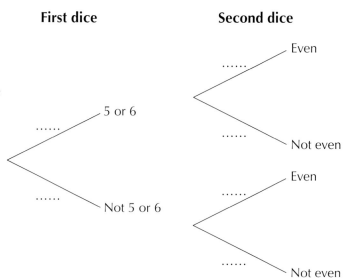

First dice   **Second dice**

...... 5 or 6

...... Even
...... Not even

...... Not 5 or 6

...... Even
...... Not even

2 A woman goes to a health club. The probability that she goes on a Saturday is $\frac{1}{4}$. The probability that she goes swimming is $\frac{2}{3}$. Each event is independent. Calculate the probability for each of the following situations.

a She does not go on a Saturday.

b She does not go swimming.

c She goes on a Saturday and she goes swimming.

3 A cube is chosen from each bag.

a Copy and complete the two-way table.

		Second bag	
		Red $\frac{1}{5}$	**Blue** $\frac{4}{5}$
First bag	**Red** $\frac{1}{2}$		
	Blue $\frac{1}{2}$		

b What is the probability of choosing two red cubes?

c What is the probability of choosing one red cube and one blue cube? (Remember that it could be red and then blue *or* blue and then red.)

A player plays three games. The probability of winning each time is $\frac{2}{3}$.

a Copy and complete the tree diagram.

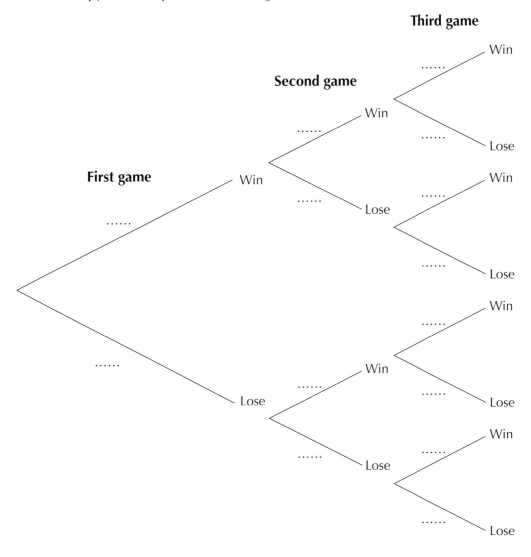

Third game

Second game

First game

b Write down the different ways of winning at least two games.

c Work out the probability of winning at least two games.

Estimates of probability

In an experiment to test whether a dice is biased, the dice was rolled 120 times. These are the results.

Number on dice	1	2	3	4	5	6
Frequency	18	25	20	22	14	21

Do you think that the dice is biased?

Number 2 was rolled 25 times out of 120. So, an **estimate of the probability** of rolling number 2 is given by:

$$\frac{25}{120} = 0.208$$

The fraction $\frac{25}{120}$ is called the **relative frequency**.

Relative frequency is an estimate of probability based on experimental data. The relative frequency may be the only way of estimating probability when events are not equally likely.

$$\text{Relative frequency} = \frac{\text{Number of successful trials}}{\text{Total number of trials}}$$

Number 2 was rolled 25 times out of 120. So, for example, you would expect it to be rolled 50 times out of 240. The expected number of successes can be calculated from the formula:

Expected number of successes = Relative frequency × Number of trials

Hence, in this case, the expected number of times number 2 is rolled is given by:

$$\frac{25}{120} \times 240 = 50$$

Example 9.9 ▷

Look again at the example above.

A dice is rolled 120 times. Here are the results.

Number on dice	1	2	3	4	5	6
Frequency	18	25	20	22	14	21

a How could you obtain a more accurate estimate than the relative frequency?

b If the dice were rolled 1000 times, how many times would you expect to get a score of 2?

a A more accurate estimate could be obtained by carrying out more trials.

b The expected number of times a score of 2 is rolled in 1000 trials is given by:

$$0.208 \times 1000 = 208$$

Example 9.10 ▷

The relative frequencies of the number of times a spinner lands on red is shown in the table below.

Number of spins	10	20	50	75	100
Relative frequency of landing on red	0.3	0.25	0.28	0.24	0.26

a Plot the relative frequencies on a graph.

b Write down the best estimate of the number of times the spinner would land on red in 1000 spins.

c Do you think the spinner is fair? Explain your answer.

Example 9.10 ▷
continued

a

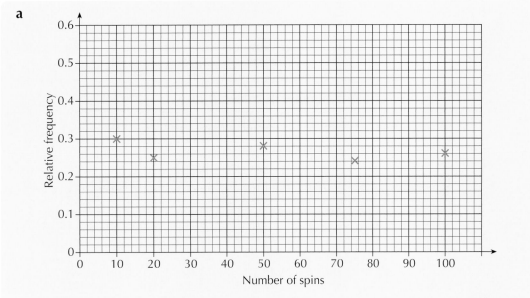

b The best estimate of the theoretical probability is 0.26 as this was the result of the most spins in the experiment. So the best estimate of the number of times the spinner would land on red is 0.26 × 1000 = 260.

c There are two out of six sections of the spinner which are red, so if the spinner were fair, the theoretical probability of landing on red would be $\frac{1}{3}$. Also, in 1000 spins the spinner would be expected to land on red 333 times ($\frac{1}{3}$ of 1000). It is likely that this spinner is biased.

Exercise 9D

1 A four-sided spinner was spun 100 times. Here are the results.

Number on spinner	1	2	3	4
Frequency	20	25	23	32

a What is the estimated probability of a score of 4?

b Do you think from these results that the spinner is biased? Give a reason for your answer.

c If the spinner were spun 500 times, how many times would you expect to get a score of 4?

2 A drawing pin is thrown and the number of times that it lands point up is recorded at regular intervals and the results shown in the table.

a Copy and complete the table for the relative frequencies.

Number of throws	10	20	30	40	50
Number of times pin lands point up	6	13	20	24	32
Relative frequency of landing point up	0.6				

b What is the best estimate of the probability of the pin landing point up?

c How many times would you expect the pin to land point up in 200 throws?

3 A bag contains yellow and blue cubes. Cubes are picked from the bag, the colour recorded and the cubes replaced.

a Copy and complete the table for the relative frequencies for the number of times a blue cube was chosen.

Number of trials	10	25	50	100
Number of times blue cube chosen	3	8	15	28
Relative frequency	0.3			

b What is the best estimate of the probability of picking a blue cube from the bag?

c You are now told that there are 75 cubes in the bag altogether. What is the best estimate of the number of blue cubes in the bag?

4 The number of times a coin lands on Heads is shown in the table below.

Number of throws	10	20	30	40	50
Number of Heads	7	12	18	22	28
Relative frequency of Heads	$\frac{7}{10}$ = 0.7				

a Copy and complete the table to show the relative frequency of Heads.
b Plot the relative frequencies on a graph.
c Write down the best estimate of the probability of a Head.
d Use your estimate to predict the number of Heads in 200 throws.
e Do you think the coin is biased towards Heads? Explain your answer.

5 The relative frequencies of the number of times a player wins a game of bowling is shown below.

Number of games	2	4	6	8	10
Relative frequency of winning	0.5	0.75	0.67	0.75	0.70
Number of wins					

a Plot the relative frequencies on a graph.
b Explain why it is not possible to tell from the graph whether the first game was a win.
c Write down the best estimate of the probability of winning a game
d Copy and complete the table to show the number of wins for 2, 4, 6, 8 and 10 games.

Extension Work

Here is a graph showing the relative frequency of the number of times a darts player hits the target.

a How many times did the darts player hit the target in the first 10 throws?

b What is the best estimate of the probability of a hit?

c How many times would you expect the darts player to hit the target in 100 throws? State any assumptions that you make.

d Why is it not appropriate to use the graph to find out how many hits there were in the first 15 throws?

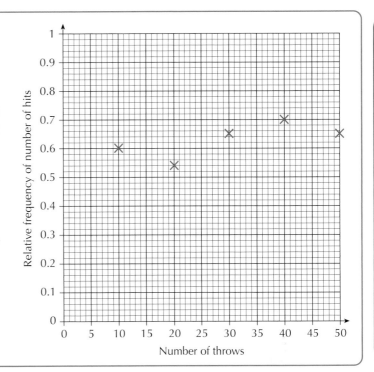

LEVEL BOOSTER

6
I can identify outcomes from two events.

I can use tables and diagrams to show outcomes.

I can solve problems involving mutually exclusive events.

I can use the fact that the total probability of all mutually exclusive events of an experiment is 1.

7
I know how to take account of bias.

I can compare outcomes of experiments.

I understand relative frequency as an estimate of probability.

8
I understand how to calculate the probability of a compound event and use this in solving problems.

National Test questions

1 *2005 Paper 2*

Here is some information about all the pupils in class 9A:A teacher is going to choose a pupil from 9A at random.

a What is the probability that the pupil chosen will be a **girl**?

b What is the probability that the pupil chosen will be **left-handed**?

c The teacher chooses the pupil at random. She tells the class that the pupil is **left-handed**.

What is the probability that this left-handed pupil is a **boy**?

	Number of boys	Number of girls
Right-handed	13	14
Left-handed	1	2

6

2 *2002 Paper 1*

I have a bag that contains blue, red, green and yellow counters. I am going to take out one counter at random.

The table shows the probability of each colour being taken out.

	Blue	Red	Green	Yellow
Probability	0.05	0.3	0.45	0.2

a Explain why the number of yellow counters in the bag cannot be 10.

b What is the smallest possible number of each colour of counter in the bag? Copy and complete the table.

Blue	Red	Green	Yellow

3 *2006 Paper 2*

A pupil wants to investigate a report that Belgian one euro coins are biased in favour of heads.

Here is her plan for the investigation.

I will spin **20** Belgian one euro coins to give one set of results.

I will do this **10 times** to give a total of **200 results** to work out an estimated probability of spinning a head.

If this probability is **greater than 56%** my conclusion will be that Belgian one euro coins are biased in favour of heads.

The table shows the 10 sets of results.

Number of each set of 20 coins that showed heads									
10	13	11	11	12	12	11	9	10	11

Using the pupil's plan, what should her conclusion be?

You **must** show your working.

4 *2006 Paper 1*

Meg and Ravi buy sweet pea seeds and grow them in identical conditions.

Meg's results:

Number of packets	Number of seeds in each packet	Number of seeds that germinate from each packet
5	20	18, 17, 17, 18, 19

Ravi's results:

Number of packets	Number of seeds in each packet	Total number of seeds that germinate
10	20	170

a Using Meg's results and Ravi's results, calculate two different estimates of the **probability** that a sweet pea seed will germinate.

Copy and complete the following.

Using Meg's results: …

Using Ravi's results: …

b Whose results are likely to give the better estimate of the probability?

State whether it is Meg's or Ravi's.

Explain why.

5 *2003 Paper 1*

a A fair coin is thrown. When it lands it shows Heads or Tails.

Game: Throw the coin three times.
   Player A wins one point each time the coin shows a Head.
   Player B wins one point each time the coin shows a Tail.

Show that the probability that player A scores three points is $\frac{1}{8}$.

b What is the probability that player B scores exactly two points? Show your working.

6 *2003 Paper 1*

A girl plays the same computer game lots of times. The computer scores each game using 1 for win, 0 for lose.

After each game, the computer calculates her overall mean score. The graph shows the results for the first 20 games.

a For each of the first three games, write W if she won or L if she lost.

First game ......
Second game ......
Third game ......

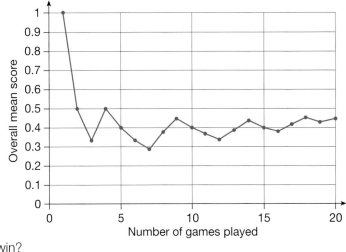

b What percentage of the 20 games did the girl win?

The graph shown right shows the girl's results for the first 100 games.

c She is going to play the game again.
Estimate the probability that she will win.

d Suppose for the 101st to 120th games, the girl were to lose each game. What would the graph look like up to the 120th game?

Show your answer on a copy of the graph below.

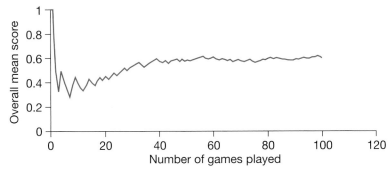

FM Class test

A Year 9 class sat some practice tests before their SATs. The following are their test results.

Name	Gender	English	Maths	Science
John Addy	M	17	45	32
Sean Allsop	M	43	37	41
Sally Emerson	F	65	54	48
Gerry Evans	M	28	65	55
Kay Gilbert	F	76	84	78
Zoe Ginn	F	49	46	57
Zahir Greer	M	87	24	43
Isabell Harding	F	93	75	68
Muhanad Hatamleh	M	72	56	51
Liah Huxter	F	69	74	78
Sahid Jallya	M	25	62	65
Molly Kenward	F	51	37	42
Brian Keys	M	48	53	49
Daniel Mann	M	55	85	73
John O'Dubhchair	M	62	39	35
Godwin Osakwe	M	38	41	27
Krishna Pallin	M	78	56	67
Joy Peacock	F	69	76	65
William Qui	M	87	92	89
Alan Runciman	M	92	34	45
Billie Speed	M	64	74	76
Robert Spooner	M	44	67	61
Joyce Tapman	F	53	43	39
Vi Thomas	F	37	57	64
Cliff Tompkins	M	48	43	51
Lesley Wallace	F	68	58	52
Madge Webb	F	74	42	44
John Wilkins	M	35	41	47
Jenny Wong	F	69	58	43
Jo Zunde	F	94	98	96

1. Draw a scatter diagram for the results in the following subjects.
   a English and maths
   b English and science
   c Maths and science

2. Draw in the lines of best fit, if there are any, and comment on the correlation shown in the three scatter diagrams you have drawn.

3. On your scatter diagrams, use colours to highlight the males and the females and comment on any gender differences now apparent from these results.

4. Two pupils were absent during the test week and only managed to do one test each.
   Isaac Fawcett sat the maths test and scored 74.
   Julie Holberry sat the English test and scored 54.

   Use the scatter diagrams to estimate what they might have scored in the other two sets.

5. Draw a stem and leaf diagram for each set of results.

6. From your stem and leaf diagrams, state the median score of each and comment on your results.

7. a Create a grouped frequency table for each set of results using the boundaries 1–20, 21–40, 41–60, 61–80 and 81–100.
   b Use the table to estimate the means for each subject.

8. Extend each grouped frequency table to create a cumulative frequency column for each set of results and draw a cumulative frequency graph for each table.

9. Use the given information and the diagrams you have produced to comment on which test appears to be the easiest and which the hardest.

CHAPTER 10

Geometry and Measures **3**

<table>
<tr>
<td>

This chapter is going to show you

- How to enlarge a shape by a fractional scale factor
- How to use trigonometry to find lengths and angles in right-angled triangles
- How to solve problems using trigonometry

</td>
<td>

What you should already know

- How to enlarge a shape by a positive scale factor
- How to recognise similar shapes
- How to use Pythagoras' theorem

</td>
</tr>
</table>

Fractional enlargements

Positive enlargement

The diagram will remind you how to enlarge triangle ABC by a **scale factor** of 3 about the centre of enlargement O to give triangle A'B'C'.

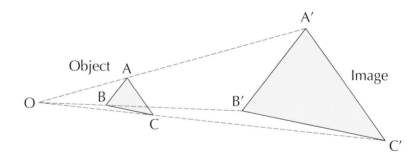

Lines called **rays** or **guidelines** are drawn from O through A, B, C to A', B', C'. Here, the scale factor is given as 3. So, OA' = 3 × OA, OB' = 3 × OB, OC' = 3 × OC. The length of each side of △A'B'C' is three times the length of the corresponding side of triangle ABC.

That is, the **object** triangle ABC is enlarged by a **scale factor** of 3 about the **centre of enlargement**, O, to give the **image** triangle A'B'C'.

The object and image are on the *same side* of O. The scale factor is positive. So, this is called **positive enlargement**.

Notice that the object and image are similar shapes, since the corresponding angles are equal and the corresponding sides are all in the ratio 1 : 3.

In the diagram below, triangle ABC is enlarged by a scale factor of $\frac{1}{2}$ to give triangle A′B′C′.

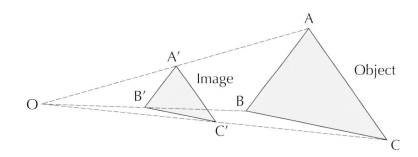

Each side of △A′B′C′ is half the length of the corresponding side of △ABC. Notice also that OA′ = $\frac{1}{2}$ of OA, OB′ = $\frac{1}{2}$ of OB and OC′ = $\frac{1}{2}$ of OC.

That is, the object △ABC has been enlarged by a scale factor of $\frac{1}{2}$ about the centre of enlargement, O, to give the image △A′B′C′.

The object and the image are on the *same side* of O, with the image *smaller* than the object. The scale factor is a fraction. This is called **fractional enlargement**.

Fractional enlargement on a grid

When fractional enlargement is on a grid, the principles are the same. The grid may or may not have coordinate axes, and the centre of enlargement may be anywhere on the grid.

The grid means that it is not always necessary to draw rays to find the image points.

Example 10.1 ▷

Enlarge △ABC on the coordinate grid by a scale factor of $\frac{1}{2}$ about the origin (0, 0).

- Draw rays, or count grid units in the *x*- and *y*-directions, from points A, B, C to the origin.
- Multiply the ray lengths or the numbers of *x*, *y* units by $\frac{1}{2}$.
- Plot these new lengths or numbers of units to obtain points A′, B′, C′.
- Join these points to give △A′B′C′.

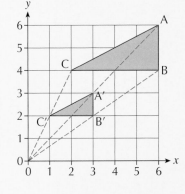

The object △ABC has been enlarged by a scale factor of $\frac{1}{2}$ about the origin (0, 0) to give the image △A′B′C′. Notice that we still use the term enlargement, even though the image is smaller than the object.

For a fractional enlargement about the *origin* of a grid, the coordinates of the object are multiplied by the scale factor to give the image coordinates. So here:

Object coordinates: A(6, 6)   B(6, 4)   C(2, 4)

Multiply each coordinate by $\frac{1}{2}$ to give: Image coordinates: A′(3, 3)   B′(3, 2)   C′(1, 2)

1 Draw copies of (or trace) the shapes below and enlarge each one by the given scale factor about the given centre of enlargement, O.

a   Scale factor $\frac{1}{2}$

b   Scale factor $\frac{1}{4}$

c   Scale factor $\frac{1}{3}$

O ×

O ×

O ×

2 Draw copies of (or trace) the shapes below and enlarge each one by the given scale factor about the given centre of enlargement, O.

a   Scale factor $1\frac{1}{2}$

b   Scale factor $2\frac{1}{2}$

c   Scale factor $-\frac{1}{2}$

O ×

O ×

×O

3 Copy the diagrams below onto a coordinate grid and enlarge each one about the origin (0, 0) by multiplying the coordinates by the given scale factor. Plot your image coordinates and check them using rays.

a   Scale factor $\frac{1}{2}$

b   Scale factor $\frac{1}{3}$

c Scale factor $\frac{1}{4}$

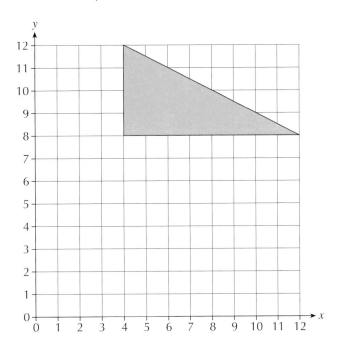

4 Copy the diagram shown onto centimetre squared paper.

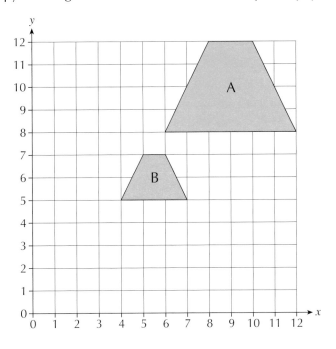

a Trapezium A is mapped onto Trapezium B by an enlargement. What is the scale factor of the enlargement?

b Find the coordinates of the centre of enlargement by adding suitable rays to your diagram.

c **i** Write down the areas of Trapezium A and Trapezium B.

    ii Use your answer to **c i** to find the ratio of the two areas in its simplest form.

d If a shape is enlarged by a scale factor of $\frac{1}{2}$, what is the area scale factor for the enlargement?

1 Working in pairs or groups, design a poster to show how the symbol on the right can be enlarged by different fractional scale factors about any convenient centre of enlargement.

2 **a** **i** Find the total surface area of the cuboid shown.
      ii Find the volume of the cuboid.

2 cm

1 cm

3 cm

   b The cuboid is enlarged by a scale factor of 2.
      i Find the total surface area of the enlarged cuboid and write down the area scale factor.
      ii Find the volume of the enlarged cuboid and write down the volume scale factor.

   c The original cuboid is now enlarged by a scale factor of 3.
      i Find the total surface area of the enlarged cuboid and write down the area scale factor.
      ii Find the volume of the enlarged cuboid and write down the volume scale factor.

   d The cuboid is now enlarged by a scale factor of k.
      i Write down the area scale factor.
      ii Write down the volume scale factor.

3 Use ICT software, such as Logo, to enlarge shapes by different fractional scale factors and with different centres of enlargement.

Trigonometry – The tangent of an angle

Trigonometry is a branch of Mathematics that is concerned with calculating the lengths of sides and the sizes of angles in right-angled triangles. Its main use is in areas of engineering, navigation and surveying.

Right-angled triangles

In a right-angled triangle, such as those shown on the right:

- The side opposite the right angle (AC) is always the longest side and is known as the **hypotenuse**.
- The side opposite the angle in question (labelled θ here) is called the **opposite** side (BC in the top triangle and AB in the bottom triangle).
- The side next to the angle in question is called the **adjacent** side (AB in the top triangle and BC in the bottom triangle).

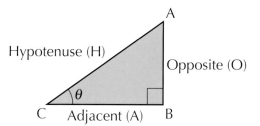

The tangent of an angle

Investigation ▶ Draw the diagram below accurately on 2 mm graph paper, with AB = 3 cm, AC = 5 cm, AD = 8 cm and AE = 10 cm.

Measure the lengths of BF, CG, DH and EI to the nearest millimetre. Copy the table below and use these measurements to complete the table, giving your answers to two decimal places.

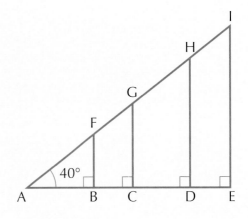

Ratio of sides	Answer to 2 dp
$\dfrac{BF}{AB}$	
$\dfrac{CG}{AC}$	
$\dfrac{DH}{AD}$	
$\dfrac{EI}{AE}$	

Using ∠A as 40°, you have found the values of the ratio of

$$\frac{\text{the opposite side}}{\text{the adjacent side}} \left(\frac{O}{A}\right) \text{ in triangles ABF, ACG, ADH and AEI.}$$

If you have measured accurately, you should have found that the four ratios have the same value – approximately 0.84. The investigation has shown that the corresponding sides are in the same ratio. This means that the triangles are similar.

The value of the ratio you have just found is called **the tangent of angle A**, and is shortened to **tanA**. The value of the tangent of every angle is stored in your calculator.

Using your calculator

Before you start any calculations in trigonometry, you need to make sure that your calculator is in **degree mode**. You can check this by looking for D or DEG in the display.

To find the value of the tangent of an angle using your calculator, you first need to find the ⊞tan⊟ key. On some calculators you have to key in the size of the angle before you press the tan button:

⊞4⊟ ⊞0⊟ ⊞tan⊟

On others you have to press the tan key before you key in the size of the angle:

⊞tan⊟ ⊞4⊟ ⊞0⊟

Find out how to use your calculator to find the tangent of an angle. The number on the display should be 0.839099631. Work through **Example 10.2** carefully to make sure you are using the keys in the correct order.

Example 10.2 ▷ | Find the value of: **a**   tan20°   **b**   tan32°   **c**   tan72.3°

Give your answers to 3 decimal places.

a   0.364   **b**   0.625   **c**   3.133

The tan key can be used to find the lengths of sides and the size of angles in right-angled triangles.

For right-angled triangles, we can use the formula **tanθ** = $\dfrac{\textbf{O}\text{pposite}}{\textbf{A}\text{djacent}}$

Once you have found the value of tan θ, you will need to be able to find the value of the angle θ itself. You can use the inverse tan button function on your calculator to do this. This is usually marked above the tan key as tan⁻¹ or arctan. Depending on your calculator, you will need to press one of the following keys to access this function:

SHIFT   INV   2ndF

You will then need to press the tan key and the number keys in the same order as before. Work through **Example 10.3** carefully to make sure you are using the correct keys on your calculator.

Example 10.3 ▷ | Find the value of θ if: **a**   tanθ = 0.3   **b**   tanθ = 0.724   **c**   tanθ = 3.764
Give your answers to 1 decimal place.

a   16.7°   **b**   35.9°   **c**   75.1°

Finding an angle   When you know the opposite and adjacent sides in a right-angled triangle, you can use tangents to calculate an angle. **Example 10.4** shows you how.

Example 10.4 ▷ | Calculate the angle marked θ in the diagram below. Give your answer to 1 decimal place.

Using the formula **tanθ** = $\dfrac{\textbf{O}\text{pposite}}{\textbf{A}\text{djacent}}$

$= \dfrac{5}{8} = 0.625$

So, θ = 32.0° (1dp)

This can be done on a calculator in one sequence. This will depend on how your calculator works.

SHIFT   tan   (5   ÷   8   )   =

Or, on some calculators you may have to key in:

5   ÷   8   =   INV   or   2ndF   tan

Finding the opposite side   You can use the same formula to calculate the length of the opposite side when you know the size of an angle and the length of the adjacent side in a right-angled triangle, as the following example shows.

Example 10.5 ▶ Calculate the length of the side marked x on the diagram below. Give your answer to 3 significant figures.

Using the formula $\mathbf{tan\theta} = \dfrac{\mathbf{Opposite}}{\mathbf{Adjacent}}$

$$\tan42° = \frac{x}{5}$$

Multiplying both sides by 5, gives: $5\tan42° = x$

So, $x = 4.50$ cm (3sf)

Depending on your calculator, this can be done in one sequence:

Exercise 10B

① Find the value of each of the following. Give your answers to 3 decimal places.

a	tan28°	**b**	tan60°	**c**	tan45°
d	tan9°	**e**	tan37.2°	**f**	tan85.1°

② Find the value of θ for each of the following. Give your answers to 1 decimal place.

a	tanθ = 0.5	**b**	tanθ = 0.23	**c**	tanθ = 0.846
d	tanθ = 1.5	**e**	tanθ = 2.33	**f**	tanθ = 10

③ Find the value of each of the following. Give your answers to 3 significant figures.

a	2tan37°	**b**	8tan25°	**c**	10tan45°
d	24tan59°	**e**	3.5tan60.1°	**f**	14.8tan80.3°

④ Calculate the angle marked θ in each of the following triangles. Give your answers to 1 decimal place.

a 3 cm, 10 cm, θ

b 4 cm, 8 cm, θ

c 5 cm, 11 cm, θ

d 2 cm, 7 cm, θ

e 12 cm, 12 cm, θ

f 8.5 cm, 19.8 cm, θ

5 Calculate the length of the side marked x in each of the following triangles. Give your answers to 3 significant figures.

a

28°
8 cm
x

b

x
18°
10 cm

c

x
45°
14 cm

d
25 cm
52°
x

e
x
30° 5.7 cm

f

18.9 cm
65°
x

6 In the $\triangle PQR$, $\angle P = 90°$, PQ = 6 cm and PR = 10 cm. Find $\angle R$. Give your answer to 1 decimal place. *Hint:* Draw a sketch to help you.

7 In the $\triangle XYZ$, $\angle Z = 90°$, $\angle Y = 56°$ and YZ = 7.2 cm. Find the length of XZ. Give your answer to 3 significant figures. *Hint:* Draw a sketch to help you.

Extension Work

1 Finding the adjacent side

You can use the same trigonometric ratio to calculate the length of the adjacent side when you know the size of an angle and the length of the opposite side in a right-angled triangle, as the following example shows.

Calculate the length marked x on the diagram to the right. Give your answer to 3 significant figures.

7 cm
36°
x

Using the formula $\tan\theta = \dfrac{\textbf{O}\text{pposite}}{\textbf{A}\text{djacent}}$

$$\tan 36° = \frac{7}{x}$$

Multiplying both sides by x, gives: $x\tan 36° = 7$

Dividing both sides by $\tan 36°$, gives $x = \dfrac{7}{\tan 36°}$

So, $x = 9.63$ cm (3sf)

Depending on your calculator, this can be done in one sequence:

7 ÷ tan 36 =   or   7 ÷ 36 tan =

Extension Work

Calculate the length of the side marked x in each of the following triangles. Give your answers to 3 significant figures.

a

b

c 7.6 cm

d
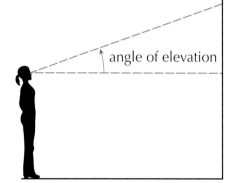

2 Angle of elevation and angle of depression

An angle of elevation is the angle measured from the horizontal when you look up to something.

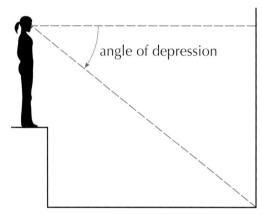

angle of elevation

An angle of depression is the angle measured from the horizontal when you look down at something.

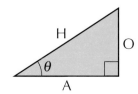

angle of depression

a The angle of elevation of the top of a tower from a point on the ground 400 m away from its base is 8°. Draw a sketch to show this and calculate the height of the tower. Give your answer to 3 significant figures.

b A boat is 250 m from the foot of vertical cliffs which are 50 m high. Draw a sketch to show this and calculate the angle of depression of the boat from the top of the cliffs. Give your answer to 1 decimal place.

Trigonometry – The sine and cosine of an angle

As you saw on page 179, for a right-angled triangle such as the one on the right, the tangent of the angle θ (tanθ) = $\frac{O}{A}$.

This is the ratio of two sides of a right-angled triangle – the opposite and the adjacent. We could just as easily have taken the ratio of any two sides such as the opposite and the hypotenuse or the adjacent and the hypotenuse.

In a right-angled triangle (such as the one on the previous page):

the value of the ratio $\dfrac{\text{Opposite}}{\text{Hypotenuse}}$ is called the **sine of the angle θ**, written as **sinθ**

the value of the ratio $\dfrac{\text{Adjacent}}{\text{Hypotenuse}}$ is called the **cosine of the angle θ**, written as **cosθ**.

The sine and cosine are used in the same way as tangent to find the lengths of sides and the sizes of angles in right-angled triangles when the length of the hypotenuse is either known or required.

The $\boxed{\text{sin}}$ and $\boxed{\text{cos}}$ keys on your calculator are used in exactly the same way as the $\boxed{\text{tan}}$ key. Check that you know how to use them correctly by working through examples 10.6–10.8.

Example 10.6 ▷

1 Find the value of: **a** sin25° **b** sin38.6° **c** cos45° **iv** cos65.3°
Give your answers to 3 decimal places.

   a 0.423   **b** 0.624   **c** 0.707   **d** 0.418

2 Find the value of θ if **a** sinθ = 0.2 **b** sinθ = 0.724 **c** cosθ = 0.36
d cosθ = 0. 895. Give your answers to 1 decimal place.

   a 11.5°   **b** 46.4°   **c** 68.9°   **d** 26.5°

Example 10.7 ▷

Calculate the angle marked θ in the diagram below.
Give your answer to 1 decimal place.

The adjacent side and the hypotenuse are given, so use cosine:

$$\cos\theta = \frac{A}{H} = \frac{5}{12} = 0.416$$

So, θ = 65.4° (1dp)

12 cm

θ

5 cm

Example 10.8 ▷

Calculate the length of the side marked x on the diagram below.
Give your answer to 3 significant figures.

The angle and the hypotenuse are given, and the opposite side is required, so use sine:

$$\sin\theta = \frac{O}{H}$$

$$\sin20° = \frac{x}{7}$$

Multiply both sides by 7 to give: $7\sin20° = x$

So, $x = 7\sin20° = 2.39$ cm (3sf)

7 cm

20°

x

Exercise 10C

1 Find the value of each of the following. Give your answers to 3 decimal places.

   a sin18°   **b** sin30°   **c** sin65.8°
   d cos29°   **e** cos60°   **f** cos85.4°

2 Find the value of θ for each of the following. Give your answers to 1 decimal place.

    a   sinθ = 0.1   **b**   sinθ = 0.53   **c**   sinθ = 0.855

    d   cosθ = 0.4   **e**   cosθ = 0.68   **f**   cosθ = 0.958

3 Find the value of each of the following. Give your answers to 3 significant figures.

    a   3sin32°   **b**   5sin45°   **c**   12.2sin86°

    d   2cos9°   **e**   3.8cos20.1°   **f**   25cos68.9°

4 Calculate the angle marked θ in each of the following triangles. Give your answers to 1 decimal place.

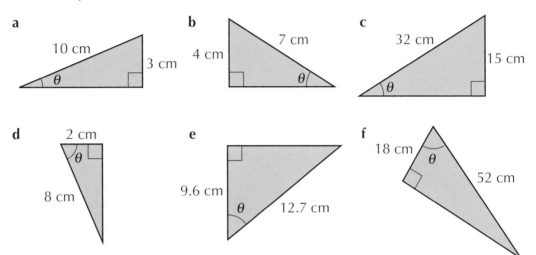

5 Calculate the length of the side marked *x* in each of the following. Give your answers to 3 significant figures.

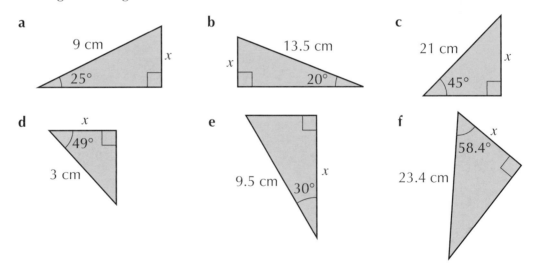

6 In the ΔABC, ∠B = 90°, ∠C = 72° and AC = 20 cm. Find the length AB. Give your answer to 3 significant figures.

7 In the ΔXYZ, ∠X = 90°, XZ = 8.6 cm and YZ = 13.2 cm. Find ∠Z. Give your answer to 1 decimal place.

8

1 Finding the hypotenuse

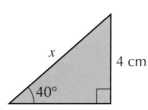

You can use the same trigonometric ratio to calculate the length of the hypotenuse when you know the size of an angle and the length of the opposite side or adjacent side in a right-angled triangle, as the following example shows.

Calculate the length of the side marked x on the diagram on the left. Give your answer to 3 significant figures.

$$\text{Using the formula } \mathbf{sin\theta°} = \frac{\mathbf{O}\text{pposite}}{\mathbf{H}\text{ypotenuse}}$$

$$\sin 40° = \frac{4}{x}$$

Multiplying both sides by x, gives: $x\sin 40° = 4$

Dividing both sides by $\sin 40°$, gives $x = \dfrac{4}{\sin 40°} = 6.22$ cm (3s.f.)

So, $x = 6.22$ cm (3sf)

Calculate the length of the side marked x in each of the following. Give your answers to 3 significant figures.

a

b

c

d

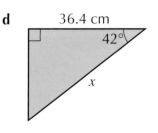

2 The graphs of $y = \sin\theta$ and $y = \cos\theta$

a Copy and complete the table below, giving your answers to two decimal places.

θ	0°	10°	20°	30°	40°	50°	60°	70°	80°	90°
$\sin\theta$										
$\cos\theta$										

b Write down anything you notice about the values of $\sin\theta$ and $\cos\theta$.

c On 2 mm graph paper and using the same axes, draw the graphs of $y = \sin\theta$ and $y = \cos\theta$, for $0° \leq \theta \leq 90°$ and $0 \leq y \leq 1$.

Solving problems using trigonometry

When solving a problem using trigonometry, the following steps should be followed.

1 Draw a sketch of the right-angled triangle in the problem. Even when an illustration or diagram accompanies the problem, it is a good idea to redraw the triangle.

2 Mark on the sketch all the known sides and angles, including the units.

3 Identify the unknown side or angle by labelling it x or θ.

4 Decide and write down which ratio you need to solve the problem.

5 Solve the problem and give your answer to a suitable degree of accuracy. This is usually three significant figures for lengths and one decimal place for angles.

Example 10.9 ▷ A window cleaner has a ladder that is 8 m long. He leans it against a wall so that the foot of the ladder is 3 m from the wall. Calculate the angle the ladder makes with the wall.

1 Draw a sketch for the problem and write on all the known sides and angles:

8 m

3 m

2 Identify the angle required by labelling it θ:

3 Decide and write down which ratio you need to use to solve the problem:

The opposite and hypotenuse are known, so sine should be used to solve the problem.

The ratio required is $\sin\theta = \dfrac{O}{H}$

8 m (H)

θ

3 m (O)

4 Solve the problem:

$$\sin\theta = \frac{3}{8} = 0.375$$

So, $\theta = 22.0°$ (1 dp)

Exercise 10D

① Simon places a ladder against a wall so that it makes an angle of 76° with the ground. When the foot of the ladder is 1.8 m from the foot of the wall, calculate how high up the wall the ladder reaches.

② Veena walks for 800 m up a road that has a uniform slope of 5° to the horizontal. Calculate the vertical height she has risen.

③ Richard's slide is 7 m long and the top of the slide is 4.5 m above the ground. Calculate the angle the slide makes with the ground.

8

8

4 A ship is 8 km east and 5 km north of a lighthouse.

Calculate the bearing of the ship from the lighthouse.

5 Pat is flying a kite on a string that is 35 m long. She holds the string at 1 m above the ground at an angle of 42° with the horizontal. Calculate the height of the kite above the ground.

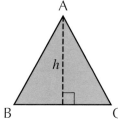

6 Calculate the acute angle between the diagonals of a rectangle which has length 18 cm and width 10 cm.

7 In the isosceles triangle ABC, AB = AC = 8 cm and ∠ABC = 64°. Calculate:

  a the perpendicular height, h, of the triangle.

  b the length of BC.

  c the area of the triangle.

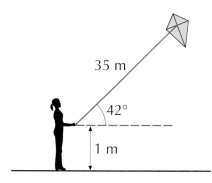

Extension **Work**

1 A plane flies for 200 km on a bearing of 135°. It then alters course and flies for 150 km on a bearing of 040°.

  a Calculate how far east the plane is from its starting point.

  b Calculate how far south the plane is from its starting point.

  c Calculate how far the plane is from its starting point.

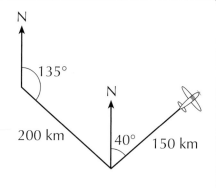

2 ABCDE is a regular pentagon of side 5 cm.

  a Calculate the perpendicular height of ΔOCD.

  b Calculate the area of ΔOCD.

  c Hence calculate the area of the pentagon.

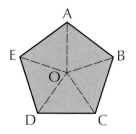

7 I can enlarge a 2-D shape by a fractional scale factor.
I can recognise similar shapes.

8 I can use sine, cosine and tangent in right-angled triangles.
I can solve problems using trigonometry.

National Test questions

1 *2002 Paper 2*

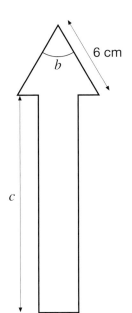

8 cm

40°

a

b

6 cm

c

Not drawn
accurately

The sketch shows two arrows.
The bigger arrow is an enlargement by scale factor 1.5 of the smaller arrow.

Write down the three missing values a, b and c.

Don't forget to include units.

2 *2002 Paper 1*

A picture has a board behind it. The drawings show the dimensions of the rectangular picture and of the rectangular board.

10 cm

8 cm

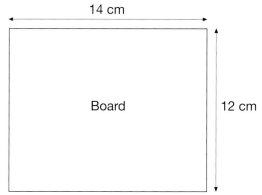

14 cm

Board

12 cm

a Show that the two rectangles are not mathematically similar.

b Suppose you wanted to cut the board to make it mathematically similar to the picture.

Keep the width of the board as 14 cm. What should the new height of the board be? Show your working.

3 *2005 Paper 2*

a Calculate the length w.

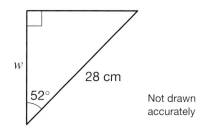

w

28 cm

52°

Not drawn accurately

b Calculate the size of angle x.

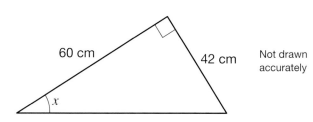

60 cm

42 cm

Not drawn accurately

x

4 *2007 Paper 1*

a Use **tan35°** as **0.7** to work out length k.

k

35°

10 cm

Not drawn accurately

b Now use **tan35°** as **0.7** to work out the **area** of this isosceles triangle.

You **must** show your working.

Not drawn accurately

35°

20 cm

5 *2000 Paper 2*

ABC and ACD are both right-angled triangles.

a Explain why the length of AC is 10 cm.

b Calculate the length of AD. Show your working.

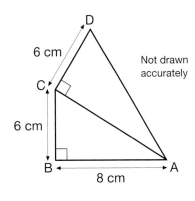

6 cm

6 cm

Not drawn accurately

8 cm

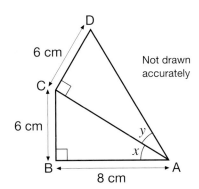

6 cm

6 cm

Not drawn accurately

8 cm

y

x

c By how many degrees is angle *x* bigger than angle *y*? Show your working.

FM Map reading

Katie and Richard go for a walk. The route they take is shown on the map. The map has a scale of 1 : 25000. They park their car at the point marked A. They walk from A to B, then B to C and so on until they arrive back at A.

Use the map to answer the questions below.

1 Copy and complete this table showing the distances that they walk.

From	To	Road or footpath	Distance on map	Distance on ground
A	B	Road	9.6 cm	2.4 km
B	C			
C	D			
D	E			
E	F			
F	G			
G	H			
H	I			
I	J			
J	K			
K	A			

2 What is the total distance that they walk on roads?

3 They walk at an average speed of 4 km/h on the roads, and 3 km/h on the footpaths. How long does the walk take them?

4 They leave their car at 10.00 am. They stop for a 1-hour lunch and a 30-minute rest. At what time do they get back to their car?

5 At point D, Katie suggests they walk in a straight line to the Cairn.

  a How far east of D is the Cairn?

  b How far north of D is the Cairn?

  c What is the bearing they must walk on to get from D to the Cairn?

  d What is the bearing they must walk on to get back from the Cairn to D?

6 On a map, symbols are used to represent different things.

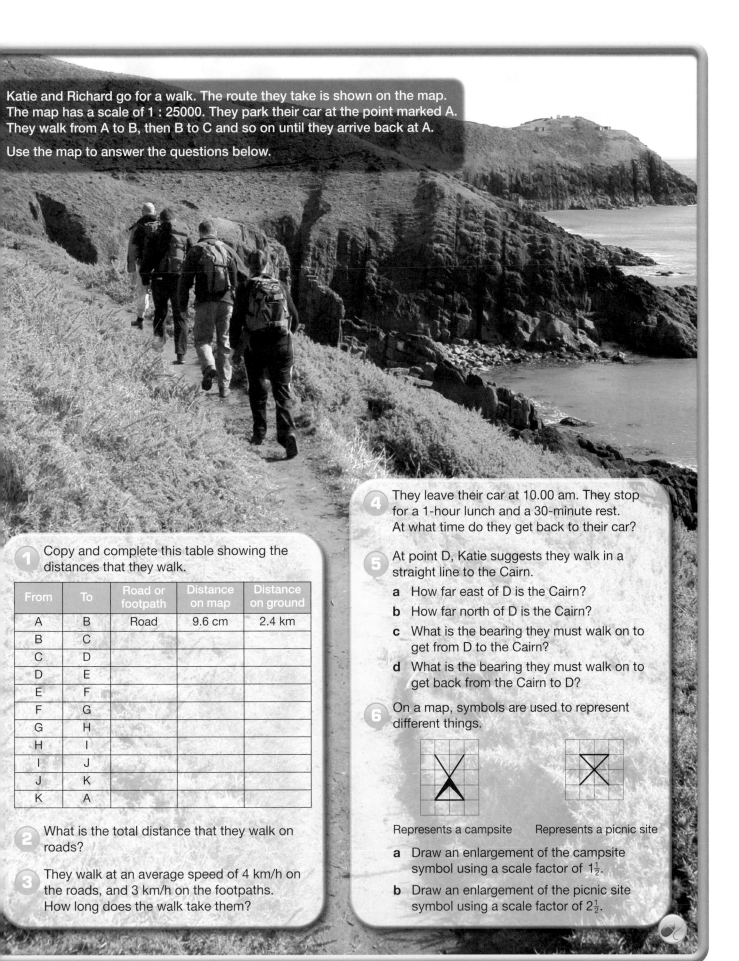

Represents a campsite   Represents a picnic site

  a Draw an enlargement of the campsite symbol using a scale factor of $1\frac{1}{2}$.

  b Draw an enlargement of the picnic site symbol using a scale factor of $2\frac{1}{2}$.

<table>
<tr>
<td>

This chapter is going to show you

- How to expand algebraic expressions
- How to factorise algebraic expressions
- How to factorise quadratic expressions
- How to change the subject of a formula

</td>
<td>

What you should already know

- How to multiply one expression by another
- How to apply the simple rules of powers

</td>
</tr>
</table>

Expansion

What is the area of this rectangle?

Split the rectangle into two smaller rectangles and find the area of each. Then the area of the original rectangle is the sum of the areas of the two smaller rectangles, as shown below:

$3x$ 4

$2x$ | $6x^2$ | $+$ | $8x$ | $2x$

Area $= 6x^2 + 8x$

This helps to illustrate the expansion of $2x(3x + 4)$, where the term outside the bracket multiplies every term of the expression inside the bracket. This is the principle of expanding brackets, which you met first in Year 8.

Take, for example, the next two expressions:

$$3(2x + 5) = 3 \boxed{6x} + \boxed{15} \; 3$$

$$= 3 \times 2x + 3 \times 5 = 6x + 15$$

$$t(8 - 3t) = t \boxed{} = t \boxed{8t} - \boxed{3t^2} \; t$$

$$= t \times 8 - t \times 3t = 8t - 3t^2$$

Manipulation

Example 11.1 ▷ Find the two missing lengths, AB and CD, of this rectangle.

From the diagram, the length of AB is given by:
$$(2p + 7) - 3 = 2p + 7 - 3$$
$$= 2p + 4$$

Hence, the length of AB is $2p + 4$.

The length of CD is given by:
$$(5m + 6) - m = 5m + 6 - m$$
$$= 4m + 6$$

Hence, the length of CD is $4m + 6$.

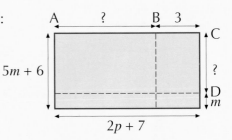

Exercise 11A

(1) Expand each of the following.

a $3(x + 2)$ **b** $5(t + 4)$ **c** $4(m + 3)$ **d** $2(y + 7)$
e $4(3 + m)$ **f** $3(2 + k)$ **g** $5(1 + t)$ **h** $7(2 + x)$

(2) Expand each of the following.

a $2(x - 3)$ **b** $4(t - 3)$ **c** $3(m - 4)$ **d** $6(y - 5)$
e $5(4 - m)$ **f** $2(3 - k)$ **g** $4(2 - t)$ **h** $3(5 - x)$

(3) Expand each of the following.

a $4(2x + 2)$ **b** $6(3t - 4)$ **c** $5(2m - 3)$ **d** $3(3y + 7)$
e $3(3 - 3m)$ **f** $4(2 + 4k)$ **g** $6(1 - 2t)$ **h** $2(2 + 3x)$

(4) Write down an expression for the area of each of the following rectangles. Simplify your expression as far as possible.

a

b

c

d

e

(5) Expand each of the following.

a $x(x + 3)$ **b** $t(t + 5)$ **c** $m(m + 4)$ **d** $y(y + 8)$
e $m(2 + m)$ **f** $k(3 + k)$ **g** $t(2 + t)$ **h** $x(5 + x)$

(6) Expand each of the following.

a $x(x - 2)$ **b** $t(t - 4)$ **c** $m(m - 3)$ **d** $y(y - 6)$
e $m(5 - m)$ **f** $k(2 - k)$ **g** $t(3 - t)$ **h** $x(6 - x)$

(7) Expand each of the following.

a $x(4x + 3)$ **b** $t(2t - 3)$ **c** $m(3m - 2)$ **d** $y(4y + 5)$
e $m(4 - 5m)$ **f** $k(3 + 2k)$ **g** $t(4 - 3t)$ **h** $x(1 + 4x)$

8 Write down an expression for the area of each of the following rectangles. Simplify your expression as far as possible.

a
2x + 3

x

b
5 − 3t

t

c
4 + 5m

m

d
k

7k − 2

9 Expand and simplify each of the following.

a $3(x + 2) + 2(4 + 3x)$ b $4(t + 3) + 3(5 + 2t)$ c $4(m + 3) + 3(2 − 4m)$

d $5(2k + 4) + 2(3 − 4k)$ e $6(2x − 3) + 2(3 − 4x)$ f $5(3x − 2) + 3(1 − 2x)$

g $3(x + 4) − 2(3 + 2x)$ h $4(x + 5) − 3(4 + 2x)$ i $4(m + 2) − 3(2 − 3m)$

j $5(2m + 1) − 2(4 − 3m)$ k $5(2x − 1) − 2(1 + 3x)$ l $6(3x − 5) − 3(2 + 4x)$

m $3(x − 2) − 2(4 − 3x)$ n $4(2x − 1) − 3(5 − 2x)$

10 Write down the missing lengths in each of the following rectangles.

a

b

c

d
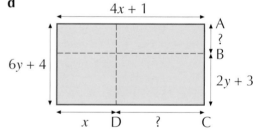

Extension **Work**

1 a Show that $\frac{1}{a} + \frac{1}{b} = \frac{(a + b)}{ab}$ is true for *all* values of a and b.

b Show that $\frac{a}{b} + \frac{c}{d} = \frac{(ad + bc)}{bd}$ is true for *all* values of a and b.

2 a Think of a number. Multiply it by 3 and add 15. Then divide the result by 3 and take away 5.

b What is the number you end up with? What do you notice? Try this with a few more numbers.

c Show by algebra that this result will *always* be the answer.

d Find another similar routine which gives a constant answer.

Factorisation

Factorisation is the opposite (inverse) process to expanding a bracket. For example, expanding $3(2x + 5)$ gives:

$$3(2x + 5) = 3 \times 2x + 3 \times 5$$
$$= 6x + 15$$

Factorisation starts with an expression, such as $6x + 15$, and works back to find the factors which, when multiplied together give that expression when simplified.

Example 11.2 ▷

Factorise $6x + 15$.

Look for a factor which will divide into each term in the expression. Here, that common factor is 3.

Now rewrite the expression using the common factor, which gives:

$$3 \times 2x + 3 \times 5$$

Insert brackets and place the common factor outside them, to obtain:

$$3(2x + 5)$$

Example 11.3 ▷

Factorise $8t - 3t^2$.

Look for a factor which will divide into each term in the expression. Here, that is t.

Now rewrite the expression using the common factor, which gives:

$$t \times 8 - t \times 3t$$

Insert brackets and place the common factor outside them, to obtain:

$$t(8 - 3t)$$

Always check your factorised expressions by expanding them. So, in the case of Example 11.2:

$$3(2x + 5) = 3 \times 2x + 3 \times 5$$
$$= 6x + 15$$

In the case of Example 11.3:

$$t(8 - 3t) = t \times 8 - t \times 3t$$
$$= 8t - 3t^2$$

Exercise 11B

(1) Factorise each of the following.

a $3x + 6$	**b** $4t + 6$	**c** $4m + 8$	**d** $5y + 10$
e $8 + 2m$	**f** $3 + 6k$	**g** $5 + 15t$	**h** $12 + 3x$

(2) Factorise each of the following.

a $2x - 4$	**b** $4t - 12$	**c** $3m - 9$	**d** $6y - 9$
e $14 - 7m$	**f** $21 - 3k$	**g** $12 - 8t$	**h** $15 - 3x$

7

3 Factorise each of the following.

a	$12x + 3$	**b**	$6t - 4$	**c**	$9m - 3$	**d**	$3y + 6$
e	$15 - 3m$	**f**	$12 + 4k$	**g**	$6 - 2t$	**h**	$27 + 3x$

4 Write down an expression for the missing lengths of each of the following rectangles. Simplify each expression as far as possible.

a

?

$\text{Area} = 3x^2 + 4x$ x

b

?

$\text{Area} = 5t + 3t^2$ t

c

?

$\text{Area} = 2m^2 - 3m$ m

d

?

$\text{Area} = 4t - 2t^2$ t

5 Factorise each of the following.

a	$x^2 + 3x$	**b**	$t^2 + 4t$	**c**	$m^2 + 5m$	**d**	$y^2 + 7y$
e	$3m + m^2$	**f**	$4k + k^2$	**g**	$3t + t^2$	**h**	$x + x^2$

6 Factorise each of the following.

a	$x^2 - 3x$	**b**	$3t^2 - 5t$	**c**	$m^2 - 2m$	**d**	$4y^2 - 5y$
e	$2m - m^2$	**f**	$4k - 3k^2$	**g**	$5t - t^2$	**h**	$7x - 4x^2$

7 Factorise each of the following.

a	$3x^2 + 4x$	**b**	$5t^2 - 3t$	**c**	$3m^2 - 2m$	**d**	$4y^2 + 5y$
e	$4m - 3m^2$	**f**	$2k + 5k^2$	**g**	$4t - 3t^2$	**h**	$2x + 7x^2$

8 Write down an expression for the missing lengths of each of the following rectangles.

a

?

$\text{Area} = 6x + 8$ 2

b

?

$\text{Area} = 6 + 9m$ 3

c

?

$\text{Area} = 12 - 8t$ 4

d

?

$\text{Area} = 8x - 2$ 2

9 **a** Write down expressions for three consecutive integers, where the smallest of them is n.

b Write down an expression for the sum of these three consecutive integers. Simplify your expression as far as possible.

c Factorise this expression.

d Use your result to explain why the sum of *any* three consecutive integers is a multiple of 3.

Extension **Work**

1 The area of a rectangle is $2x^2 + 4x$. Write down *three* different pairs of expressions for the possible lengths of two adjacent sides of the rectangle.

2 Show, by substitution of $x = 1$, $x = 2$ and $x = 3$, that each pair of values generates the *same* values of areas.

3 The area of another rectangle is $12x^2 + 18x$. Write down *seven* different pairs of expressions for the possible lengths of two adjacent sides of the rectangle.

Quadratic expansion

What is the area of this rectangle?

It is $(x + 3)(x + 2)$.

Its area can also be found by splitting each side into two sections, as shown below. The original rectangle is thus divided into four smaller rectangles.

The area of each smaller rectangle is then found, giving the area of the original rectangle as the sum of the areas of the four smaller rectangles.

	x	3	
	x^2	$3x$	x
	$2x$	6	2

The area of the four rectangles $= x^2 + 3x + 2x + 6 = x^2 + 5x + 6$

The area of the original rectangle $= (x + 3)(x + 2)$

Hence:

$$(x + 3)(x + 2) = x^2 + 5x + 6$$

This illustrates the expansion of $(x + 2)(x + 3)$, where every term in the first bracket is multiplied by every term in the second bracket, as shown below.

$$(x + 3)(x + 2) = x^2 + 3x + 2x + 6$$
$$= x^2 + 5x + 6$$

Using this method of curved arrows makes dealing with negative signs inside the brackets much easier, as Example 11.4 shows.

Example 11.4

Expand $(x - 3)(x - 4)$.

$$(x - 3)(x - 4) \quad \begin{aligned} &= x^2 - 4x - 3x + 12 \\ &= x^2 - 7x + 12 \end{aligned}$$

Example 11.5

Expand $(x + 3)^2$.

$$(x + 3)^2 = (x + 3)(x + 3) = x^2 + 3x + 3x + 9 = x^2 + 6x + 9$$

Exercise 11C

Expand each of the following expressions.

1 $(x + 3)(x + 4)$

2 $(x + 5)(x + 1)$

3 $(x + 2)(x + 7)$

4 $(x + 2)(x - 4)$

5 $(x + 4)(x - 3)$

6 $(x + 1)(x - 5)$

7 $(x - 3)(x + 2)$

8 $(x - 1)(x + 6)$

9 $(x - 4)(x + 3)$

10 $(x - 1)(x - 2)$

11 $(x - 3)(x - 6)$

12 $(x - 4)(x - 5)$

13 $(4 + x)(1 - x)$

14 $(5 + x)(2 - x)$

15 $(3 + x)(6 - x)$

16 $(x + 5)^2$

17 $(x - 3)^2$

18 $(2 - x)^2$

19 **Investigation**

a Take a square piece of card or paper and label the two adjacent sides, x.

The area of the square is x^2.

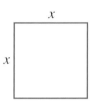

b In the unlabelled corner, draw a smaller square and label each side.

The area of the smaller square is y^2.

c Cut out this square of side y, and then label the remaining parts of the two sides $x - y$.

The area of this remaining shape must be $(x^2 - y^2)$.

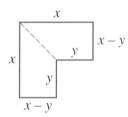

d Now cut this remaining shape diagonally, as indicated by the dashed line. Fit the two parts together, as shown.

The area remains, as before, $(x^2 - y^2)$.

e This makes a rectangle of side $(x + y)$ and $(x - y)$.

Hence:
$$(x + y)(x - y) = x^2 - y^2$$

f It has been shown that the above identity is true geometrically. Now show it is also true algebraically.

20 The result $x^2 - y^2 = (x + y)(x - y)$ from Question **19** is called the **difference of two squares**, and can be used to solve certain arithmetic problems. For example, find the value of $32^2 - 28^2$ without squaring any numbers.

$$32^2 - 28^2 = (32 + 28)(32 - 28)$$
$$= 60 \times 4 = 240$$

Use this method to calculate each of the following.

a $54^2 - 46^2$ **b** $25^2 - 15^2$ **c** $17^2 - 3^2$

d $38^2 - 37^2$ **e** $29^2 - 21^2$ **f** $18^2 - 17^2$

g $8.1^2 - 1.9^2$ **h** $7.9^2 - 2.1^2$ **i** $999^2 - 998^2$

Expand each of the following quadratic expressions.

1 $(2x + 3)(4x + 1)$

2 $(3x + 2)(4x + 5)$

3 $(4x + 3)(2x - 1)$

4 $(5x - 2)(2x + 6)$

5 $(4x - 3)(2x - 4)$

6 $(5x - 3)^2$

Quadratic factorisation

Expansion removes brackets, so $(x + 2)(x + 4)$ gives $x^2 + 6x + 8$. Factorisation is the opposite of expansion and involves putting an expression back into the brackets from which it was derived.

This generally requires the application of what is called 'intelligent trial and improvement'.

Let's look at a few examples of factorising expressions in the form of $x^2 + Bx + C$.

Example 11.6

Factorise $x^2 + 6x + 8$.

Given the x^2 and both signs being +, the arrangement of brackets must be of the form $(x + a)(x + b)$. So, the question is what are the values of a and b?

The product ab is equal to 8. So, a and b must be a factor pair of 8. The choices are 8, 1 and 4, 2.

The sum of a and b is 6. So the pair required is 2 and 4. Hence:

$x^2 + 6x + 8 = (x + 2)(x + 4)$

Example 11.7

Factorise $x^2 - 9x + 20$.

Look at the signs. The second sign is a plus which means that the two signs in the brackets will be the same. The first sign is a minus which means that both signs are minuses.

From the x^2 and the signs, the arrangement of the brackets must be of the form $(x - a)(x - b)$. The question is what are the values of a and b?

The product ab is equal to 20. So, a and b must be a factor pair of 20. The choices are 20, 1; 10, 2; 5, 4.

The sum of a and b is –9. So, the pair required is –5 and –4. Hence:

$x^2 - 9x + 20 = (x - 5)(x - 4)$

Example 11.8

Factorise $x^2 - 5x - 24$.

Look at the signs. The second sign is a minus which means that the signs in the brackets will be different. The first sign is also a negative, which means that the larger number will need to be negative.

From the x^2 and the signs, the arrangement of the brackets must be of the form $(x + a)(x - b)$. The question is what are the values of a and b?

The product ab is equal to 24. So a and b must be a factor pair of 24. The choices are 24, 1; 12, 2; 8, 3; 6, 4.

The sum of a and b is -5. As the signs are different, this means that the *difference* of a and b is -5, with the larger number being negative. So, the pair required is 3 and -8. Hence:

$$x^2 - 5x - 24 = (x + 3)(x - 8)$$

Exercise 11D

Factorise each of the following.

1 $x^2 + 10x + 24$ **2** $x^2 + 14x + 24$ **3** $x^2 + 9x + 18$

4 $x^2 - 11x + 18$ **5** $x^2 - 7x + 12$ **6** $x^2 - 8x + 12$

7 $x^2 + 2x - 24$ **8** $x^2 + 7x - 44$ **9** $x^2 + 4x - 12$

10 $x^2 - 7x - 44$ **11** $x^2 - 2x - 63$ **12** $x^2 - x - 90$

13 $x^2 + 10x + 25$ **14** $x^2 - 12x + 36$ **15** $x^2 - 2x + 1$

16 $x^2 - 4$ **17** $x^2 - 25$ **18** $x^2 - 100$

Extension Work

Factorise each of the following. Take note of the coefficient of x^2.

1 $3x^2 + 4x + 1$ **2** $3x^2 - 5x - 2$ **3** $9x^2 + 12x + 4$

4 $2x^2 - 11x + 5$ **5** $4x^2 - 15x - 25$ **6** $6x^2 - 7x - 20$

Change of subject

The cost, in pounds sterling, of advertising in a local paper is given by the formula:
$$C = 10 + 4A$$

where A is the area (in cm^2) of the advertisement.

To find the cost of a 7 cm^2 advertisement, substitute $A = 7$ into the formula to give:
$$C = 10 + 4 \times 7 = £38$$

To find the size of the advertisement you would get for, say, £60, you would take these two steps.

- Rearrange the formula to make it read $A = \dfrac{C - 10}{4}$
- Substitute $C = 60$ into this formula

When a formula is rearranged like this, it is called **changing the subject** of the formula. The subject of a formula is the variable (letter) in the formula which stands on its own, usually on the left-hand side of the equals sign. So, in this case, C is the subject in the original formula. In the rearranged formula, A becomes the subject.

To change the subject of a formula, use the same method as in solving equations. That is, do the same thing to both sides of the equals sign in order to isolate the variable which is to be the new subject. So, in this example:

$$C = 10 + 4A$$

- First, subtract 10 from both sides: $C - 10 = 4A$
- Then divide both sides by 4: $\dfrac{C - 10}{4} = A$
- Now switch the formula so that the subject is on the left-hand side:

$$A = \dfrac{C - 10}{4}$$

Hence, to find the size of an advertisement costing £60, substitute $C = 60$ to give:

$$A = \dfrac{60 - 10}{4} = 12.5 \text{ cm}^2$$

Exercise 11E

1 Change the subject of each of the following formulae as indicated.

- **a**   **i**   Make I the subject of $V = IR$.
  - **ii**   Make R the subject of $V = IR$.
- **b**   **i**   Make U the subject of $S = U + FT$.
  - **ii**   Make F the subject of $S = U + FT$.
  - **iii**   Make T the subject of $S = U + FT$.
- **c**   **i**   Make b the subject of $P = 2b + 2w$.
  - **ii**   Make w the subject of $P = 2b + 2w$.
- **d**   **i**   Make b the subject of $A = \dfrac{bh}{2}$.
  - **ii**   Make h the subject of $A = \dfrac{bh}{2}$.

2 The formula $F = \dfrac{9C}{5} + 32$ is used to convert temperatures in degrees Celsius, C, to degrees Fahrenheit, F.

- **a**   Make C the subject of the formula.
- **b**   Use this formula to find the Celsius value of each of the following Fahrenheit temperatures. Give your answers to 1 decimal place.
  - **i**   Temperature on the planet Corus, -65 °F
  - **ii**   Body temperature of a reptile, 66.5 °F
  - **iii**   Recommended temperature for a tropical fish tank, 56.5 °F

3 The Greek mathematician Hero showed that the area A of a triangle with sides a, b and c is given by the formula:

$$A = \sqrt{S(S - a)(S - b)(S - c)}$$

where $S = \dfrac{a + b + c}{2}$

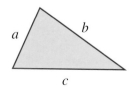

Use Hero's formula to find the area of the following triangles to 1 decimal place.

a

5 cm 10 cm

12 cm

b

8 m

3 m

8 m

4 The estimated cost, £*C*, of making a pizza of radius *r* cm and depth *d* cm is given by:

$$C = \frac{r^2d}{20}$$

a What is the estimated cost of making a pizza of radius 8 cm with a depth of 0.5 cm?

b i Rearrange the formula to make *d* the subject.

ii What is the depth of a 10 cm radius pizza whose estimated cost to make is £3.75?

5 The area, *A* cm², of an ellipse is given by $A = \pi ab$.
Calculate to one decimal place each of these.

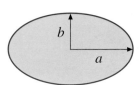

a Find the area of an ellipse with *a* = 8 cm and *b* = 5 cm.

b i Rearrange the formula to make *a* the subject.

ii Find the length of *a* when *A* = 150 cm² and *b* = 5 cm.

c i Rearrange the formula to make *b* the subject.

ii Find the length of *b* when *A* = 45 cm² and *a* = 9.5 cm.

6 Euler's theorem, which connects the number of nodes (*N*), the number of regions (*R*) and the number of arcs (*A*) of a figure, is stated as:

$$N + R - A = 2$$

Take, for example, the figure on the right. This shows 5 nodes, 3 regions (two inside and one outside the figure) and 6 arcs.

a Show that Euler's theorem is correct for the shape shown.

b Show that Euler's theorem is correct by drawing a shape with 6 nodes and 5 regions.

c i Rearrange the formula to make *A* the subject.

ii How many arcs will there be in a shape which has 10 nodes and 9 regions?

Extension Work

1 a Make *r* the subject of $A = \pi r^2$, where *A* is the area of a circle.

b Make *r* the subject of $V = \pi r^2 h$, where *V* is the volume of a cylinder.

c Make *r* the subject of $V = \frac{4\pi r^3}{3}$, where *V* is the volume of a sphere.

2 What is the radius of a circle with an area of 100 cm²?

3 What is the radius of a cylinder with a volume of 200 cm³ and a height of 9 cm?

Graphs from equations in the form $Ay \pm Bx = C$

You have already met the linear equation $y = mx + c$ which generates a straight-line graph. It is this equation which is seen here as $Ay \pm Bx = C$. When the graph is plotted, it will, of course, still produce a straight line.

To construct the graph of $Ay + Bx = C$, follow these steps.

- Substitute $x = 0$ into the equation so that it becomes $Ay = C$
- Solve for y, i.e. $y = \dfrac{C}{A}$ so that one point on the graph is $\left(0, \dfrac{C}{A}\right)$
- Substitute $y = 0$ into the equation so that it becomes $Bx = C$
- Solve for x, i.e. $x = \dfrac{C}{B}$ so that one point on the graph is $\left(\dfrac{C}{B}, 0\right)$
- Plot the two points on the axes and join them up.

Example 11.9

Draw the graph of $4y - 5x = 20$.

Substitute $x = 0 \Rightarrow 4y = 20$
$\qquad\qquad\qquad\quad y = 5$

So the graph passes through $(0, 5)$.

Substitute $y = 0 \Rightarrow -5x = 20$
$\qquad\qquad\qquad\quad x = -4$

So the graph passes through $(-4, 0)$.

Plot the points and join them up.

Note that this method is sometimes called the 'cover-up' method as all you have to do to solve for x or y is cover up the other term:

i.e. $4y$ $= 20 \Rightarrow y = 5$

$\qquad$ $- 5x = 20 \Rightarrow x = -4$

Exercise 11F

1 Draw graphs of these straight lines. Use a grid that goes from 0 to +10 on both the x- and y-axis.

    a $2y + 3x = 6$ **b** $4y + 3x = 12$ **c** $y + 2x = 8$

    d $y + x = 6$ **e** $5y + 2x = 10$ **f** $2y + 5x = 20$

7

2 Draw graphs of these straight lines. Use a grid that goes from –10 to +10 on both the x- and y-axis.

a	$y - 5x = 10$	**b**	$2y - 3x = 12$	**c**	$x - 3y = 9$
d	$2y + 3x = -6$	**e**	$2y - 5x = 10$	**f**	$2x - 3y = 6$
g	$y + 3x = -9$	**h**	$3x - 4y = 12$	**i**	$y - 2x = 8$
j	$y + x = -8$	**k**	$5y - 2x = 10$	**l**	$x - 4y = 10$

Extension Work

1 Show clearly that when $4x + 5y = 20$ is rearranged to make y the subject, the answer is $y = -\frac{4}{5}x + 4$.

2 Describe how you would plot the graph $4x + 5y = 20$ using the 'cover-up' method.

3 Describe how you would plot the graph $y = -\frac{4}{5}x + 4$ using the gradient–intercept method.

4 Compare the advantages or disadvantages of rearranging into the form $y = mx + c$ to draw the graph over using the cover-up method.

LEVEL BOOSTER

5 I can expand simple brackets.

6 I can expand and simplify expressions with two or more brackets.

7 I can factorise expressions by taking out a common factor.
I can rearrange formulae to change the subject.
I can multiply a pair of linear brackets to get a quadratic expression.
I can draw linear graphs using the cover-up method.

8 I can factorise a quadratic expression into two linear brackets.

National Test questions

1 *2000 Paper 1*

a Two of the expressions below are equivalent. Write them down.

$5(2y + 4)$ $5(2y + 20)$ $7(y + 9)$ $10(y + 9)$ $2(5y + 10)$

b One of the expressions below is not a correct factorisation of $12y + 24$. Which one is it? Write down your answer.

$12(y + 2)$ $3(4y + 8)$ $2(6y + 12)$ $12(y + 24)$ $6(2y + 4)$

c Factorise this expression: $7y + 14$.

d Factorise this expression as fully as possible: $6y^3 - 2y^2$.

2 *2005 Paper 2*

Multiply out the brackets in these expressions.

$y(y - 6)$

$(k + 2)(k + 3)$

3 *2006 Paper 2*

Multiply out these expressions.

Write your answers as simply as possible.

$5(x + 2) + 3(7 + x)$

$(x + 2)(x + 5)$

4 *2006 Paper 1*

a Copy and complete these factorisations.

$x^2 + 7x + 12 = (x + 3)(\ldots + \ldots)$

$x^2 - 7x - 30 = (x + 3)(\ldots - \ldots)$

b Factorise these expressions.

$x^2 + 7x - 18$

$x^2 - 49$

5 *2005 Paper 1*

To change temperatures measured in °C to °F you can use an exact formula or an approximate formula.

Exact formula

$F = \frac{9C}{5} + 32$

Approximate formula

$F = 2C + 30$

F is the temperature in °F

C is the temperature in °C

At what temperature in °C do these formulae give an **equal** value of F?

You **must** show an algebraic method.

6 *2007 Paper 2*

I am thinking of a number.

When I subtract 25 from my number, then square the answer, I get the **same result as** when I square my number, then subtract 25 from the answer.

What is my number?

You **must** show an algebraic method.

Trip to Rome

Tom and his wife Geri live in Silkstone. Their friends Stan and his wife Olive live in Barlborough. They both want to take a 7-day holiday in Rome. There are two airports in Rome, Ciampino (CIA) and Fiumicino (FCO).

The diagram shows the local airports, the costs of flights on the days they want to fly and the cost of parking a car for 7 days. Prices for flights are per person and include all taxes and fees.

The diagram also shows the main roads from their homes to the airports.

Motorways and dual carriageways are shown solid and minor roads are shown dotted.

Junctions are marked with arrows and the distances between arrows are shown in miles.

Leeds/Bradford (LBA) to Rome (FCO)

Out	£48.99
Return	£73.76
Parking	£39.60

Liverpool (LPL) to Rome (CIA)

Out	£52.79
Return	£15.79
Parking	£36.50

Manchester (MAN to Rome (FCO)

Out	£85.99
Return	£43.76
Parking	£23.92

East Midlands (EMA) to Rome CIA)

Out	£64.99
Return	£64.99
Parking	£29.00

Birmingham (BHX) to Rome (FCO)

Out	£62.34
Return	£20.34
Parking	£19.92

Transfers from Rome airports to City Centre

Fiumicino – Train to Termini station €10 each way
Ciampino – Bus to Termini station €9 each way, €14 return

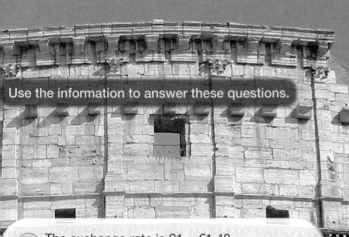

Use the information to answer these questions.

1. The exchange rate is £1 = €1.40.
   a How much would it cost to get a return transfer from each airport to Rome city centre in pounds?
   b Which is the cheapest of the five airports for two people to fly to Rome and back and park their car for seven days? Include the cost of return transfers from the airport to the centre of Rome.

2. a How far is it from Silkstone to Leeds/Bradford airport?
   b How much of this distance is on minor roads?

To calculate the driving time to the airports the following rules are used.
- On motorways assume an average speed of 60 miles per hour.
- On minor roads assume an average speed of 30 miles per hour.
- Allow 15 minutes to park the car and get to the terminal.

3. How long will it take Stan to drive to each of the airports by the shortest routes?

4. A flight from Manchester is scheduled to leave at 08.30. The airline asks passengers to check in 2 hours before the flight. What is the latest time Stan should leave home to be sure of being at the terminal for 06.30?

5. Another flight from Birmingham is scheduled to leave at 06.45.
   What time would Stan need to leave home to be sure of being at the terminal in time?

Tom knows that the running cost of his car is 80p per mile.

Stan knows that the running cost of his car is 90p per mile.

The friends decide to travel together. They work out two possible arrangements.

Plan 1: Stan and Olive will pick up Tom and Geri and the four will fly from Leeds/Bradford.
Plan 2: Tom and Geri will pick up Stan and Olive and the four will fly from East Midlands.

6. a Work out the cost of each plan taking into account all possible costs.
   b The flight from Leeds/Bradford leaves at 09.00. The flight from East Midlands leaves at 06.30. Allow 10 minutes to pick up friends at their house.
      i What time would Stan need to leave home for Plan 1?
      ii What time would Tom need to leave home for Plan 2?
   c Which plan would you advise the friends to go for? Give reasons for your choice.

7. Devise a **Plan 3** which would be much cheaper than either Plan 1 or Plan 2.

A local taxi company called 'Jane's taxis' operates from Silkstone. The table shows their charges.

Airport	LBA	MAN	LPL	EMA	BHX
Drop off	£28	£28	£35	£28	£42
Pick up	£28	£28	£35	£28	£42

8. Stan and Olive intend to drive to Silkstone, park their car and the 4 friends will then take Jane's taxi's to Manchester airport to fly to Rome and back, then get Jane's taxis to pick them up.

   How much will this cost in total?

   Include the cost of Stan's drive from Barlborough to Silkstone and the transfers from the airport in Rome.

9. Using all the available data, find the cheapest possible way for the four friends to fly to Rome and back.

This chapter is going to give you practice in National Test questions about

- Number – fractions, percentages and decimals
- Number – the four rules, ratios and standard form
- Algebra – the basic rules and solving linear equations
- Algebra – graphs
- Geometry and measures
- Statistics

Number 1 – Fractions, percentages and decimals

Exercise 12A **Do not use a calculator for the first two questions.**

1 Calculate the following, giving your answers as fractions.

a $\dfrac{3}{5} + \dfrac{1}{3}$ **b** $\dfrac{5}{9} - \dfrac{1}{6}$ **c** $2\dfrac{3}{4} + 1\dfrac{2}{5}$

2 The following method can be used to work out 11.5% of 320:

$$10\% \text{ of } 320 = 32$$
$$1\% \text{ of } 320 = 3.2$$
$$\tfrac{1}{2}\% \text{ of } 320 = 1.6$$
$$\overline{11.5\% \text{ of } 320 = 36.8}$$

Use a similar method or a method of your own to work out $28\tfrac{1}{2}\%$ of 480.

You may use a calculator for the rest of the exercise unless told otherwise.

 FM **3** Jack's Jackets is having a sale.

Calculate the original price of a jacket with a sale price of £36.21.

4 This table shows the populations (in thousands) of the eight largest towns in the UK in 1991 and in 2001. It also shows the percentage change in the populations of the towns over that 10-year period.

	London	Birmingham	Leeds	Glasgow	Sheffield	Liverpool	Manchester	Bristol
1991	6 800	1 007	717	660	529	481	439	407
2001	7 200	1 017	731	692	531	456		423
% change	5.9%	1%	2.0%	4.8%	0.3%	−5.2%	−3.2%	

    a How many more people lived in Leeds than Sheffield in 2001?

    b Calculate the population of Manchester in 2001.

    c Calculate the percentage change in the population of Bristol over the 10 years.

 5 A garage records the sales of fuel in one morning.

Fuel	Number of litres sold	Takings
Premium	345	£334.72
Ultimate 102	180	£189.56
Diesel	422	£417.48
LP Gas	25	£14.60
Total	**972**	**£956.36**

    a What percentage of the total litres sold was Ultimate 102?

    b What percentage of the total money taken was for Diesel?

    c Which is cheaper per litre, Diesel or Premium?

6 **Do not use a calculator for this question.**

    a Calculate: **i** 0.2×0.4 **ii** $600 \div 0.3$

    b Estimate the answer to $\dfrac{479 \times 0.48}{0.59}$

 7 Some bathroom scales measure in stones and pounds, whilst others measure in kilograms. One way to change from stones and pounds to kilograms is shown below.

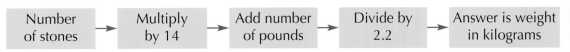

| Number of stones | → | Multiply by 14 | → | Add number of pounds | → | Divide by 2.2 | → | Answer is weight in kilograms |

    Use the flowchart to help you convert 70 kg to stones.

8 The train fare for a child on a journey to London is £13. This child's fare is 35% less than an adult fare. How much is an adult's fare?

9 The table shows the number of mobile phones per thousand of the population in the USA and the UK.

	2003	2007
USA	830	980
UK	800	

a Between 2003 and 2007 the use of mobile phones in the UK increased by 48.5%. How many people per 1000 had mobile phones in the UK in 2007?

b What was the percentage increase in mobile phone use in the USA between 2003 and 2007?

 10 On Sunday, an Internet auction site posted some computers for sale. Each day the price of the computers is reduced by 12% of the price the day before.

a A computer was priced at £950 on Sunday. Derek bought it on Monday. How much did he pay for it?

b Another computer sold for £439.12 on Monday. What was its price on Sunday?

c A computer was priced at £560 on Sunday. It was eventually sold on Friday. How much did it sell for?

d John decides to take a chance on a computer that is priced at £1500 on Sunday, and wait until it is less than half the original price. How many days will he have to wait?

8

11 **Do not use a calculator for this question.**

a Which calculation below gives the answer to this question?

In a sale, Tomb Taker III, which is priced at £45, is reduced by 15%. The sale price is then reduced by a further 10%. How much is Tomb Taker III now?

$$45 \times 0.15 \times 0.10 \quad 45 \times 1.15 \times 1.1 \quad 45 \times 0.85 \times 0.9 \quad 45 \times (0.85 + 0.9)$$

b What value do you multiply by to increase a quantity by 13%?

12 For each part of the question, where n is always an integer, write down the answer that is true and explain your choice. Do not use a calculator.

a When n is even, $\dfrac{n(n + 1)(n + 2)}{4}$ is:

Always odd Always even Sometimes odd, sometimes even

b When n is even, $\dfrac{n(n + 1)(n + 2)}{6}$ is:

Always an integer Always a fraction Sometimes an integer, sometimes a fraction

13 The following formula can be used to calculate the area of a triangle with sides a, b and c.

$$A = \sqrt{s(s - a)(s - b)(s - c)} \quad \text{where } s = \tfrac{1}{2}(a + b + c)$$

a If a triangle has sides of length $a = 4.5$ cm, $b = 7.5$ cm and $c = 9.5$ cm, calculate the area of the triangle. Write down all the digits shown on your calculator.

b Round off your answer to three significant figures.

Number 2 – The four rules, ratios and standard form

6

Exercise 12B

Do not use a calculator for the first three questions.

 1 Litter bins cost £29 each. A school has a budget of £500 to spend on bins. How many bins can the school afford?

 2 Alf and Bert are paid £48 for doing a job. They decide to share the money in the ratio 3 : 5. How much does Alf get?

3 Work out: **a** 24×0.6 **b** $54 \div 0.6$ **c** 0.2×0.3

You may use a calculator for the rest of the exercise unless told otherwise.

 4 A car company wants to move 700 cars by rail. Each train can carry 48 cars.

  a How many trains will be needed to move the 700 cars?
  b Each train costs £3745. What is the total cost of the trains?
  c What is the cost per car of transporting them by train?

 5 a A bus travels 234 miles in 4 hours and 30 minutes. What is the average speed of the bus?

  b A car travels 280 miles at an average speed of 60 miles per hour. How long was the car travelling for? Give your answer in hours and minutes.

 6 Concrete is made by mixing cement and sand in the ratio 1 : 4.

  a What weight of sand is needed to mix with four bags of concrete, each weighing 25 kg?
  b Frank needs one tonne of concrete. How many 25 kg bags of cement will he need?

 7 Parking tickets cost £1.25 each. In one day a ticket machine takes the coins listed in the table.

How many tickets were sold that day?

Coin	Number of coins
£1	126
50p	468
20p	231
10p	185
5p	181

8 Without using a calculator, find the values of a, b and c.

  a $81 = 3^a$ **b** $256 = 2^b$ **c** $64 = (2^2)^c$

7

9 Look at the six cards with numbers on below. Do not use a calculator.

$(-1)^2$ 4^4 $(-2)^6$ 8^2 5^9 $(-3)^4$

   a Which card has the largest value?

   b Which two cards have the same value?

   c Which card is equal to 2^8?

   d Which cards have values that are cube numbers?

10 A litre jug contains orange squash and water in the ratio 1 : 4. A 900 ml jug contains orange squash and water in the ratio 2 : 7. Both jugs are poured into a two-litre jug. This is then topped up with water. What is the ratio of orange squash to water in the two-litre jug now?

11 **Do not use a calculator for this question.**

   a Which of these statements is true?

     i $3^2 \times 10^3$ is smaller than $3^3 \times 10^2$

     ii $3^2 \times 10^3$ is equal to $3^3 \times 10^2$

     iii $3^2 \times 10^3$ is larger than $3^3 \times 10^2$

   b Which two numbers below are equal?

     360×10^2 3.6×10^3 36×10^2 0.36×10^5 $(3.6 \times 10)^2$

   c Two of these numbers have the same value as 5.4×10^{-2}. Which two?

     0.54×10^{-3} 54×10^{-3} 0.54×10^{-1} 54×10^{-1} 540×10^{-5}

12 The diameter of a virus is 0.000 001 cm.

   a Write this number in standard form.

   b How many viruses would fit across a full stop which has a diameter of 0.05 cm? Give your answer in standard form.

FM **13** The table below shows the population of some areas of the world in 2000 together with their yearly population growth.

Continent	Population (2000)	Growth per year
Asia	8.25×10^8	2.5%
Australia	1.92×10^7	0.7%
Pacific Islands and New Zealand	1.4×10^7	1.1%

   a Australia, the Pacific Islands and New Zealand form the continent of Oceania. Work out the population of Oceania.

   b If the growth rate of Asia continues at the same rate, work out the population of Asia in 2005. Give your answer in standard form to three significant figures.

   c If the growth rate of Australia continues at the same rate, work out the population of Australia in 2010. Give your answer in standard form to three significant figures.

Algebra 1 – Rules of algebra and solving equations

Do not use a calculator for this exercise.

1 The diagram shows a square with sides of length $(n + 4)$ cm.

The square has been split into four smaller rectangles. The area of one rectangle is shown.

	n	4
n	......	$4n$
4	......	......

a On a copy of the diagram, fill in the three missing areas with a number or an algebraic expression.

b Write down an expression for the total area of the square.

2 Expand each of the following brackets and simplify each expression if possible.

a $4(x - 5)$ **b** $3(2x + 1) + 5x$ **c** $3(x - 2) + 2(x + 4)$

d $5(3x + 4) + 2(x - 2)$ **e** $4(2x + 1) - 3(x - 6)$

3 a When $x = 4$ and $y = 6$, work out the value of each of the three expressions below.

    i $3x + 9$ **ii** $4x - y$ **iii** $2(3x + 2y + 1)$

b Solve the equations below to find the value of z in each case.

    i $5z + 9 = 24$ **ii** $\dfrac{z - 8}{2} = 7$ **iii** $5z + 9 = 3z + 7$

4 Two friends, Selma and Khalid are revising algebra.

Selma says: 'I am thinking of a number. If you multiply it by 6 and add 3, you get an answer of 12.'

Khalid says: 'I am thinking of a number. If you multiply it by 3 and subtract 6, you get the same answer as adding the number to 7.'

a Call Selma's number x and form an equation. Then solve the equation.

b Call Khalid's number y and form an equation. Then solve the equation.

5 Solve each of the following equations.

a $3x + 7 = x + 10$ **b** $5x - 6 = 10 - 3x$ **c** $3(x + 3) = x + 8$

6 a You are told that $2a + 4b = 15$ and that $2b - c = 13$.

Write down the values of the following.

    i $6a + 12b = \dots$ **ii** $4b - 2c = \dots$ **iii** $2a + 2c = \dots$

b Factorise each of the following.

    i $3x + 6y$ **ii** $x^2 + x$ **iii** $4ab + 6a$

7 For each equation below, write down the missing expression to make the equation true.

a $\boxed{3n - 1} + \boxed{\dots\dots} = \boxed{5n + 3}$ **b** $\boxed{6n + 9} - \boxed{\dots\dots} = \boxed{5n + 3}$

c $\boxed{6n + 1} + \boxed{\dots\dots} = \boxed{5n + 3}$ **d** $\boxed{8n + 2} - \boxed{\dots\dots} = \boxed{5n + 3}$

8 a Two of the expressions below are equivalent. Which ones are they?

$3(4x - 6)$ $2(6x - 4)$ $12(x - 3)$ $6(2x - 3)$ $8(4x - 1)$

b Factorise this expression: $6y - 12$

c Factorise this expression as fully as possible.

$9y^2 - 6y$

9 a Find the value of these expressions when $x = 2$.

i $\dfrac{3x^3}{8}$

ii $\dfrac{2x^2(x + 3)}{5x}$

b Simplify this expression: $\dfrac{4x^2y^3}{6xy}$

c Simplify these expressions.

i $4(x - 3) - 3(x + 4)$

ii $2(3y + 4x) + 3(y - 2x)$

10 Look at this sequence of fractions:

$\dfrac{2}{5}$ $\dfrac{4}{7}$ $\dfrac{6}{9}$ $\dfrac{8}{11}$ $\dfrac{10}{13}$ …

a What is the nth term of this sequence ?

b Another sequence has an nth term of $\dfrac{n^2}{n^2 + 1}$. The first term is $\dfrac{1}{2}$.
Write down the next three terms.

c The sequence in part **b** goes on forever and reaches a limit. What is the limit?

11 Solve the following equations.

a $5 - 3y = 12 - 4y$

b $\dfrac{7y}{y - 1} = 5$

c $\dfrac{4}{y - 2} = y - 2$

12 Simplify these expressions.

a $(x - 4)(x - 4)$

b $(x - 4)(x + 5)$

c $(3x - 2)(4x + 1)$

13 The triangle and the rectangle have the same area.

Find the value of z.

$2z + 2$ $2z$ z $4z - 2$

Algebra 2 – Graphs

Exercise 12D   **Do not use a calculator for this exercise.**

You will need graph paper or centimetre-squared paper.

For all the graphs you are asked to draw, axes the size of those in Question 4 will be large enough.

1 In a house, the hot-water tank automatically refills with cold water whenever hot water is taken out. The heating system then heats the water to a pre-set temperature.

Dad always has a shower in the morning. Mum always has a bath and the two children get up so late that all they do is wash their hands and faces.

The graph shows the temperature of the water in the hot-water tank between 7 am and 9 am one morning.

a At what time did Dad have his shower?

b At what time did Mum have her bath?

c At what time did the first child wash?

d Gran likes to have as hot a bath as possible, once everyone else has left the house at 9 am. Estimate at what time the water will be back to its maximum temperature.

2 For every point on the graph of $x + y = 6$, the x- and y-coordinates add up to 6. Which of the following points lie on the line?

a **i** $(3, -3)$ **ii** $(6, 0)$
iii $(-7, -1)$ **iv** $(-1, 7)$

b On a grid draw the graph of $x + y = 6$.

 3 The prison population of a country was increasing rapidly, as is the use of illegal drugs. These graphs show the changes in prison population and drug use between 2003 and 2006.

 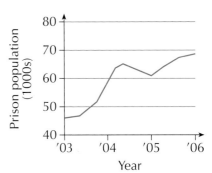

Use the graphs to decide for each of the following statements, **a**, **b** and **c**, if:

● the statement is true.

● the statement is false.

● you cannot be sure if it is true or false from the information given.

Use only the information given in the graphs. Do not use any facts that you might already know about the subject. Explain your answers.

a There is a positive correlation between prison population and illegal drug use.

b The prison population will reach 70 000 before 2013.

c Reducing illegal drug use will decrease the prison population.

4 The graph shows the line $y = 2x + 2$.

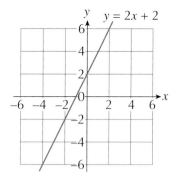

a   Copy the graph and draw and label the line $y = 2x - 1$ on the same axes.

b   Draw and label the line $y = x + 2$ on the same axes.

c   Write down the coordinates of the point where the graphs $y = 2x - 1$ and $y = x + 2$ intersect.

5 The diagram shows a rectangle ABCD.

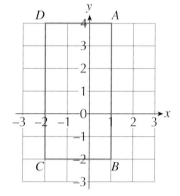

a   The equation of the line AB is $x = 1$. What is the equation of the line CB?

b   The equation of the diagonal AC is $y = 2x + 2$. What is the equation of the diagonal BD?

c   Write down the equations of the two lines of symmetry of the rectangle.

6 a   On the same axes, draw and label the graphs of $y = -3$, $x = 2$ and $y = 3x$.

b   The three lines you have drawn enclose a triangle. Work out the area of this triangle in square units.

7 Here are the equations of six graphs.

A $y = 2x - 1$ B $y = x$ C $y = 2$ D $x = 2$

E $y = 2x + 3$ F $y = \frac{1}{2}x - 1$

a   Which two graphs are parallel?

b   Which two graphs are perpendicular?

c   Which pair of graphs cross the y-axis at the same point?

d   Which pair of graphs cross the x-axis at the same point?

8 The graph on the right shows the journey of a train from Leeds to London, stopping at Doncaster.

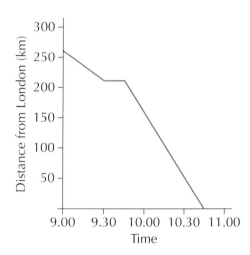

a   What time did the train arrive at Doncaster?

b   What was the average speed of the train for the whole journey?

9 The diagram shows two graphs, A and B.

    a Show that the equation of line A is $x + 2y = 8$.

    b Write down the equation of line B.

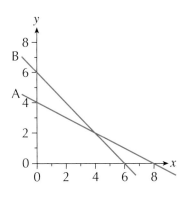

10 The graph on the right shows the equation $y = x^2 - 4$.
Use the graph to solve the equation $x^2 = 6$.

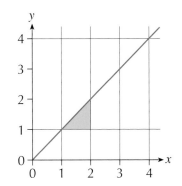

11 Copy the diagram exactly and number both axes from 0 to 4.

    a Write down three inequalities that describe the shaded region shown on the right.

    b Mark the region described by the following inequalities with the letter R.

        $y \geq x$

        $y \leq 4$

        $3 \leq x \leq 4$

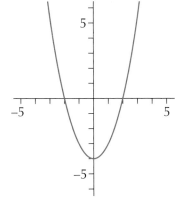

Geometry and measures

Exercise 12E

Do not use a calculator for Questions 1, 2, 6, 7 and 8.

You will find squared paper useful for Question 5.

1 Find the values of angles a, b and c in this diagram. The lines marked with arrows are parallel.

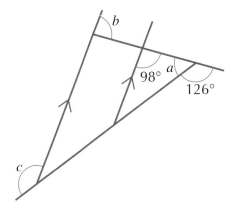

2 Calculate the area of the trapezium shown on the right.

4.8 cm

5 cm

6.2 cm

You may use a calculator for the rest of this exercise unless told otherwise.

3 This car speedometer shows speed in both miles per hour (mph) and kilometres per hour (kph). Use the speedometer to answer the following questions.

a How many kilometres are equivalent to 50 miles?

b Is someone travelling at 100 kph breaking the speed limit of 70 mph? Justify your answer.

c About how many miles is 150 km? Explain your answer.

4 ABCD is an isosceles trapezium.

a Work out the size of angles a, b and c in the diagram.

b Explain how you know that BE is parallel to AD.

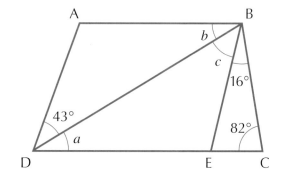

5 Copy the diagram onto squared paper and enlarge the shape by a scale factor of 3, using the point O as the centre of enlargement.

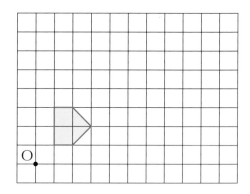

6 **Do not use a calculator for this question.**

a What is the volume of the prism shown on the right?

b The prism below has the same volume as the prism in part **a**. What is the cross-sectional area?

13 cm

5 cm

10 cm

Cross section

12 cm

7 **Do not use a calculator for this question.**

The two triangles shown are similar. Calculate the values of *x* and *y*.

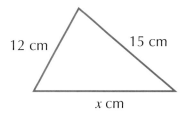

8 **Do not use a calculator for this question.**

a A rectangle measures 24 cm by 12 cm.
What is its area?

b The rectangle is folded in half several times until it measures 6 cm by 3 cm.
How many times was it folded?

c What is the ratio of the areas of the original rectangle and the smaller rectangle?
Give your answer in its simplest form.

9 **a** Make an accurate construction of this triangle.

b Measure the angle at A.

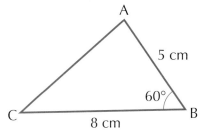

10 The diagram shows a cuboid and a triangular prism. Both solids have the same volume. Use this information to calculate the length of the prism.

11 **a** Calculate the length of the side marked *x* in this right-angled triangle.

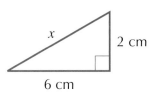

b Calculate the length of the side marked *y* in this right-angled triangle.

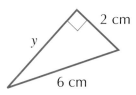

12 a What is the area and perimeter of this sector of a circle?

b A semicircle of radius 5 cm has the same perimeter as a circle of radius, r. Calculate the value of r. Give your answer to 3 sf.

60°
8 cm

13 In the two triangles shown below, the lengths AB and PQ are equal. Calculate the value of the length x and the angle y.

A
20 cm
34°
C
x cm
B

P
$y°$
Q
15 cm
R

Statistics

Exercise 12F   **Do not use a calculator for Questions 1 to 5, 9 and 10.**

1 A bag contains only red and blue marbles. A marble is to be taken from the bag at random.

It is twice as likely that the marble will be red as blue. Give a possible number of red and blue marbles in the bag.

2 Paul's marks for his last nine maths homeworks are:

9   3   5   4   4   7   5   8   6

a What is the range of his marks?

b What is the median mark?

c After checking his final homework, Paul realised that his teacher did not mark one of the questions. Once this had been marked, Paul's mark increased from 6 to 8.

Say whether each of the statements, **i**, **ii** and **iii** are true, false or if it is not possible to say. Explain your answers.
i The mode of the marks has increased.
ii The median mark has increased.
iii The mean mark has increased.

3 The probability that a ball taken at random from a bag is black is 0.7. What is the probability that a ball taken at random from the same bag is *not* black?

4 Lee and Alex are planning a survey of what pupils at their school prefer to do at the local entertainment complex, where there is a cinema, a bowling alley, a games arcade and a disco.

    a   Alex decides to give out a questionnaire to all the pupils in a Year 7 tutor group. Explain why this may not give reliable results for the survey.

    b   Lee decides to include this question in his questionnaire:

        How many times in a week do you go to the entertainment complex?

        Never ☐   1–2 times ☐   2–5 times ☐   Every day ☐

    Explain why this is not a good question.

5 x is a whole number bigger than 1. For the five values on the cards below:

    a   what is the median value?

    b   what is the mean value?

| $3x$ | $2x + 1$ | $x + 1$ | $3x + 2$ | $6x + 1$ |

You may use a calculator for the rest of the exercise unless told otherwise.

6 The scatter diagram shows the value and the mileage for a number of cars. The mileage is the total distance a car has travelled since new. The value of a car is given as a percentage of its value when it was new.

A line of best fit has been drawn on the scatter diagram.

    a   What does the scatter diagram show about the relationship between the value of a car and its mileage?

    b   A car has a mileage of 45 000. Estimate its value as a percentage of its value when new.

    c   A car cost £12 000 when it was new. It is now worth £7800. Use this information to estimate how many miles it has travelled.

7 The table shows the National Test Levels awarded to a class in Mathematics.

Level	3	4	5	6
Number of pupils	2	7	13	8

    a   How many pupils were there altogether in the class?

    b   Work out the mean National Test score for the class.

8 A teacher records how long it takes her class to do a test. The table shows the results.

Work out the mean time taken to do the test.

Time, t minutes	Frequency
$0 < t \le 2$	9
$2 < t \le 4$	12
$4 < t \le 6$	15
$6 < t \le 8$	3
$8 < t \le 10$	1

9 **Do not use a calculator for this question.**

Look at the two spinners on the right.

Use a tree diagram to help you calculate the probability of spinning the same colour on both spinners.

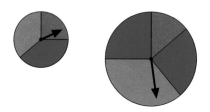

10 **Do not use a calculator for this question.**

The diagram shows the cumulative frequency graph for the marks that 1000 pupils received on a GCSE maths paper.

a Find the median mark.

b Find the interquartile range.

c Pupils who score 65 or over get a grade A. Approximately what percentage of pupils is this?

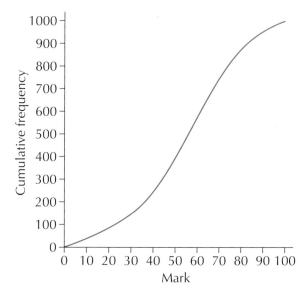

11 A bag contains 4 red and 6 blue marbles. A marble is taken from the bag at random and replaced. Another marble is then taken from the bag.

A tree diagram may help to answer these questions.

a What is the probability that both marbles are blue?

b What is the probability that there is one marble of each colour?

c A marble is taken from the bag. The colour is recorded and the marble is then replaced. This is done 200 times. How many red marbles would you expect to get?

 More National Test practice provided in the Interactive Book.

<table>
<tr><th></th><th>This chapter is going to show you</th></tr>
</table>

This chapter is going to show you

- Some of the statistical techniques you have met before
- How to make a hypothesis
- How to carry out a handling data investigation

What you should already know

- How to carry out a survey
- How to write a questionnaire
- How to collect data
- How to construct and interpret two-way tables
- How to construct and interpret frequency diagrams
- How to construct and interpret scatter graphs
- How to compare data
- How to draw and interpret cumulative frequency graphs
- How to calculate statistics for large sets of data

Statistical techniques

This lesson will remind you of the statistical techniques that you have met before. You will be using these to carry out a handling data project.

The following tables show the vocabulary you should know before you start an investigation.

Handling data vocabulary

Collecting data

	Definition	Example
Questionnaire	A set of questions used to collect information from people	Here is an example of a poor question: How old are you? ☐ 0–10 ☐ 10–20 ☐ 20–30 ☐ over 30 It is poor because the categories overlap, so that both 10 and 20 are in two response sections.
Population	The set of people or objects being investigated	A school with 1000 pupils
Sample	Part of the whole population being used for analysis	50 pupils picked from the 1000 in a school
Survey	The collection of data from a sample of the population	Investigating the favourite colour of pupils in a school by asking 50 pupils

	Definition	Example
Census	The collection of data from an entire population	Investigating the favourite colour of pupils in a school by asking *every* pupil in the school
Data collection sheet or Observation sheet	A form for recording results	Favourite colours of 50 pupils: Blue ⊞⊞ ⊞⊞ ⊞⊞ Red ⊞⊞ ⊞⊞ ⊞⊞ III
Tally	A means of recording data quickly	Green ⊞⊞ ⊞⊞ IIII Other ⊞⊞ III
Raw data	Data which has not been sorted or analysed	Ages of 10 pupils: 12, 14, 13, 11, 12, 12, 15, 13, 11, 12
Primary data	Data that *you* have collected, usually by observation, surveys or experiments	Colours of cars on your street
Secondary data	Data collected by someone else and then used by you	Acceleration times of different cars
Two-way table	A table for combining two sets of data	(see table below)
Frequency table	A table showing the quantities of different items or values	(see table below)
Frequency diagram	A diagram showing the quantities of different items or values	(see diagrams below)

Two-way table example:

	Ford	Vauxhall	Peugeot
Red	3	5	2
Blue	1	0	4
Green	2	0	1

Frequency table example:

Weight of parcels W (kg)	Number of parcels (frequency)
$0 < W \leq 1$	5
$1 < W \leq 2$	7
$W > 2$	3

HISTOGRAM (Journey times)

BAR CHART (Pupils' favourite colours)

PIE CHART (Reasons for absence)

	Definition	Example
Frequency diagram (*continued*)		**Mean temperature for two cities** **LINE GRAPH**
Stem-and-leaf diagram	A way of grouping data, in order	**Recorded speeds of 16 cars** 2 | 3 7 7 8 9 9 3 | 1 2 3 5 5 5 7 4 | 2 2 5 Key: 2 | 3 means 23 miles per hour
Population pyramid	A statistical diagram often used for comparing large sets of data	**Age distribution in France (2000)**
Scatter graph or scatter diagram including line of best fit	A graph to compare two sets of data	
Cumulative frequency diagram	A graph used to estimate median and interquartile range for large sets of data	

Processing data

	Definition	Example
Mode	The value that occurs *most* often	Find the mode, median, mean and range of this set of data 23, 17, 25, 19, 17, 23, 21, 23
Median	The *middle* value when the data is written in order (or the average of the middle two values)	Sorting the data into order, smallest first, gives: 17, 17, 19, 21, 23, 23, 23, 25 Mode = 23
Mean	The sum of all the values divided by the number of items of data	Median = $\dfrac{21+23}{2}$ = 22 Mean = $\dfrac{17+17+19+21+23+23+23+25}{8}$ = 21
Range	The difference between the largest and smallest values	Range = 25 − 17 = 8
Lower quartile	One quarter of the values lie below the lower quartile	From the stem-and-leaf diagram find the median and the interquartile range
Upper quartile	Three quarters of the values lie below the upper quartile	**Ages of a team of 11 footballers** 1 | 7 7 7 8 9 9 2 | 0 5 6 3 | 1 5
Interquartile range	The difference between the upper quartile and the lower quartile	Key: 1 | 7 means 17 years old There are 11 footballers Median = $\dfrac{(11+1)}{2}$ = 6th value = 19 years Lower quartile = 3rd value = 17 years Upper quartile = 9th value = 26 years Interquartile range = 26 − 17 = 9 years

Exercise 13A

1 Criticise each of the following questions that were used in a questionnaire about travelling to school.

   a How do you travel to school?

      ☐ Walk   ☐ Bus   ☐ Car

   b How long does your journey take?

      ☐ 0–5 minutes   ☐ 5–10 minutes

      ☐ 10–15 minutes   ☐ 15–20 minutes

   c At what time do you usually set off to school?

      ☐ Before 8.00 am   ☐ 8.00–8.15 am

      ☐ 8.15–8.30 am   ☐ Other

2 A school quiz team is made up of pupils from four different classes. The table shows the number of pupils in the team from each class.

Class	Number of pupils
A	4
B	3
C	8
D	5

   a Represent this information in a pie chart.

   b Holly says: 'The percentage of pupils chosen from class C is double the percentage chosen from class A.' Explain why this might not be true.

3 19 pupils take a test. The total marks available were 20. Here are the results.

    17, 16, 12, 14, 19, 15, 9, 16, 18, 10, 6, 11, 11, 14, 20, 8, 12, 19, 5

   a Use the data to copy and complete this stem-and-leaf diagram:

$$
\begin{array}{c|l}
0 & \\
1 & \\
2 & \\
\end{array}
$$

    Key: ☐ | ☐ means ☐

   b Work out the median mark.

   c State the range of the marks.

   d How many pupils scored 75% or more in the test?

4 Look at the population pyramid for France in the year 2000 on page 227.

   a Compare the number of females and males alive in the year 2000 who were born during or before World War II, which lasted from 1939 to 1945.

   b Suggest some possible reasons for the difference in the number of males and females in this age range.

5 In a spelling test for a class of 30:

   ● six scored between 0 and 2

   ● fifteen scored between 3 and 7

   ● nine scored between 8 and 10

  Estimate the mean score.

6 Below are the times taken (T seconds) by 20 pupils to run 100 m.

Boys	13.1	14.0	17.9	15.2	15.9	17.5	13.9	21.3	15.5	17.6
Girls	15.3	17.8	16.3	18.0	19.2	21.4	13.5	18.2	18.4	13.6

   a Copy and complete the two-way table to show the frequencies.

   b What percentage completed the 100 m in less than 16 seconds?

   c Which is the modal class for the girls?

   d In which class is the median time for the boys?

	Boys	Girls
$12 \leq T < 14$		
$14 \leq T < 16$		
$16 \leq T < 18$		
$18 \leq T < 20$		
$20 \leq T < 22$		

7 Use the table of data in **Question 8** below to estimate the mean height of the group of Year 9 pupils.

8 The table below shows the heights of 100 pupils in Year 9.

  a Copy and complete the cumulative frequency table.

  b Draw the cumulative frequency graph.

  c Use your graph to estimate the median and interquartile range.

Height, h (cm)	Number of pupils	Height, h (cm)	Cumulative frequency
$0 < h \leq 100$	0	$h \leq 100$	
$100 < h \leq 120$	7	$h \leq 120$	
$120 < h \leq 130$	32	$h \leq 130$	
$130 < h \leq 140$	41	$h \leq 140$	
$140 < h \leq 150$	17	$h \leq 150$	
$150 < h \leq 160$	3	$h \leq 160$	

Extension Work

FM

It was estimated that there were 58 836 700 people living in the UK in mid-2001. This was an increase of 1.4 million people (2.4 per cent) since 1991.

The graph shows the population (in thousands) of the UK between 1991 and 2001. Explain why it may be misleading.

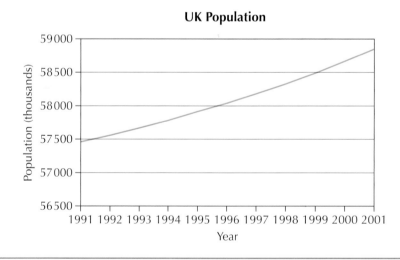

UK Population

A handling data project

In this section you are going to plan and write a handling data investigation. Look at the handling data cycle below. This shows the basic steps in an investigation.

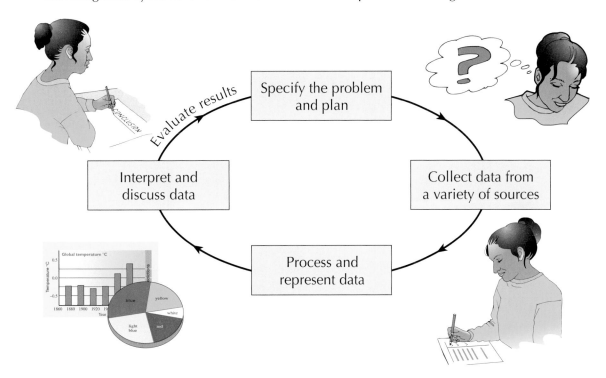

More detail is given about each step below. Follow this checklist when doing your investigation and writing your report.

- **Specify the problem and plan**
    - Statement of problem or topic to investigate
    - Hypothesis stating what you think the investigation will show
    - How you will choose your sample and sample size
    - Any practical problems you foresee
    - Identify any sources of bias and plan how to minimise them
    - How you will obtain your data
    - Identify what extra information may be required to extend the project

- **Collect data from a variety of sources**
    - Follow initial plan and use a suitable data collection sheet

- **Process and represent data**
    - Analysis of your results using appropriate statistical calculations and diagrams

- **Interpret and discuss data**
    - Comparison of results with your original hypothesis
    - List of any factors which might have affected your results and how you could overcome these in future
    - Consider the limitations of any assumptions made
    - A final conclusion

Exercise 13B

In small groups investigate one of the following topics.

 1 Compare people's hand-span with their shoe size.

 2 Compare the reaction times of two different groups of people: for example, girls and boys.

 3 Investigate the ability of people to estimate the lengths of lines (straight or curved) and to estimate the size of angles.

 4 Compare the word lengths in a newspaper with those in a magazine, or compare the word lengths in two different newspapers.

5 "How fair do the people of the UK feel that Society is? Does their opinion change with age?"

Ask about 40 people of various ages, trying to ask about 20 female and 20 male.

Use the simple recording sheet below:

● Enter the gender, F, female or M, male

● Enter Age, years (Be sensitive to the older generation!)

● Ask the question "How fair do you think the UK society is as a whole, please give a score between 1 and 20, where:

      1   = Not fair at all

      10 = Sometimes fair and sometimes not fair

      20 = Very fair

Sex F/M   **Age**   **How fair is our society?**

Not all fair   Sometimes fair   Very
                                      Sometimes not fair   fair

● Once you have all results, create scatter graphs using:

   ● Age on a vertical scale

   ● Fairness score on the horizontal axis

● You should create three different scatter diagrams for the following.

   i   Both sexes

   ii Just male

   iii Just female

● Look at the scatter graphs and see if there are any relationships to be seen between age and how fair they feel society is.

Choose one of the following tasks.

1   Working individually, write a report of your investigation using the checklist. Look again at the limitations of your investigation. Think how you could overcome these: for example, by increasing your sample size or choosing your sample using a different method.

2   In your small group, create a display which can be used as part of a presentation to show the other groups in your class how you carried out your investigation and what results you obtained. Look again at the limitations of your investigation. Think how you could overcome these: for example, by increasing your sample size or choosing your sample using a different method.

3   If you have completed your report, then consider a different problem from the list in Exercise 13B. Write a plan of how you would investigate it, including how to overcome any problems encountered in your first project.

 More National Test practice provided in the Interactive Book.

Geometry and Measures **4** and Revision

This chapter is going to show you

- Some of the methods already met to determine shapes and their properties
- How to carry out a shape and space investigation
- How to carry out a symmetry investigation

What you should already know

- How to find the surface area of 2-D shapes
- How to find the volume of 3-D shapes
- How to use reflective and rotational symmetry

Geometry and measures revision

Before starting an investigation into geometry and measures, you must be familiar with all the formulae and terms which you have met so far.

This section provides a checklist before you start your investigation.

Perimeter and area

Square	Rectangle	Parallelogram	Triangle	Trapezium	Circle

$P = 4l$

$A = l^2$

$P = 2l + 2w$

$A = lw$

$A = bh$

$A = \frac{1}{2}bh$

$A = \frac{1}{2}(a + b)h$

$C = \pi d = 2\pi r$

$A = \pi r^2$

Volume and surface area

Cube	Cuboid	Prism	Cylinder

$V = l^3$

$A = 6l^2$

$V = lwh$

$A = 2lw + 2lh + 2hw$

$V = Al$

$V = \pi r^2 h$

Exercise 14A

1 For each of the following shapes, find:　**i** the perimeter.　**ii** the area.

a

3 cm

3 cm

b

5 cm

9 cm

c
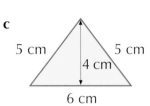

5 cm　　5 cm

4 cm

6 cm

d

16 cm

10 cm

8 cm　10 cm

16 cm

e

6 cm

5 cm

3 cm

5 cm

14 cm

2 For each of the following circles, calculate:　**i** the circumference.　**ii** the area.

Take π = 3.14 or use the 　π 　key on your calculator. Give your answers to one decimal place.

a　　**b**　　**c**　　**d**
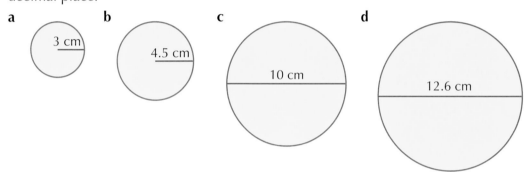

3 cm

4.5 cm

10 cm

12.6 cm

3 A circle has a circumference of 20 cm.

a Calculate the diameter of the circle.

b Calculate the area of the circle.

Take π = 3.14 or use the 　π 　key on your calculator. Give each answer to one decimal place.

4 For each of the following 3-D shapes, calculate:　**i** the surface.　**ii** the volume.

a

5 cm

5 cm

5 cm

b

2 cm

10 cm

5 cm

c

5 cm

4 cm

8 cm

3 cm

d
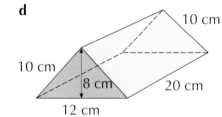

10 cm

10 cm

8 cm

20 cm

12 cm

5 Calculate the volume of each of the following cylinders. Give each answer to three significant figures. (Take π = 3.142 or use the $\boxed{\pi}$ key on your calculator.)

a

3 cm

8 cm

b

15 cm

5 cm

c

2.8 m

1.2 m

6 A cylinder has a volume of 200 cm³ and a height of 5 cm. Calculate the diameter of the cylinder. Give your answer to one decimal place.

Extension **Work**

Calculate the perimeter and the area of the shape on the right.

Take π = 3.14 or use the $\boxed{\pi}$ key on your calculator. Give your answers to three significant figures.

40 m

120 m

Geometry and measures investigations

When undertaking an investigation, you should carry out the following.

- Draw some easy examples first, making all diagrams clear with all measurements shown.
- Put your results in a table with suitable headings.
- Look for any patterns among the entries in the table.
- Describe and explain any patterns you spot.
- Try to find a rule or formula to explain each pattern.
- Try another example to see whether your rule or formula does work.
- Summarise your results with a conclusion.
- If possible, extend the investigation by introducing different questions.

Exercise 14B

Working in pairs or small groups, investigate one of the following.

1 Investigate whether the perimeter and the area of a square can have the same value. Extend the problem by looking at rectangles.

2 For the growing squares on the grid opposite, investigate the ratio of the length of a side to the perimeter and the ratio of the length of a side to the area.

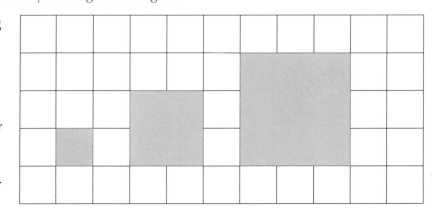

3 A coin is stamped from a square sheet of metal. Investigate the percentage waste for coins of different sizes.

4 The diagram below represents a 6 × 2 snooker table with a pocket at each corner, A, B, C and D.

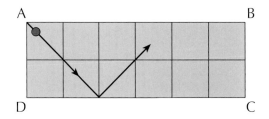

A snooker ball is hit from the corner at A at an angle of 45° and carries on bouncing off the sides of the table until it goes down one of the pockets.

a   How many times does the ball bounce off the sides before it goes down a pocket?

b   Down which pocket does the ball go?

c   Investigate for different sizes of snooker tables.

Symmetry revision

Before starting an investigation into symmetry, you must be familiar with terms which you have met so far.

This section provides a checklist before you start your investigation.

There are two types of symmetry: **reflection symmetry** and **rotational symmetry**.

Some 2-D shapes have both types of symmetry, while some have only one type.

All 2-D shapes have rotational symmetry of order 1 or more.

Reflection symmetry

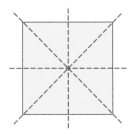

A square has 4 lines of symmetry

A parallelogram has no lines of symmetry

Remember that tracing paper or a mirror can be used to find the lines of symmetry of a shape.

Rotational symmetry

A 2-D shape has rotational symmetry when it can be rotated about a point to look exactly the same in its new position.

The **order of rotational symmetry** is the number of different positions in which the shape looks the same when rotated about the point.

A square has rotational symmetry of order 4

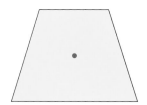

This trapezium has rotational symmetry of order 1

Remember that tracing paper can be used to find the order of rotational symmetry of a shape.

A **plane of symmetry** divides a 3-D shape into two identical parts. Each part is a reflection of the other in the plane of symmetry.

A cuboid has three planes of symmetry, as shown below.

Each plane of symmetry is a rectangle.

Exercise 14C

1 Copy each of these shapes and draw its lines of symmetry. Write below each shape the number of lines of symmetry it has.

a   b   c   d   e

2 Write down the number of lines of symmetry for each of the following shapes.

a   b   c   d

3 Copy each of the following diagrams and write the order of rotational symmetry below each one.

a   b   c   d   e

4 Write down the order of rotational symmetry for each of the following shapes.

a   b   c   d

5 Write down the number of planes of symmetry for each of the following 3-D letters.

a   b   c   d

6 Draw a 3-D shape that has five planes of symmetry.

Extension Work

Find pictures in magazines which have reflection or rotational symmetry.

Make a poster of your pictures to display in your classroom.

Symmetry investigations

When undertaking a symmetry investigation, you should carry out the following.

- Draw some easy examples first, showing any lines of symmetry and/or stating the order of rotational symmetry on the diagrams.
- Explain anything you notice from the diagrams.
- Describe and explain any patterns which you spot.
- Summarise your results with a conclusion.
- If possible, extend the investigation by introducing different questions.

Exercise 14D

Working in pairs or small groups, investigate one of the following.

1 Three squares are shaded on the 3×3 tile shown so that the tile has one line of symmetry.

     a   Investigate the line symmetry of the tile when three squares are shaded.

     b   Investigate the line symmetry when different numbers of squares are shaded.

Extend the problem by looking at different sizes of tiles.

2 Pentominoes are shapes made from five squares which touch edge to edge. Here are two examples.

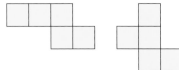

Investigate line symmetry and rotational symmetry for different pentominoes.

Extend the problem by looking at hexominoes. These are shapes made from six squares which touch edge to edge.

3 In how many ways will the T-shape fit inside the 3 × 3 grid?

Investigate the number of ways the T-shape will fit inside a 10 mm square grid of any size.

4 The **symmetry number** for a 3-D solid is the number of ways the solid can be placed through a 2-D outline of the solid.

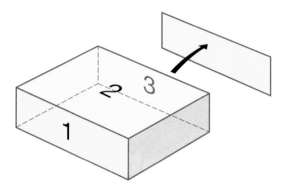

For example, the outline of a cuboid is a rectangle and the cuboid can be 'posted' (so that it fits exactly) through the rectangle in four different ways. These are:

- Side 3 first, with side 2 facing up (shown above)
- Side 3 first, with 2 facing down
- Side 1 first, with 2 facing up
- Side 1 first, with 2 facing down

So, the symmetry number for a cuboid is 4.

Investigate the symmetry number for other 3-D solids.

 More National Test practice provided in the Interactive Book.

CHAPTER 15

Statistics **4** and Revision

This chapter is going to show you

- Different topics within probability
- How to use probability to make a hypothesis
- How to carry out a handling data investigation using experimental and theoretical probabilities

What you should already know

- Probabilities are numbers between 0 and 1
- How to work out simple probabilities
- How to calculate probabilities for two or more outcomes using sample spaces
- How to calculate probabilities for two or more outcomes using tree diagrams
- The difference between experimental and theoretical probability
- The vocabulary of probability

Revision of probability

Make sure that you are familiar with the vocabulary of probability, which is listed in the table below.

Probability vocabulary

	Example
Probability scale Chance/likelihood Equally likely Certain Uncertain Very likely Unlikely Fifty–fifty chance/evens	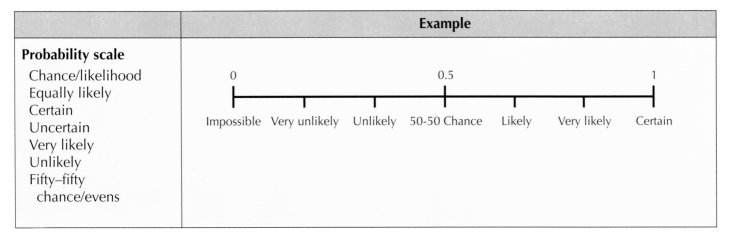

	Example
Probability Event Outcome Random Experimental probability Theoretical probability Relative frequency Expectation Bias Fair	**Example 1** A fair spinner is numbered 1, 2, 3. **a** The spinner is spun twice. List all the outcomes. **b** How many possible outcomes are there if the spinner is spun 3 times? **a** 1, 1 1, 2 1, 3 2, 1 2, 2 2, 3 3, 1 3, 2 3, 3 **b** $3 \times 3 \times 3 = 27$ **Example 2** A six-sided dice is rolled 60 times. It lands on six 15 times. **a** What is the experimental probability of landing on a 6? **b** If the dice were rolled 300 times, how many times would you expect it to land on 6? **c** If the dice were fair, what would be the theoretical probability of landing on 6? **a** $\dfrac{15}{60} = \dfrac{1}{4}$ **b** $\dfrac{1}{4} \times 300 = 75$ times **c** $\dfrac{1}{6}$
Probability diagram Sample Sample space	**Example 3** A coin is thrown and a dice is rolled. **a** Draw a sample space diagram. **b** Write down the probability of getting a Head and a 6. **a** <table><tr><td colspan="2" rowspan="2"></td><td colspan="6">Dice</td></tr><tr><td>1</td><td>2</td><td>3</td><td>4</td><td>5</td><td>6</td></tr><tr><td rowspan="2">Coin</td><td>Head</td><td>H,1</td><td>H,2</td><td>H,3</td><td>H,4</td><td>H,5</td><td>H,6</td></tr><tr><td>Tail</td><td>T,1</td><td>T,2</td><td>T,3</td><td>T,4</td><td>T,5</td><td>T,6</td></tr></table> **b** $\dfrac{1}{12}$
Tree diagram	**Example 4** The probability that it rains on one day = 0.6. **a** Draw a tree diagram to show the probabilities of rain on two consecutive days. **b** Use the tree diagram to calculate the probability that it rains on only one of the two days.

a

1st day   2nd day

```
                              0.6      Rain
              0.6   Rain
                              0.4      Does not rain

              0.4              0.6     Rain
                   Does not rain
                              0.4      Does not rain
```

b   Probability of rain on only one day is given by:

P(Rain on 1st day and does not rain on 2nd day) OR
P(Does not rain on 1st day and rains on 2nd day)

$= 0.6 \times 0.4 + 0.4 \times 0.6$

$= 0.24 + 0.24$

$= 0.48$

Estimate of probability (relative frequency)

Example 5

The number of times a javelin successfully sticks in the ground is shown.

Number of throws	10	20	30	40	50
Number of successes	8	19	27	36	45
Relative frequency of success	$\frac{8}{10}$ = 0.8				

a   Complete the table to show the relative frequency of success.

b   Plot the relative frequencies on a graph.

c   Write down the best estimate of the probability of success.

d   Use your estimate to predict the number of times a javelin successfully sticks in the ground in 500 throws.

a

Number of throws	10	20	30	40	50
Number of successes	8	19	27	35	45
Relative frequency of success	$\frac{8}{10}$ = 0.8	$\frac{19}{20}$ = 0.95	$\frac{27}{30}$ = 0.9	$\frac{35}{40}$ = 0.875	$\frac{45}{50}$ = 0.9

	Example
Estimate of probability (relative frequency) *(continued)*	**b**

c   Best estimate of probability = 0.9 (50 throws)

d   0.9 × 500 = 450 successes

| **Event** Exhaustive Independent Mutually exclusive | **Example 6** In a raffle there are blue, green and yellow tickets. The table shows the probability of each colour being chosen. **a** What is the probability of picking a blue or a yellow ticket? **b** What is the probability of picking a green ticket? **a** $\frac{1}{2} + \frac{1}{8} = \frac{5}{8}$ **b** $1 - \frac{5}{8} = \frac{3}{8}$ | <table><tr><th>Ticket colour</th><th>Probability</th></tr><tr><td>Blue</td><td>$\frac{1}{2}$</td></tr><tr><td>Green</td><td>?</td></tr><tr><td>Yellow</td><td>$\frac{1}{8}$</td></tr></table> |
| **Probability notation** P(Event) | $P(\text{Green}) = \frac{3}{8}$ | |

Exercise 15A

1 Three coins are thrown.

    a How many different outcomes are there? Make a list to show all the possibilities.

    b Work out the probability of getting no Heads.

    c Work out the probability of getting exactly one Head.

    d Work out the probability of getting at least one Head.

2 Matthew is either late, on time or early for school. The probability that he is late is 0.1 and the probability that he is on time is 0.3.

    a What is the probability that he is late or on time?

    b What is the probability that he is early?

3 A group of 50 pupils are told to draw two straight lines on a piece of paper. Seven pupils draw parallel lines, twelve draw perpendicular lines and the rest draw lines which are neither parallel nor perpendicular.

Use these results to estimate the probability that a pupil chosen at random has:
a drawn parallel lines.
b drawn perpendicular lines.
c drawn lines that are neither parallel nor perpendicular.

4 A five-sided spinner is spun 50 times. Here are the results.

Number on spinner	1	2	3	4	5
Frequency	8	11	10	6	15

a Write down the experimental probability of the spinner landing on the number 4.
b Write down the theoretical probability of a fair, five-sided spinner landing on the number 4.
c Compare the experimental and theoretical probabilities and say whether you think the spinner is fair.
d How many fours would you expect if the spinner were spun 250 times?

5 The relative frequencies of the number of wins of a football team are shown in the table below.

Number of games	5	10	15	20	25
Relative frequency of wins	0.8	0.7	0.67	0.75	0.76
Number of wins	4				

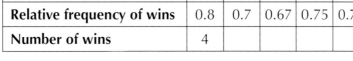

Goal!

a Plot the relative frequencies on a graph.
b Explain why it is not possible to tell from the graph whether the first game was a win.
c Write down the best estimate of the probability of winning the next game.
d Copy and complete the table to show the number of wins for 10, 15, 20 and 25 games.

6 Geoff is building a wall. The probability that Geoff completes the wall by Saturday is $\frac{4}{5}$.

Andy is building a patio. The probability that Andy completes the patio by Saturday is $\frac{1}{3}$. Calculate the probability that by Saturday:
a both the wall and the patio are completed.
b the wall is completed but the patio is not completed.
c neither the wall nor the patio are completed.

1   State whether each of the following pairs of events are independent or not independent. Explain your answers.

   a   Rolling a dice and getting 6
      Rolling the dice a second time and getting 6

   b   Picking out a winning raffle ticket
      Picking out a second winning raffle ticket

   c   It raining in London on Monday
      It raining in London on Tuesday

2   State whether each of the following pairs of outcomes are mutually exclusive or not mutually exclusive. Explain your answers.

   a   An ordinary, six-sided dice landing on an even number
      The dice landing on a prime number

   b   Two coins being thrown and getting at least one Head
      The two coins being thrown and getting two Tails

   c   Two coins being thrown and getting at least one Tail
      The two coins being thrown and getting two Tails

3   State whether each of the following outcomes are exhaustive or not exhaustive. Explain your answers.

   a   A dice landing on an odd number
      The dice landing on a multiple of 2

   b   A spinner numbered 1, 2, 3, 4, 5 landing on a number greater than 3
      The spinner landing on a number less than 3

   c   A spinner numbered 1, 2, 3, 4, 5 landing on a number greater than 3
      The spinner landing on a number less than 4

A probability investigation

Look again at the handling data cycle.

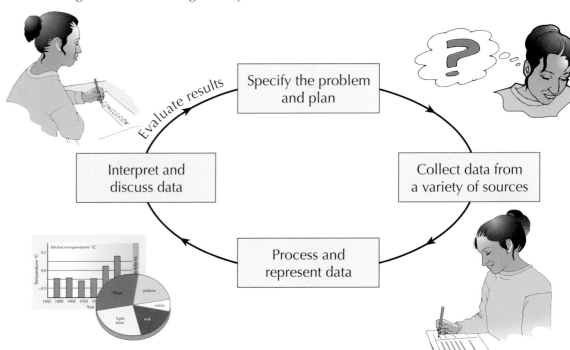

Use the handling data cycle to help you when completing your probability investigation. More detail is given about each step below.

- **Specify the problem and plan**
  - Statement of problem or topic to investigate
  - Hypothesis stating what you think the investigation will show
  - How you will choose your sample and sample size
  - Any practical problems you foresee
  - Identify any sources of bias and plan how to minimise them
  - How you will obtain your experimental data
  - Identify what extra information may be required to extend the project

- **Collect data from a variety of sources**
  - Follow initial plan and use a suitable data collection sheet

- **Process and represent data**
  - Analysis of your results using appropriate statistical calculations and diagrams

- **Interpret and discuss data**
  - Comparison of results with your original hypothesis
  - List of any factors which might have affected your results and how you could overcome these in future
  - Consider the limitations of any assumptions made
  - A final conclusion

Exercise 15B

In small groups carry out an experiment to investigate one of the following.

1. Organise a class lottery. Get each person to choose ten numbers, from 1 to 20. Have 10 separate draws and record who has a winning number each time (there may be more than one winner for each draw). Compare the theoretical and experimental probabilities of each player winning.

2. Investigate whether a drawing pin will land point up more often than point down. Use different-sized drawing pins to test whether the results are always the same.

3. Ask a member of your group to put 10 coloured cubes in a bag, so that the rest of the group do not know what the colours are. Investigate how many times you need to pick a cube out and replace it in order to be able to predict accurately the contents of the bag.

4. Some people are luckier than others when rolling a dice.

5. A playing card usually lands face-up when dropped.

Extension Work

Choose one of the following tasks.

1   Working individually, write a report of your experiment using the checklist. Look again at the limitations of your experiment and think how you could overcome these: for example, by increasing your sample size or choosing your sample using a different method.

2   In your small group, create a display which can be used as part of a presentation to show the other groups in your class how you carried out your experiment and what results you obtained. Look again at the limitations of your experiment and think how you could overcome these: for example, by increasing your sample size or choosing your sample using a different method.

3   If you have completed your report, then consider a different problem from the list in Exercise 15B. Write a plan of how you would investigate it, including how to overcome any problems encountered in your first project.

 More National Test practice provided in the Interactive Book.

This chapter is going to

- Get you started on your GCSE course

Solving quadratic equations

Example 16.1 ▷ Substitute into the quadratic expression $x^2 - 5x + 6$.

a $x = 2$ **b** $x = 3$

a $(2)^2 - 5(2) + 6 = 4 - 10 + 6 = 0$
b $(3)^2 - 5(3) + 6 = 9 - 15 + 6 = 0$

The values 2 and 3 are known as the roots of the quadratic equation $x^2 - 5x + 6 = 0$ since they solve the equation exactly.

Example 16.2 ▷ **a** $p \times q = 0$
What are the possible values of p and q?
b $(x - 2)(x - 3) = 0$
What are the possible values of x?

a Either $p = 0$, so $0 \times q = 0$, or $q = 0$, so $p \times 0 = 0$.
b Either $x - 2 = 0$, so $0 \times (x - 3) = 0$, in which case $x = 2$; or $x - 3 = 0$, so $(x - 2) \times 0 = 0$, in which case $x = 3$.

To solve a quadratic equation, firstly **factorise** the left hand side.

For example, solve $x^2 - 5x + 6 = 0$.

Factorising the left hand side gives $(x - 2)(x - 3) = 0$.

The values of the brackets multiplied together can only give 0 if one or the other brackets equals 0. So either $x - 2 = 0$ or $x - 3 = 0$.

Therefore the roots of $x^2 - 5x + 6 = 0$ are $x = 2$ or $x = 3$.

Example 16.3 ▷ Solve these quadratic equations using the above rule.

a $(x - 5)(x + 2) = 0$ **b** $x^2 + 5x - 14 = 0$ **c** $x^2 - 4x + 4 = 0$

a Either $x - 5 = 0$, so $x = 5$; or $x + 2 = 0$, so $x = -2$.
The roots are $x = 5$ or $x = -2$.

b $x^2 + 5x - 14 = 0$ factorises into $(x + 7)(x - 2) = 0$.
Either $x + 7 = 0$, so $x = -7$; or $x - 2 = 0$, so $x = 2$.
The roots are $x = -7$ or $x = 2$.

Sometimes the roots of a quadratic equation are the same.

c $x^2 - 4x + 4 = 0$ factorises into $(x - 2)(x - 2) = 0$.
As both brackets are the same, $x - 2 = 0$, so $x = 2$.
Hence the quadratic equation has just one root, $x = 2$.

Exercise 16A

1 Solve these equations.

a $(x + 1)(x - 1) = 0$ **b** $(x - 2)(x + 5) = 0$ **c** $(x - 3)(x + 6) = 0$

d $(x + 4)(x + 3) = 0$ **e** $(x + 2)(x + 7) = 0$ **f** $(x - 3)(x - 8) = 0$

g $(x - 8)(x + 1) = 0$ **h** $(x + 3)(x + 3) = 0$ **i** $(x - 4)(x - 4) = 0$

2 First factorise then solve these equations.

a $x^2 + 3x + 2 = 0$ **b** $x^2 + 11x + 30 = 0$ **c** $x^2 + 6x + 8 = 0$

d $x^2 - 5x + 6 = 0$ **e** $x^2 - 7x + 10 = 0$ **f** $x^2 - 5x + 4 = 0$

g $x^2 + 10x + 25 = 0$ **h** $x^2 - 8x + 16 = 0$ **i** $x^2 - 2x - 15 = 0$

j $x^2 + 2x - 15 = 0$ **k** $x^2 - 2x - 24 = 0$ **l** $x^2 - x - 6 = 0$

m $x^2 - 10x + 9 = 0$ **n** $x^2 - 3x - 18 = 0$ **o** $x^2 + 2x + 1 = 0$

Quadratic expressions of the form $ax^2 + bx + c$

Example 16.4

Expand these brackets.

a $(2x + 3)(x - 1)$ **b** $(3x - 4)(2x + 3)$ **c** $(3x - 2)^2$

a $(2x + 3)(x - 1) = 2x(x - 1) + 3(x - 1) = 2x^2 - 2x + 3x - 3 = 2x^2 + x - 3$

b $(3x - 4)(2x + 3) = 3x(2x + 3) - 4(2x + 3) = 6x^2 + 9x - 8x - 12 = 6x^2 + x - 12$

c $(3x - 2)^2 = (3x - 2)(3x - 2) = 9x^2 - 6x - 6x + 4 = 9x^2 - 12x + 4$

Example 16.5

Factorise:

a $3x^2 + 7x + 2$ **b** $6x^2 - 17x + 12$

a We know that there will be two brackets. The factors of 3 are 3 and 1, so the brackets must start $(3x \quad)(x \quad)$. The factors of 2 are 2 and 1. Now it is a matter of finding a combination of both sets of factors to give $7x$. By trial we can find that $(3x + 1)(x + 2)$ works.

b Factors of 6 are 1 and 6 or 3 and 2. Factors of 12 are 1 and 12, 2 and 6 or 3 and 4.

We now have to find a pair of factors of 6 that combine with a pair of factors of 12 to give -17.

Factors of 6		Factors of 12		
1	2	1	2	3
6	3	12	6	4

We can see that combining the following factors gives $(2 \times -4) + (3 \times -3) = -17$.

$$\begin{matrix} 2 & & 3 \\ & \times & \\ 3 & & 4 \end{matrix}$$

So, the factorisation is $(2x - 3)(3x - 4)$.

1 Expand the brackets into quadratic expressions.

a $(2x + 1)(x + 5)$ b $(3x - 3)(x + 4)$ c $(2x - 5)(2x - 4)$

d $(3x + 3)(2x - 7)$ e $(2x + 6)^2$ f $(3x - 4)^2$

g $(2x - 8)(3x + 1)$ h $(4x - 1)(2x + 3)$ i $(2x - 1)(2x + 1)$

2 Factorise these quadratic expressions.

a $2x^2 + 7x + 3$ b $2x^2 + 9x + 10$ c $3x^2 + 13x + 4$

d $2x^2 - x - 1$ e $6x^2 + 7x + 2$ f $2x^2 - x - 6$

g $2x^2 + 3x - 9$ h $4x^2 + 4x + 1$ i $4x^2 + 7x - 2$

j $5x^2 + 11x + 2$ k $3x^2 + 2x - 1$ l $8x^2 + 6x + 1$

m $3x^2 - 5x - 2$ n $6x^2 + x - 1$ o $4x^2 - 11x - 3$

p $4x^2 + 4x - 15$ q $2x^2 - 9x - 35$ r $2x^2 - 5x - 25$

s $3x^2 + 14x - 5$ t $9x^2 + 6x + 1$ u $10x^2 + 13x - 3$

Quadratic equations

Example 16.6

Solve these equations.

a $2x^2 + 7x + 3 = 0$ b $4x^2 + 4x - 15 = 0$

a $2x^2 + 7x + 3 = 0$ factorises to $(2x + 1)(x + 3) = 0$

Either $2x + 1 = 0$ so, $x = -\frac{1}{2}$ or $x + 3 = 0$ so, $x = -3$

The solutions are $x = -\frac{1}{2}$ or $x = -3$

b $4x^2 + 4x - 15 = 0$ factorises to $(2x - 3)(2x + 5) = 0$

Either $2x - 3 = 0$ so, $x = 1\frac{1}{2}$, or $2x + 5 = 0$ so, $x = -2\frac{1}{2}$

The solutions are $x = 1\frac{1}{2}$ or $x = -2\frac{1}{2}$

Example 16.7

Solve the following equations.

a $x^2 + 6x = 7$ b $2x(x + 2) = 3(x + 1)$

a This equation is not in the correct form to factorise and solve. It needs to be rearranged.

$x^2 + 6x = 7$

So, $x^2 + 6x - 7 = 0$

Factorising gives $(x + 7)(x - 1) = 0$

So, $x = -7$ or $x = 1$

b Expanding and rearranging the brackets gives $2x^2 + 4x = 3x + 3$

So, $2x^2 + x - 3 = 0$

Factorising gives $(2x + 3)(x - 1) = 0$

So, $x = -1\frac{1}{2}$ or $x = 1$

1 First factorise then solve these equations.

a	$2x^2 - 7x + 3 = 0$	**b**	$3x^2 - 5x - 2 = 0$	**c**	$2x^2 + 7x - 4 = 0$
d	$4x^2 + 4x - 3 = 0$	**e**	$2x^2 + 11x - 6 = 0$	**f**	$4x^2 + 7x - 2 = 0$
g	$6x^2 + 17x + 5 = 0$	**h**	$6x^2 + x - 1 = 0$	**i**	$4x^2 + 12x + 9 = 0$
j	$20x^2 - 9x + 1 = 0$	**k**	$6x^2 - 19x + 10 = 0$	**l**	$9x^2 + 6x + 1 = 0$
m	$4x^2 - 4x + 1 = 0$	**n**	$6x^2 - x - 5 = 0$	**o**	$3x^2 - x - 10 = 0$

2 Solve these equations.

a	$x^2 + x = 2$	**b**	$x(x - 1) = 1 - x$	**c**	$2x(x - 1) = 1 - x$
d	$3x^2 = x + 2$	**e**	$4x(x - 1) = 5x - 2$	**f**	$4x(4x - 3) = 4(x - 1)$
g	$x(x + 5) = 5x + 25$	**h**	$6x(x + 1) = x + 4$	**i**	$1 - x = 20x^2$

The quadratic formula

Another way to solve quadratic equations in the form $ax^2 + bx + c = 0$ is by using the following formula:

$$x = \frac{-b \pm \sqrt{b^2 - 4ac}}{2a}$$

This formula is used when quadratic equations do not factorise, although it will work with any quadratic equation. The symbol '±' means that you firstly add the values to find one root to the equation, and then subtract the values to find the other root.

Example 16.8 ▶

Solve these equations.

a $2x^2 + 7x + 3 = 0$ **b** $x^2 - 16 = 0$

a First, identify a, b and c.

For this equation, $a = 2$, $b = 7$ and $c = 3$.

Substitute these values into the formula $x = \dfrac{-(7) \pm \sqrt{(7)^2 - 4(2)(3)}}{2(2)}$

Now evaluate the square root $x = \dfrac{-(7) \pm \sqrt{25}}{4} = \dfrac{-(7) \pm 5}{4}$

So the solutions are $x = \dfrac{-7 + 5}{4} = \dfrac{-2}{4} = -\dfrac{1}{2}$ or $\dfrac{-7 - 5}{4} = \dfrac{-12}{4} = -3$

b For this equation, $a = 1$, $b = 0$ and $c = -16$.

Substitute into the formula $x = \dfrac{-(0) \pm \sqrt{(0)^2 - 4(1)(-16)}}{2(1)}$

Now evaluate the square root $x = \dfrac{0 \pm \sqrt{64}}{2} = \dfrac{\pm 8}{2}$

So the solutions are $x = 4$ or -4

Example 16.9 ▷ Solve these equations.

a $2x^2 + 3x - 4 = 0$, giving your answer to 2 decimal places

b $3x^2 - 4x - 1 = 0$, giving your answer in **surd** form. Surd form means leaving square roots in your answer.

These equations will not factorise. The 'clue' is that you are asked for your answers to 2 decimal places or in surd form.

a In this equation, $a = 2$, $b = 3$ and $c = -4$

Substituting into the formula gives $x = \dfrac{-(3) \pm \sqrt{(3)^2 - 4(2)(-4)}}{2(2)}$

Therefore $x = \dfrac{-(3) \pm \sqrt{41}}{4} = \dfrac{-3 \pm 6.4031}{4}$

So the answers are $x = 0.85$ and -2.35

b In this equation, $a = 3$, $b = -4$ and $c = -1$

Substituting into the formula gives $x = \dfrac{-(-4) \pm \sqrt{(-4)^2 - 4(3)(-1)}}{2(3)}$

Therefore $x = \dfrac{4 + \sqrt{28}}{6}$ or $\dfrac{4 - \sqrt{28}}{6}$

Exercise 16D

1 Solve these equations using the quadratic formula. All of the answers are whole numbers or fractions.

  a $x^2 + 2x - 24 = 0$ **b** $x^2 + 6x - 7 = 0$ **c** $2x^2 + 3x - 2 = 0$

  d $2x^2 + 3x - 20 = 0$ **e** $x^2 + 5x = 0$ **f** $x^2 - 36 = 0$

2 Solve these equations, giving your answers to 2 decimal places.

  a $2x^2 + 3x - 6 = 0$ **b** $3x^2 - x - 6 = 0$ **c** $x^2 + 4x - 7 = 0$

  d $2x^2 - 4x - 1 = 0$ **e** $x^2 + 6x - 1 = 0$ **f** $2x^2 + 5x - 1 = 0$

  g $3x^2 - 6x + 1 = 0$ **h** $2x^2 - 3x - 3 = 0$ **i** $x^2 - 5x + 2 = 0$

3 Solve these equations, giving your answer in surd form.

  a $x^2 - 3x + 1 = 0$ **b** $x^2 + 4x - 1 = 0$ **c** $x^2 + 4x + 1 = 0$

  d $x^2 + 6x + 1 = 0$ **e** $x^2 + 10x + 2 = 0$ **f** $x^2 + 2x - 1 = 0$

Completing the square

Another way of factorising quadratic expressions is called **completing the square**. This is based on the expansion $(x + a)^2 = x^2 + 2ax + a^2$, which can be rearranged to:

$$x^2 + 2ax = (x + a)^2 - a^2$$

Example 16.10 ▷ Complete the square for these quadratic expressions.

    a $x^2 + 4x$ **b** $x^2 - 10x$

To find the value that goes with x inside the bracket, halve the x coefficient (the coefficient is the number in front of a letter), and then subtract the square of this.

a In this expression, half of 4 is 2.
So, $x^2 + 4x = (x + 2)^2 - 2^2 = (x + 2)^2 - 4$

b $x^2 - 10x = (x - 5)^2 - 5^2 = (x - 5)^2 - 25$

Example 16.11 ▷ By completing the square, rewrite these quadratic expressions.

    a $x^2 + 6x - 4$ **b** $x^2 - 4x + 1$

Firstly, complete the square for the x^2 and x term. Then 'tidy up' the rest of the expression.

a $x^2 + 6x - 4 = (x + 3)^2 - 9 - 4 = (x + 3)^2 - 13$

b $x^2 - 4x + 1 = (x - 2)^2 - 4 + 1 = (x - 2)^2 - 3$

Example 16.12 ▷ Solve these quadratic equations by completing the square.

    a $x^2 + 6x - 1 = 0$ **b** $x^2 - 2x - 15 = 0$

a $x^2 + 6x - 1 = 0$

Complete the square	$(x + 3)^2 - 9 - 1 = 0$
Tidy up	$(x + 3)^2 - 10 = 0$
Take constant term to right hand side	$(x + 3)^2 = 10$
Square root both sides	$x + 3 = \pm \sqrt{10}$
Make x the subject	$x = -3 \pm \sqrt{10}$

So, the answer is $x = -3 + \sqrt{10}$ or $x = -3 - \sqrt{10}$
The answer should be left in surd form.

b $x^2 - 2x - 15 = 0$

Complete the square	$(x - 1)^2 - 1 - 15 = 0$
Tidy up	$(x - 1)^2 - 16 = 0$
Take constant term to right hand side	$(x - 1)^2 = 16$
Square root both sides	$x - 1 = \pm 4$
Make x the subject	$x = +1 \pm 4$

So, the answer is $x = 5$ or $x = -3$

A

Exercise 16E

  1 Complete the square for these quadratic expressions.

    a $x^2 + 8x$ **b** $x^2 - 2x$ **c** $x^2 - 12x$
    d $x^2 - 14x$ **e** $x^2 + 4x$ **f** $x^2 + 2x$

2 By completing the square, rewrite these quadratic expressions.

   a $x^2 + 8x - 1$ **b** $x^2 - 2x + 3$ **c** $x^2 - 12x + 5$

   d $x^2 - 14x + 7$ **e** $x^2 + 4x - 3$ **f** $x^2 + 2x - 5$

   g $x^2 + 6x - 2$ **h** $x^2 + 10x - 9$ **i** $x^2 - 6x + 3$

3 Solve these quadratic equations by completing the square method.

   a $x^2 + 8x - 1 = 0$ **b** $x^2 - 2x - 3 = 0$ **c** $x^2 - 12x + 5 = 0$

   d $x^2 - 14x + 7 = 0$ **e** $x^2 + 4x - 5 = 0$ **f** $x^2 - 6x - 2 = 0$

   g $x^2 - 10x + 1 = 0$ **h** $x^2 - 6x + 4 = 0$ **i** $x^2 - 8x + 5 = 0$

   j $x^2 - 2x - 1 = 0$ **k** $x^2 + 2x - 5 = 0$ **l** $x^2 + 12x - 7 = 0$

The difference of two squares

Example 16.13

Expand these brackets.

   a $(x + 3)(x - 3)$ **b** $(a - b)(a + b)$

   a $(x + 3)(x - 3) = x(x - 3) + 3(x - 3) = x^2 - 3x + 3x - 9 = x^2 - 9$

   b $(a - b)(a + b) = a(a + b) - b(a + b) = a^2 + ba - ba - b^2 = a^2 - b^2$

Example 16.13 demonstrates the rule known as the difference of two squares. Reversing the result in part **b** gives:

   $a^2 - b^2 = (a - b)(a + b)$

Example 16.14

Factorise these expressions.

   a $x^2 - 16$ **b** $x^2 - 4y^2$ **c** $9x^2 - 4$

Once you know the above rule, you can use it to factorise expressions like these.

   a $x^2 - 16 = x^2 - 4^2 = (x - 4)(x + 4)$

   b $x^2 - 4y^2 = x^2 - (2y)^2 = (x - 2y)(x + 2y)$

   c $9x^2 - 4 = (3x)^2 - 2^2 = (3x - 2)(3x + 2)$

Exercise 16F

1 Expand and simplify these brackets into quadratic expressions.

   a $(x + 1)(x - 1)$ **b** $(x - 5)(x + 5)$ **c** $(x - y)(x + y)$

   d $(2x + 1)(2x - 1)$ **e** $(x + 2y)(x - 2y)$ **f** $(2x - 3y)(2x + 3y)$

2 Factorise these quadratic expressions.

   a $x^2 - 100$ **b** $x^2 - 4$ **c** $x^2 - 36$

   d $x^2 - 81$ **e** $x^2 - 64$ **f** $x^2 - 121$

   g $x^2 - z^2$ **h** $4x^2 - 25$ **i** $x^2 - 9y^2$

   j $16x^2 - 9$ **k** $4x^2 - 25y^2$ **l** $25x^2 - 64$

   m $9 - x^2$ **n** $4x^2 - 36$ **o** $36x^2 - 1$

C
B
A

Edexcel, Question 4, Paper 13, March 2005

1 Expand and simplify $(x - 9)(x + 4)$

AQA, Question 13, Paper 1, November 2005

2 Solve $x^2 + 7x + 12 = 0$

EDEXCEL, Question 8, Paper 19, June 2005

3 The diagram shows a 6-sided shape.
All the corners are right angles.
All measurements are given in centimetres.
The area of the shape is 25 cm².

Show that $6x^2 + 17x - 39 = 0$

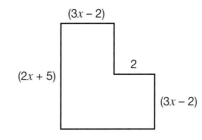

OCR, Question 4c, Paper 3, January 2004

4 Solve $x^2 + 7x + 5 = 0$ giving the roots correct to two decimal places.

AQA, Question 13, Paper 1, November 2005

5 Solve the equation $x^2 - 6x - 3 = 0$

Give your answer in the form $p \pm q\sqrt{3}$ where p and q are integers.

AQA, Question 12, Paper 2, November 2006

6 **a** Show clearly that $(p + q)^2 \equiv p^2 + 2pq + q^2$

  b Hence, or otherwise, write the expression below in the form $ax^2 + bx + c$

  $(2x + 3)^2 + 2(2x + 3)(x - 1) + (x - 1)^2$

AQA, Question 19, Paper 2, June 2007

7 Solve the equation

  $2x^2 - 6x - 1 = 0$

Give your answers to two decimal places.

You must show your working.

EDEXCEL, Question 7, Paper 13 March 2005

8 For all values of x

  $x^2 + 6x + 4 = (x + p)^2 + q$

  a Find the value of p and the value of q.

  b Hence, or otherwise, solve the equation $x^2 + 6x + 4 = 0$

  Give your solutions in the form $a \pm \sqrt{b}$, where a and b are integers.

EXEXCEL, Question 7, Paper 13, January 2005

9 Solve $x^2 + 6x = 4$

Give your answers in the form $p \pm \sqrt{q}$, where p and q are integers.

EDEXCEL, Question 25, Paper 3, June 2005

10 Simplify fully

a $(2x3y)^5$

b $\dfrac{x^2 - 4x}{x^2 - 6x + 8}$

OCR, Question 25, Paper 3, January 2004

11 a By completing the square find the integers p and q such that

$$x^2 + 6x - 1 = (x + p)^2 + q$$

b Hence solve $x^2 + 6x - 1 = 0$, leaving the roots in surd form.

OCR, Question 20c, d, Paper 3, January 2004

12 Simplify

a $2x(x - 5y) - y(2x + 5y)$

b $\dfrac{x - x^2}{x^2 + 5x - 6}$

AQA, Question 16, Paper 1, November 2006

13 The diagram shows a graph of the form $y = x^2 + qx + r$

a The graph crosses the x-axis at A $(-2, 0)$ and B $(8, 0)$.

Show that this is the graph of $y = x^2 - 6x - 16$

b Point P is the lowest point of the graph.

What are the coordinates of P?

c Solve the equation $(x + 3)^2 - 6(x + 3) - 16 = 0$

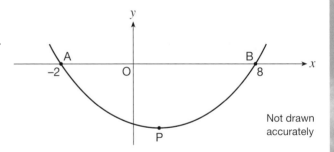

Not drawn accurately

AQA, Question 21, Paper 1, June 2007

14 a Find the value of a and b such that

$$x^2 + 6x - 11 \equiv (x + a)^2 + b$$

b Hence, or otherwise, solve the equation $x^2 + 6x - 11 = 0$

Give your answer in surd form.

1 The Eden Project business plan expected 700 000 visitors in the first year, followed by a 9% increase in visitor numbers each year for each of the next 8 years.

How many visitors did they expect to get in the fifth year?

Round your answer to a sensible number.

2 The Schools Visit Manager at the Eden Project estimates that the ratio of men : women : children visiting the project is 1 : 2 : 4.

On the first Wednesday in March, there were 7700 visitors to the project.

a How many of the 7700 visitors were children?

b Every person visiting that day was given a ticket with a number on, and one was chosen at random for a prize.

What is the probability that a child won the prize?

6 The extract below is part of a UK website.

> The largest greenhouse in the world is the 'Humid Tropics Biome' (HTB) at the Eden Project, Cornwall, England.
>
> The HTB covers 1,559 hectares, is 55 m high, 100 m wide and 200 m long.

This information needs to be placed in an American web page.

The standard unit used in the USA for this type of measurement is feet (not metres).

Rewrite the website information for the American web page using the information below.

1 acres = 0.405 hecatres, 1 meter = 39.37 inches, 1 foot = 12 inches

4 The thermometer on a wall in the Humid Tropics Biome shows 24°C.

Lorna remembers the formula she used in her science lesson last week to change a temperature in degrees Celsius to degrees Fahrenheit:

$$°F = 1.8 \times °C + 32$$

Change 75.2°F into °C.

5 'The People's £50 million National Lottery Grant' was held on ITV in December. The Eden Project's 'The Edge' got 34 560 votes. This equated to approximately 12% of all the votes cast. How many people voted altogether in this programme?

6 Rio asked 100 people he met in the Warm Temperature Biome how long it took them to get to the Eden Project that morning. He put his results in the grouped frequency table as on the right:

Time taken, T (hrs)	Number of people
$0 < T \le 1$	8
$1 < T \le 2$	20
$2 < T \le 3$	42
$3 < T \le 4$	17
$4 < T \le 5$	8
$5 < T \le 6$	5

a Draw a cumulative frequency diagram illustrating this data.

b Use your cumulative frequency diagram to estimate the median time taken.

c Use your cumulative frequency diagram to estimate the interquartile range of the time taken.

7 In one of the restaurants, two friends bought some food.

Zafira bought 3 packs of sandwiches and 4 small fruit juices for £11.55.

Cordoba bought 1 pack of sandwiches and 3 small fruit juices for £5.10.

Use simultaneous equations to find the cost of:

a a pack of sandwiches.

b a small fruit juice.

8 The graph below shows the change in temperature for part of one day last June in the Humid Tropics Biome (HTB).

a What time did the Sun rise?

b The Sun went behind a cloud in the morning. For how long?

c The automatic vents start working when the temperature rises too high. At what time did they start working?

d What was the minimum temperature in the HTB?

e What was the maximum temperature in the HTB?

f What do you think happens to the temperature in the HTB after 7 pm?

9 A node is a large piece of cast iron which can weigh up to 80 kg. Three beams are attached to each node to make a structure.

The nodes are similar. Find the volume of the smaller node below.

Diameter = 90 cm   Diameter = 45 cm
Volume = 9500 cm³   Volume = _____ cm³

10 Bambusa Gigantica, a type of bamboo, can grow up to 45 cm a day.

Diameter of bamboo = 11 cm

A display shows one week's growth from one of the large bamboo plants. This piece has a diameter of 11 cm.

Calculate the volume, in cm³, of bamboo that grew in one week from this bamboo plant.

11 The percentage humidity is the amount of water vapour in the air.

The 'apparent' temperature is people's average guess of the temperature.

A biology pupil compared the percentage humidity in different parts of the different biomes with the 'apparent' temperature, and also with the number of plants per square metre (m²).

Her results are shown on the two scatter diagrams given.

a Describe the type of correlation between humidity and apparent temperature.

b Describe the type of correlation between humidity and the number of plants per square metre (m²).

c Describe the relationship between the apparent temperature and the number of plants per square metre (m²).

d Draw a scatter diagram to show the correlation between the apparent temperature and the number of plants per square metre (m²). Plot about 10 points on your graph.

12 All regular hexagons are similar to each other.

Calculate the length of the diagonal shown in the smaller hexagon.

13 One of the longest cylindrical beams used in the biomes is 18.6 m long and has a diameter of 40 cm. The steel it is made from has a density of 7.9 g/cm³.

Find, correct to 3 significant figures, the weight of the beam in tonnes.

14 Fabia is watching an exit door from a biome. She notices that the probability of a man leaving through this door is 0.4 and the probability of a woman leaving through it is 0.6.

a Draw a tree diagram to show the probabilities of the next two people leaving through the exit.

b Use your tree diagram to calculate the probability that the next two people leaving through the exit are both men.

15 One type of automated vent is an equilateral triangle within a regular hexagon.

Find the area of the triangular vent.

16 Using a ruler and protractor, draw a regular hexagon of perimeter 42 cm.

17 The total site of the Eden Project covers 502 022 m², of which 97 843 m² is landscaped and 1231 m² is a man-made lake.

a What percentage of the total site has been landscaped? Give your answer correct to 2 significant figures.

b What percentage of the total site is the man made lake? Give your answer correct to 2 decimal places.

1 Here are some road signs.

For each part, copy the sign and draw in all the lines of symmetry.

a
Minimum 30 mph

b
Road narrows

c
Clearway

2 Here are some road signs.

For each part, state the order of rational symmetry.

a
Roundabout

b
Clearway

c
No entry

3 Here are three advertisements for driving schools.

Fast Pass

First four lessons £8 each
Then £20 per lesson
All lessons 1 hour

Easy Drive

Standard hourly rate £20
First five hours £60
Block bookings
10 hours £150
15 hours £225

Safe Motoring

First lesson free
Normal price £20 per hour
£2 off per hour for block booking
of 10 or more lessons

a Work out the cost of 40 hours of lessons using Fast Pass.

b Work out the cost of 40 hours of lessons using Easy Drive. Remember to save money by using the block booking prices.

c Work out the cost of 40 hours of lessons using Safe Motoring. Remember to save money by using the block booking prices.

d Which driving school is the cheapest for 40 hours of lessons?

4 The table shows the percentage of casualties in road accidents for different age groups.

Age	Percentage
17–25 years	33%
26–39 years	28%
40–59 years	24%
60 years and over	15%

a Draw a pie chart to show this information.

b Give a reason why there are more casualties in the 17–25 years age group.

5 Research shows that it is safer for pedestrians to walk facing traffic than walking with their back to traffic on rural roads.

10% of those involved in an accident when walking with their back to traffic are killed or seriously injured.

6% of those involved in an accident when facing traffic are killed or seriously injured.

a If 2000 pedestrians are involved in accidents when walking with their back to traffic, how many of these are likely to be killed or seriously injured?

b If 2000 pedestrians are involved in accidents when facing traffic, how many of these are likely to be killed or seriously injured?

6 The driving test is made up of two parts: the theory test and the practical test.

A learner has to pass the theory test before taking a practical test.

In April 2008, the theory test cost £30 and the practical test cost £56.50 for weekdays and £67 for weekday evenings or weekends.

a The probability that a driver passes the theory test is 0.9. What is the probability that the driver fails the theory test?

b A driver passes her theory test first time and the practical test on the third attempt. How much more does it cost if the practical tests are taken at the weekend than if they are taken on a weekday?

7 A practical test lasts for 40 minutes and covers 12 miles. Work out the average speed in miles per hour.

8 The table shows the number of attempts that some drivers take to pass their driving test.

Number of attempts to pass	Number of drivers
1	16
2	9
3	7
4	4
5	3
6	1
	Total = 40

a What fraction of the drivers pass at the first attempt?

b Work out the median number of attempts to pass.

c Work out the mean number of attempts to pass for these drivers.

9 The scatter diagram shows the relationship between the age and the number of driving lessons taken by students at a driving school.

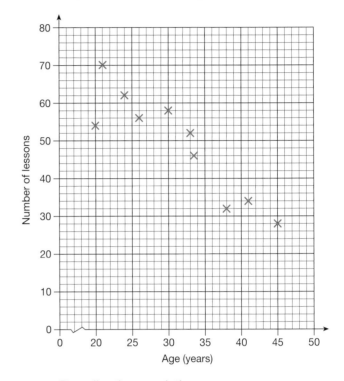

a Describe the correlation.

b Estimate the number of lessons taken by a 36-year-old person at this driving school.

c Explain why it would not be sensible to use the scatter diagram to estimate the number of lessons needed by a 50-year-old person.

10 Here is a formula for working out stopping distance, d (feet), when travelling at speed, v (mph).

$$d = v + \frac{v^2}{20}$$

a Work out the stopping distance in feet when $v = 20$ mph.

b By working out the stopping distance in feet when $v = 30$ mph, show that a car would travel almost twice as far when stopping from 30 mph than 20 mph.

Red squirrels are native to Britain. In 1870 some North American grey squirrels were released in the North of England. The grey squirrel thrived in the conditions in Britain and slowly took over the habitats of the red squirrel, reducing their numbers dramatically.

1 Today it is estimated that there are 180 000 red squirrels and 2.7 million grey squirrels in Britain.

   a Write 2.7 million in figures.

   b Write the ratio number of red squirrels : number of grey squirrels in its simplest form.

2 The population of red squirrels in England, Wales and Scotland is estimated as:

Country	Number of red squirrels
England	35 000
Scotland	120 000
Wales	25 000

Draw a fully-labelled pie chart to show this information.

3 A study on the body weights of squirrels gave the following data for red squirrels over a 12-month period.

Month	Jan	Feb	Mar	Apr	May	Jun	Jul	Aug	Sep	Oct	Nov	Dec
Average weight (g)	273	265	274	280	285	290	310	325	345	376	330	290

This graph shows the same data for grey squirrels.

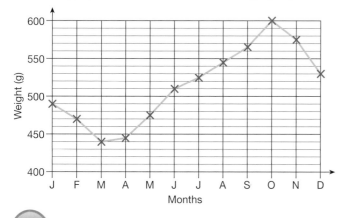

a On a copy of the graph, draw a line graph to show the average body weight of the red squirrels.

b Why do you think the weights of the squirrels increase in the autumn?

c Comment on the differences in the weights of the red and grey squirrels over the year.

4 One reason that grey squirrels do better than red squirrels is that they are more aggressive feeders. This table shows how many of each type can be supported in different types of habitats.

Grizedale forest in Cumbria has an area of 2445 hectares. The table also shows the percentage of Grizedale forest given over to different habitats.

Type of habitat	Number of grey squirrels per hectare	Number of red squirrels per hectare	Land use (%) of forest
Broad-leaved woodland	8	1	65
Coniferous woodland	2	0.1	12
Agricultural	0	0	10
Wildlife management	10	2	2
Open areas	0	0	11

a How many hectares of Grizedale forest are broad-leaved woodland?

   Give your answer to an appropriate degree of accuracy.

b Assuming no red squirrels live in the forest, estimate how many grey squirrels the forest could support.

c In fact the ratio of grey to red squirrels in the forest in n : 1.

   Show that the value of n is approximately 8.

10 adult male red and 10 adult male grey squirrels are trapped and studied.

This is the data obtained

Red squirrels

	A	B	C	D	E	F	G	H	I	J
Body length (mm)	202	185	215	192	205	186	186	199	235	222
Tail length (mm)	185	164	198	175	182	173	162	184	210	203
Weight (g)	320	292	340	305	335	341	295	325	360	357

Grey squirrels

	A	B	C	D	E	F	G	H	I	J
Body length (mm)	272	243	278	266	269	280	251	272	278	281
Tail length (mm)	223	196	220	218	218	222	198	220	226	225
Weight (g)	530	512	561	512	542	551	520	530	558	564

 5 a Work out the mean and range of the weights of the red squirrels.

b Work out the mean and range of the weights of the grey squirrels.

c Comment on the differences in the weights of each species.

6 For red squirrel A the tail length is 92% (to the nearest percentage) of the body length and for grey squirrel A the tail length is 82% of the body length.

a Work out the same data for red and grey squirrels D, G and J.

b The data for another squirrel is:

Body length: 240 mm   Tail length: 215 mm

Unfortunately the species was not recorded.

Is the squirrel a red or grey squirrel? Give a reason for your answer.

7 The scatter diagram below shows the relationship between the body length and tail length of red squirrels.

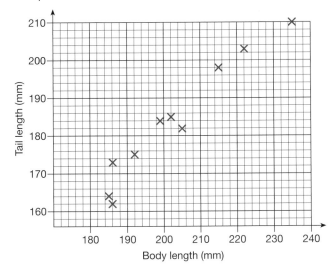

a Estimate the tail length of a red squirrel with a body length of 210 mm.

b Describe the correlation between the body length and tail length of red squirrels.

c i Using the data for grey squirrels, draw a scatter diagram to show the relationship between body length and tail length.

Use a horizontal axis for body length from 240 mm to 290 mm and a vertical axis for tail length from 190 mm to 230 mm.

ii Draw a line of best fit on the diagram.

iii Use your line of best fit to estimate the body length of a grey squirrel with a tail length of 205 mm.

iv Explain why the diagram could not be used to estimate the tail length of a young grey squirrel with a body length of 180 mm.

8 The normal diet of red squirrels is mainly seeds and pine cones with some fungi and plant shoots.

This table shows the percentage of each type of food in the diet of some red squirrels.

Food	Seeds	Pine cones	Fungi	Shoots
Percentage	42%	34%	14%	10%

Copy and complete a percentage bar chart to show the information.

9 This is an extract from a newspaper article.

> By 1998 on the Welsh island of Anglesey grey squirrels had almost totally wiped out the native red squirrels. Since then due to a policy of removing grey squirrels from the island the red squirrel population has recovered and in 2007 was 180. This is a 720% increase on the population in 1998. By 2010 it is expected that the grey squirrel will be completely removed from the island and the population of red squirrels to be over 300.

a What is the expected percentage increase in the red squirrel population between 2007 and 2010?

b What was the population of red squirrels on Anglesey in 1998?

10 Red squirrels are affected by the Parapoxvirus. A colony of red squirrels numbering 1250 was infected by the virus and lost 15% of its numbers each month for 5 months. How many squirrels were left in the colony after 5 months?

FM Mobile shop

Mobile shops were very common in the 1960s but as supermarkets started to open and people had access to cars, they fell out of favour. Nowadays, with people wanting fresher produce and concerned about driving long distances to shop, they are returning to some remote rural areas.

Jeff and Donna decide to start a Mobile shop in a rural area of North Devon.

1 This is a map of the villages they decide they will serve with the distances between villages shown.

The distances are in kilometres.

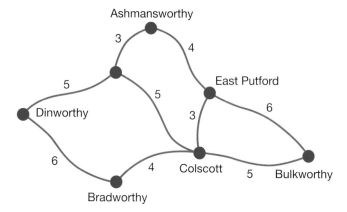

They plan this route: Ashmansworthy – Dinworthy – Bradworthy – Colscott – Bulkworthy – East Putford – Ashmansworthy.

a How many kilometres is this route?

b They plan a timetable.

They intend to be open for 30 minutes in each village.

It takes 5 minutes to pack all the groceries safely after they close before they can drive off.

It takes 5 minutes to unpack the groceries after they arrive and before they can open.

They know they need to allow 2 minutes per kilometre on the rural roads.

They intend to open the shop at 9 am in Ashmansworthy.

This is the timetable for the first two villages.

Copy and complete the timetable for the opening times at each village.

Event	Time
Open Ashmansworthy	9.00
Close Ashmansworthy	9.30
Leave Ashmansworthy	9.35
Arrive Dinworthy	9.51
Open Dinworthy	9.56
Close Dinworthy	10.26
Leave Dinworthy	10.31

c What time do they arrive back in Ashmansworthy?

2 Most mobile shops are often converted single-decker buses.

Jeff and Donna see this advert and decide to buy this bus.

1983 Leyland Tiger – Mid engine, Plaxton Paramount 3200, Semi-automatic, 53 seats with belts, Air Door, Very clean inside and out. Drives well, MOT Jan 2008. Length: 12 metres, height 3.2 metres, width 2.5 metres. Price: £2500.
For more photos please visit our website www.usedcoachsales.co.uk

They know that fitting out the bus will cost £5000.

Insuring and taxing the bus will cost £1500.

Buying the initial stock for the bus will be £2000.

They have savings of £7500.

a What is the minimum amount they need to borrow from the bank to get started?

b The bank agrees to lend them up to £10 000 at an interest rate of 7.5% per annum.

   i How much will the interest be on £10 000 for one year?

   ii If they only borrow the minimum amount they need and decide to pay the loan back over one year, what will be the approximate monthly payment?

3 Health and Safety rules state that they must have adequate lighting, hot water for washing hands, a fridge for storing chilled foods and heating for the winter. They consult an electrician who estimates the power for each item to be:

Lighting	500 W
Water heater	2 kW
Fridge	1 kW
Heating	kW

a W stands for Watts.
What does k stand for?

b What is the total maximum power needed? Answer in Watts.

4 Before they go ahead with the plan, Jeff and Donna decide to do a survey of the villages to see if there will be enough business to make the venture worthwhile.

a Jeff says, 'We need to find out the population of each village and survey about 20% of the residents in each of them'.

Donna says, 'We need to find out how many households there are in each village and survey about 20% of them'.

Who is correct and why?

b The number of households in each village is given in the table.

How many households in each village should be surveyed?

Village	Households
Ashmansworthy	322
Dinworthy	178
Bradworthy	476
Colscott	150
Bulkworthy	483
East Putford	189

c This is one of the questions that Jeff prepares for the survey.

> How much do you spend each week?
> Up to £20 ☐   £20 – £30 ☐   More than £30 ☐

Give two criticisms of this question.

d This is a question that Donna prepares for the survey.

Please tick the appropriate box.
How much do you spend each week on:

Item	£0 to £9.99	£10 to £19.99	£20 to £29.99	£30 or more
Meat				
Fruit				
Vegetables				
Cleaning products				
Other household items				

Give two reasons why this is a good question.

5 The bus is 12 m long and 2.5 m wide.

This is a scale drawing of the bus with 1 cm representing 1 m.

a What is the total area of the bus?

b What is the actual width of the counter?

c The area behind the counter is the 'shop area'. What percentage of the total area is the 'shop area'?

Give your answer to the nearest percentage.

d The fridge is $1\frac{1}{2}$ m high. What is the volume of the fridge?

6 Donna uses the following formula to work out the profit the shop will make each week.

P is the profit. T is the total amount taken over the counter in pounds in a week.

$$P = \frac{T}{5} - 150$$

a What does 150 represent?

b What is the profit if the weekly takings are £1600?

c Jeff says that they need to make a weekly profit of £400.

How much do they need to take each week to do this?

d They apply for a grant to the European Union community fund who agree to subsidise them by 10% of their takings each week.

i How much profit do they make when their weekly takings are £1000 and they receive a subsidy?

ii Show that they need to take between £1800 and £1850 each week to make a profit of £400 taking the subsidy into account.

7 A council survey shows that in a month the bus will drive about 1200 km with a CO_2 emission of 390 g/km.

At the same time, the number of miles driven by people living in the village to travel to supermarkets will reduce by about 6000 km with an average CO_2 emission of 170 g/km.

Estimate the saving in CO_2 emissions in a year if the mobile shop starts to operate. Answer in kilograms.

Index

Long South fence

← 7 m →

5 m

Chicken
run

?

West fence

Short South fence

TREE
SEAT

.TREE

North West fence

BBQ
AREA

East fence

Scale
1 cm = 1 m

HOUSE

William Collins' dream of knowledge for all began with the publication of his first book in 1819. A self-educated mill worker, he not only enriched millions of lives, but also founded a flourishing publishing house. Today, staying true to this spirit, Collins books are packed with inspiration, innovation and practical expertise. They place you at the centre of a world of possibility and give you exactly what you need to explore it.

Collins. Freedom to teach.

Published by Collins
An imprint of HarperCollins*Publishers*
77–85 Fulham Palace Road
Hammersmith
London
W6 8JB

Browse the complete Collins catalogue at
www.collinseducation.com

© HarperCollins*Publishers* Limited 2008

10 9 8 7 6 5

ISBN 978-0-00-726626-5

Keith Gordon, Kevin Evans, Brian Speed and Trevor Senior assert their moral rights to be identified as the authors of this work.

British Library Cataloguing in Publication Data
A Catalogue record for this publication is available from the British Library.

Extra Functional Maths material written by Greg and Lynn Byrd
Commissioned by Melanie Hoffman and Katie Sergeant
Project managed by Priya Govindan
Edited by Karen Westall
Index by Michael Forder
Proofread by Amanda Dickson
Design and typesetting by Jordan Publishing Design
Covers by Oculus Design and Communications
Covers managed by Laura Deacon
Illustrations by Nigel Jordan, Tony Wilkins and Barking Dog Art
Printed and bound by Printing Express, Hong Kong
Production by Simon Moore

Acknowledgments

The publishers thank the Qualifications and Curriculum Authority for granting permission to reproduce questions from past National Curriculum Test papers for Key Stage 3 Maths.

The publishers have sought permission from AQA, OCR and EDEXCEL to reproduce past GCSE exam papers.

The map on page 192 is reproduced by permission of Ordnance Survey on behalf of HMSO. © Crown copyright 2008. All rights reserved. Ordnance Survey Licence number 100048274.

The publishers wish to thank the following for permission to reproduce photographs:

p.14–15 (main image) © VisualHongKong / Alamy, p.40–41 (main image) © Gilbert Iundt / TempSport / Corbis and (inset image of flag) © Andrew Paterson / Alamy, p.80–81 (main image) © V. J. Matthew / istockphoto.com, p.106–107 (main image) © Brandon Alms / istockphoto.com, p.124–125 (main image) © Josef Philipp / istockphoto.com, p.144–145 (main image) © Elena Schweitzer / istockphoto.com, p.156–157 (main image) © Comstock / Corbis and (inset image of violin case) © Nancy Louie / istockphoto.com, p.172–173 (main image) © Laurence Gough / istockphoto.com, p.192–193 (main image) © Guy Nicholls / istockphoto.com, p.208–209 (main image) © Cornel Stefan Achirei / istockphoto.com, p.260 (main image) © Brian Kelly / istockphoto.com and (inset image) © Kevin Jarratt / istockphoto.com, p.262 (main image) © Chris Elwell / istockphoto.com, p.264 (main images) © Sharon Day / istockphoto.com, p.266 (main image) © David Lyons / Alamy

Every effort has been made to trace copyright holders and to obtain their permission for the use of copyright material. The authors and publishers will gladly receive any information enabling them to rectify any error or omission at the first opportunity.